A MOTHER'S STORY

A Mother's Story

The Fight To Free My Son David

Joyce Milgaard
with Peter Edwards

SEAL BOOKS

Seal Books and colophon are trademarks of Random House of Canada Limited.

A MOTHER'S STORY
Seal Books/published by arrangement with Doubleday Canada
Doubleday Canada hardcover edition published 1999
Seal Books edition published April 2000

ISBN 0-7704-2817-7

Seal Books are published by Doubleday Canada, a division of Random House of Canada Limited. "Seal Books" and the portrayal of a seal, are the property of Random House of Canada Limited.

Cover photograph by Gerard Kwiatkowski
Cover design by Susan Thomas/Digital Zone

PRINTED AND BOUND IN CANADA

TRAN 10 9 8 7 6 5 4 3 2 1

To my family and to God, who supported us all
Joyce Milgaard

To Sarah and James
You are my strength
Peter Edwards

CONTENTS

ACKNOWLEDGEMENTS

I would like to acknowledge all the people who supported our family through their prayers, letters and their financial support to free David, the churches of all denominations that held special services and prayer days for us, the David Milgaard support group volunteers in communities across the country who worked so tirelessly, and the many organizations, too numerous to mention, that helped to right this wrong. It could not have happened without each and every one of you.

Special thanks to Leslie Bland, and to Lawrie Cherniack for their editing expertise, and to Peter Edwards for helping me turn my thoughts so wonderfully into words.

Joyce Milgaard

I would never have become involved in this once-in-a-career story if not for my *Toronto Star* colleague Harold Levy, whose energy and social conscience make him a joy to work with.

Star editor Joe Hall encouraged the story in its early phases, and editors Alan Christie and Fred Kuntz continued to see the value in it. The *Star* switchboard team, which once included Joyce Milgaard, lived up to its superb reputation once again.

My agent, Daphne Hart of the Helen Heller Agency, and editor, Jennifer Glossop, were professional and a joy to work with, as usual, as were John Pearce and Lesley Grant of Doubleday Canada.

Special thanks to Sher Kariz, John Findley, Lisa Priest, and Laurie Dover and Sam Goldstein for their support during a difficult time, and to Joyce Milgaard, whose intensely positive outlook is truly a marvel to behold.

Peter Edwards

"Somebody must have made a false accusation against Joseph K., for he was arrested one morning without having done anything wrong."
Franz Kafka, *The Trial*

"God and my mother were the two strongest hopes that I clung to, and they still are."
David Milgaard

"Trust in the Lord with all thine heart;
and lean not unto thine own understanding.
In all thy ways acknowledge him,
and he shall direct thy paths."
Proverbs 3:6–7

FOREWORD

IT IS OCTOBER 15, 1998, and I have just spent another one and a half hours on the telephone with Mother giving her my input on this book. Another one and a half hours we have each lost of our lives to this lie.

When we talked, I asked who was going to write her foreword. She replied she didn't know. I decided I would write it for her. I realized then that I didn't even know what should be in it. But what follows is true, honest emotion.

Guilty is what they said David was.

Guilty is what they have made each of us feel. Try living one day on the outside knowing you have your freedom and your brother is locked away and you can do *nothing* to change that. Then do that for twenty-three years.

Guilty is how David feels because he has seen us spend all these years with our lives on hold trying to free him.

Guilty is how my mother feels because she was not there for the rest of us while we were growing up.

Guilty is how we felt whenever we walked out the prison doors after visiting David and hearing the metal clang of the door as it shut behind you, leaving him there. It is a sound you never forget.

Guilty is how we would feel any time something wonderful would happen in our lives, knowing David couldn't be there to share in the happiness.

Guilty is how we each felt every time we sat together on holidays, birthdays or family get-togethers and David couldn't be there with us.

Guilty is how we'd feel when we just couldn't be there for him because they had moved him so far away.

Guilty is how we would feel every time he was beaten or hospitalized.

Guilty is how we would feel knowing we were helpless to try and free him.

I detest the word *guilty*.

I have always been known as the pessimist. You're right I am. For so many years, we would be waiting for something, anything, to make that phone ring or letter come with some iota of good news. Always hoping deep down that I would be wrong and that something good could happen in the Milgaard family. I grew up believing that being a Milgaard meant having no happiness.

My mother, the eternal optimist, would always have such high hopes and expectations about what would happen today, tomorrow, soon. Her belief in God and man gave her that.

David's incarceration took it away from me. I became a devil's advocate. Actually, I still am. I have become a full-time resident of the Land of If. If they do this then we can do that. If they do that then we can do this. Always looking for how the "system" was going to screw us again and again, and regretfully, I was usually right. My mother would always say, "Don't say garbage like that" or "Susan, you can't be right."

Each time we got a negative reply to something, it made me so angry to see my mother bent over and crying about how she kept failing David. No matter how many times we told her it was not her but the system that had failed him, I still don't think she believes it herself.

I have seen the sacrifices she has had to make not only for David but for each of us. She has always put us ahead of herself and her needs.

She had always been there any time one of us shared our problems. It was our choice not to always tell each other about what was happening in our lives. I do not believe that it is only because we didn't want to burden her. We didn't want to burden anyone in the family. So we each lived our difficult times in privacy and shared the good ones so we could all benefit from them.

There are times that I have not wanted to be "Joyce Milgaard's daughter" or "David Milgaard's sister" but just Susan. The reality of it all is that I don't even know who Susan is. They took that away from me too.

I am so very grateful that my mother has had Christian Science to support her all of these years. Even though my faith was destroyed, my mother's never faltered. I must admit though that in the toughest times, I would say a prayer for her. It may have been just to get a phone call she was waiting for or to have a peaceful sleep, but more often than not it was so she would have the strength to keep going for one more day. I knew I couldn't.

In reading this book, you will see how her faith in God and her undying love and belief in David changed her from a housewife in a small town to a dynamic, articulate, courageous and tenacious woman. I could go on forever listing my mother's qualities, but most of you have already come to know them as you have followed our case over the years.

I am so very proud of my mother. I am happy for the person she has become. I am even happier to see that she is starting to live her life now. Her dedication to us will never cease. Her dedication to God will never cease. Her dedication to *any* wrongfully convicted person will never cease. How can you not be proud to say, "I am Joyce Milgaard's daughter"?

In ending, I would like you to do something immediately before you begin and immediately after you have finished reading her book. Hug your child like you have never hugged him or her before. What happened to David could happen to anyone with the system that still exists and they could be gone tomorrow.

I love you, Mom.

Susan

No scenes in this book have been fabricated, and tapes, reports, interviews and documents have been used to reconstruct conversations. Some have been shortened and some spelling and punctuation has been corrected to make the story more readable.

Joyce Milgaard
Peter Edwards

ONE

POLICE AT OUR DOOR

"Are you David Milgaard's mother?"
Police officers at our door

I WAS PUZZLED BUT NOT overly concerned when the two plainclothes police detectives knocked on the door of my home in the tiny prairie town of Langenburg, Saskatchewan, and asked, "Are you David Milgaard's mother?"

It was a late afternoon in May 1969, and I was about to prepare dinner for Chris, Susan and Maureen, my three youngest children, while my husband, Lorne, was getting ready for his job as night-shift foreman of a potash mine. My oldest child, sixteen-year-old David, was selling magazines door to door in Prince George, B.C. We weren't used to detectives at the door of our little house, but we weren't afraid of the law either. I had a simple, happy life then, tending a big garden, making my own pickles and learning to bake bread from a neighbour. I was taking figure-skating lessons with my daughters and had no complaints. Life was good.

1

I invited the City of Saskatoon detectives in and served them coffee as they asked their questions about David. They were polite enough as they told me that David and two of his friends had been seen in Saskatoon in January, the same day a twenty-year-old nurse's aide named Gail Miller was raped and murdered.

I hadn't heard of the Gail Miller murder case until then. We didn't read the Saskatoon newspaper, the *Star Phoenix*, and in those days, television news was not nearly as important as it is today. The officers described a horrible crime, and the more we heard of it, the sadder we felt, as Gail Miller sounded like a sweet, caring girl. She grew up in a large farm family of six sisters and three brothers near the prairie village of Laura. Her grandmother had paid for her move to Saskatoon so she could study to be a nurse's aide and someday work with babies. She had lived in a drab one-room apartment in a boarding house. On January 31, 1969, at eight-thirty in the morning, schoolchildren found her facedown in a snowbank near her boarding house. Her white uniform was torn and stained with blood from dozens of stab and slash wounds. Whoever attacked her had clearly been in a rage.

The grisly crime had hit sleepy Saskatoon hard. The city had had only one murder in the past two years, and naturally, residents were shocked and eager for justice. There had been a good deal of fear in the city in the months before the murder, I would later learn. On December 14, the *Star Phoenix* had published a police warning that women should not walk in dark areas of the city because of a series of rapes and assaults. The article said the rapist first talked to women, then took them into alleys and attacked them. Since I hadn't followed the news reports, I was blissfully unaware when the police officers arrived at our door.

It seemed ridiculous to me that the police suspected that David might be Gail Miller's killer. I knew David was no angel, and that he had been in plenty of trouble, but nothing involving violence. Over the past couple of years, David had run away a few times with his girlfriend. They had travelled over much of Canada and the north-western United States, living mostly through panhandling, scrounging and welfare. Each time we had called the police and they had hauled him back, but even through this unsettled time, there were no charges related in any way to violence. That simply wasn't David. I was grateful that his younger brother, Chris, did not follow in his footsteps. Chris was always so good and dependable; I never had to worry about him. As a mother I would often say to David, "Why can't you be more like your brother? He has made friends here. He's doing well. Why can't you be satisfied?"

He was a free spirit, a hippie, experimenting, like so many others in the 1960s, with soft drugs and free love. David's friends had even nicknamed him Hoppy, because he hopped in and out of bed with a number of girls. David wasn't much of a drinker. He liked soft drugs more. He had smoked marijuana from age thirteen and took LSD occasionally from age fourteen. There had also been some experimenting with amphetamines, barbiturates and, a couple of times, even heroin. We had huge arguments about his use of drugs and his choice of friends. I prayed that he would be shown that he was walking down the wrong road. At the time, I could only hope it would pass with him, as my own unsettled times had passed with me.

One day early in 1968, a man had come to the door selling magazines for Maclean Hunter. David could do this, I thought. So I asked the salesman to come back and meet my son. I realized David was very young, but I used to sell magazines for Maclean Hunter, and it had been good for me. David got the job and was an instant success. Like me, he was a natural at selling magazine subscriptions, and really enjoyed trying to talk people into buying them. Our second son, Chris, also got involved in selling magazines in May of 1969, after he finished the school year. Chris and David went out on the road together. Sometimes they'd be gone a month at a time, although if they were in Saskatchewan, they came home for the weekends. It was good money and they were getting to travel. I knew that Maclean Hunter had a reputation for running very good crews, and that supervisors didn't take any kind of nonsense from the kids. To me, it was a wonderful answer to David's problems, because in a small town like ours, there weren't many places young people could find work. I felt he was well on his way by the time the police officers came to our door.

I was upset when the police left, and Lorne comforted me, as he always did. However, deep down, I felt it was no more than a mistake that would be sorted out before long. Things can't go that crazy.

A couple days after the police visit, David phoned from Prince George to say he had heard the police were looking for him and he was going to turn himself in to clear the matter up quickly. I agreed that this was a good idea. David told me a little about his trip to Saskatoon that January. He and his friends Ron Wilson and Nichol John had spent the last money they had fixing up the car so they were broke when they left Regina. They went to get his friend Albert (Shorty) Cadrain because they were sure he would have some money. As soon as I knew that they had no money for drugs or alcohol, I knew there was no possible way he might be guilty.

The next day, David went to the police in Prince George. True to his easygoing nature, he hadn't been worried when they questioned him earlier about Gail Miller's rape and murder. He wasn't an innocent choir-boy type, but he didn't see how anyone could seriously think he was a killer. To help police, he voluntarily gave them blood, saliva, semen and hair samples and drew maps of the area for investigators. The sooner they finished with him, the sooner they could catch the real killer.

"Why didn't you tell us?" I asked months later, when David finally told me.

"I didn't think anything of it," David said. "It wasn't me. I didn't do it."

As David later said, "Naive isn't the word. I really believed it. I was trying my best as a young person to help the police. This had to be resolved. It was a terrible crime." Despite his hippie lifestyle, David had a typically Canadian faith in the system, and trusted that the police would catch the real killer.

He couldn't have been more wrong.

TWO

GROWING UP

"My family had a great deal of difficulty with me too."
I see similarities between myself as a child and David

I WAS BORN IN 1930, the youngest of four children, and I was brought up to believe the police are good people. My dad was a firefighter in Peterborough, Ontario, and I always thought you could trust firefighters and police officers. My mother was a homemaker, a war bride from a very good family in Wimbledon, England. She liked to tell everyone how her brother, my uncle George, had been the Lord Mayor of London at one time, and his picture with Princess Margaret at some official function was prominently displayed in our living room. I was never told how my parents met, except that it was during the First World War. They married in England, and my oldest brother, Norman, was born there.

Dad was gassed by the German army in France the first time chlorine was used in wartime. He was sent for treatment to England, and I still have a little gold case for chocolates that he was given by a member of the royal family while he was in hospital. His sickness lingered after he was discharged from hospital. And, like many soldiers, he also brought horrible memories and a drinking problem home from the war. Alcohol was considered a manly way to deal with problems back then. My father was just a youth when he went out onto the battlefield, although he pretended to be older. It wasn't until after she moved to Canada that my mother found out Dad was only sixteen when he went off to war. Later, I'd lie about my age too, so I guess that runs in the family.

My dad was a physically imposing man, about six-foot-two and heavily muscled, while my mother was barely five feet tall and she quickly became pleasantly plump. We used to joke that she could walk under the coffee table without bending over. Her well-to-do family named her Ethel, but Dad called her the more common-sounding Molly. I think he wanted to make her sound ordinary.

My family had a great deal of difficulty with me too. When I was four, my mother kept me in a big cardboard box on the front yard, as they didn't have playpens back then. I would climb to the top of the box and then fall out. I would holler bloody murder if anyone was walking by, but if no one was around, I would sneak off. Most of the time, I would end up at the school across the street. Dad would come in the big firetruck to take me home, and I just loved that. Eventually, the principal told my parents that I could stay and go to kindergarten, because I was always there anyway.

I remember once there was this lady in Peterborough who had beautiful, beautiful tulips and I cut off all of the tops and put them in my little wagon to take to my mother. This was the day before a flower show. Years later, when David was a toddler and we were visiting Peterborough from Winnipeg, he went out and beheaded the flowers in the same woman's flowerbed. You can imagine her outrage.

As the baby of the family, I was spoiled by everyone. My sister, Peggy, was nine years older than me and I looked up to her. I was pretty, but she was beautiful. I had a good singing voice, but Peggy could sing better. In fact, she could do everything better than I could. It was impossible to hate her, though. We remained close as young adults, and it seemed once she moved out we could actually communicate without the telephone. I would know when she needed to talk to me and vice versa, and we would contact one another.

I would probably have been considered an abused child by today's terms because my father used to beat me when he was drunk. When he was sober and happy, his voice had a deep, rich, reassuring timbre to it, but when he was drinking, there was an anger and an edge when he spoke. All I would have to do then was say the slightest thing wrong and I would get a beating. So whenever he came home drunk I would run to Peggy's house. I remember him coming home drunk one night and I climbed out the window and ran all the way in my bare feet in the wintertime to Peggy's. She wasn't home, so I climbed in her basement window. She had two collie dogs, and my voice sounded like Peggy's, so the collies let me in. I would have been nine or ten at the time.

Aside from the drinking, my father truly was a fine man. Most of the time Dad couldn't remember being drunk the next day. He was very good to me the rest of the time, but it was hard on my mother. I used to blame my mother because she would natter at him so much that he would get upset and then I would get in between them when he went after her. But she wouldn't let him alone. So I always swore that I would never, ever get involved with anyone who drank, and if they did, I wouldn't natter at him. I wanted to be like my sister, Peggy.

I had a temper of my own. Once, I was sitting at the dining-room table when my dad said something to me. I picked up an ashtray and threw it at him. It went past him and through a plate-glass window. I took off, since I knew I would get a beating for doing that. I had good qualities too. I was bright. I was inquisitive. I was a fantastic storyteller. I could babysit children and have them totally enthralled just by making up tales about princes and princesses and fantastic adventures in faraway lands. I was a bit of a tomboy and used to boss the boys around and heaven help anyone if they were picking on my friends.

By the time I was eleven, I was out working. I would use the fact that I had a job and an income to keep my parents in line. My attitude was that they owed me because I put bread on the table. Thinking back on it, in many ways, I was just a selfish and single-minded little person. Because I started school young, I was already in grade nine when I was eleven years old. That was also the year I started smoking and set up the first professional babysitting service in Peterborough. I contracted out the services of women in the neighbourhood, taking orders, paying the babysitters and collecting a commission. I placed advertisements in the *Peterborough Examiner*, listing the family phone number. I didn't bother to tell Dad, but he found out soon enough because of the constant ringing of the phone. He was very upset with me but also, I think, proud of my initiative.

Dad broke his leg when I was eleven, and lost his job as a firefighter. Money was scarce, and Mom tried to help make ends meet by running a boarding house. I thought I could help support the family by working in a weaving mill, so I lied about my age, saying I was sixteen, and went off to work full-time. But the mill was hot, noisy, dry and dusty, and I kept getting dizzy and fainting. Understandably, the employers didn't want me once they saw I had trouble staying conscious. My working concerned Dad too. He had listed me as a dependent child and a tax deduction on his income tax form, but since I was paying my own income tax, Dad was terrified the tax department would catch up with us.

My next job was in the Eaton's department store as a salesclerk. One day when working in the hardware department, I made great efforts to sell some items to a gentleman who told me he was visiting from Toronto. I kept pulling out things to show him that would make wonderful gifts to bring home for his family. Later, I was called up into the general manager's office and, much to my surprise, the customer was there. I was soon put at ease to find that he was offering me a transfer to the

Toronto store. He was impressed with my ability as a salesperson, and he felt that he would like his staff to copy my sales manner. I let him call my mother to see if she would agree. Instead, she blurted out my real age, and that I was only a baby. That was the end of not only the job offer but also my employment at Eaton's.

I was soon helping Peggy at a hairdresser's. That career was cut short, however, when I told one of the city's elite ladies that she had bugs in her hair. The owner said either Peggy or I would have to go, and I was quickly out the door. Peggy had married young to get away from my dad, but it turned out well. She had always had just this one boyfriend and loved him from the word go. When Peggy's husband, Arnold, went overseas to war, I went to live with her in their general store and cabin in Lakefield, near Peterborough. I helped out by working as a switchboard operator in the country, working those old-style switchboards with the plug-ins. I would have been about fourteen, and I worked all night one or two nights a week.

I learned a lot about mothering from Peggy, as she was a very good parent. She was close with her two daughters, and neither strict nor lax but balanced. They had a good life. They seemed to have everything that I didn't have. They made good money and had a really nice house in a very nice neighbourhood. We were so close, and went out more as girlfriends than as sisters.

Peggy's husband came home from war and it was time to move on. At fifteen, I enrolled in a business college. About two weeks later, nuns from St. Joseph's Hospital phoned the college to ask if a competent switchboard operator was available who was close to finishing the course. "Yes," I replied, "there is." Then I called back, disguising my voice and lining up the job for myself. It took the nuns only a couple of days to catch on that something wasn't right. My typing skills were nonexistent, not something one would expect from someone close to graduation. Sister Theophanie, who ran the hospital, quietly approached me and asked if by any chance I had answered a call from the sisters about a telephone operator. "Yes," I replied, worried that I'd lose my new job. But Sister Theophanie just laughed and let me stay on since I was fast on the switchboard.

They were also amused later when, at sixteen, I solemnly told them I had decided to become a nun. I made a point of not wearing makeup that day as I told Sister Theophanie of my decision. I can still hear her hysterical laughter. I shouldn't have been too surprised. I was smoking two packs of cigarettes a day then, and drinking as well, and was confident enough to tell fortunes for charity.

By going to work as an adolescent, I had benefits that other kids didn't and, of course, I had money. I wasn't really very mature, but I thought I was. I thought I could do anything, and I could do a lot of things simply because I thought I could.

It wasn't long before until I was off to Toronto, to live with my aunt Sue on Logan Avenue near Danforth Avenue. I landed a job as a switchboard operator at the *Toronto Star*, and I enjoyed travelling, socializing, drinking with friends, flirting with boys and wearing nice clothes. Sometimes I helped reporters track down people who didn't wish to be found and cajoling them to talk. Decades later, those skills would be extremely important for helping David.

During the summer, I rented a place on Toronto Island, and one day, I saw the horrific burning of the cruise boat *Noronic* in Lake Ontario. I tried to pull one man from the water, but he wouldn't let me because he was modest and had lost his pants. A young girl was on deck, frozen in fear as the smoke and flames swirled towards her. Everyone shouted for her to jump but she was petrified. I can still see her as her clothes caught fire and I'll never forget what burning flesh smells like. I grabbed a notebook and began writing notes. I got my first byline for that story.

My social life was busy also. I was a hard drinker and a real party-goer. I could swear and drink with the best — and worst — of them. Once, at the Press Club in Toronto, I bet one of the reporters that I could drink him under the table. Every couple of drinks, I would go to the washroom to get sick, and so I beat him. Although I shudder to think about it now, I know that if there had been drugs available in those days, I would have been a user. I was interested in guys only until they became interested in me. Why? The thrill of the chase, I guess. When I think back, I realize that I used people. My family couldn't believe how many times I was engaged. It never entered my mind that I was hurting people and that it would make me seem like a shallow person. I did use people, but I was also generous to a fault and loved to give to others.

After a year at the *Star*, I was offered a job selling advertisements for magazines, with the promise that I might make $200 a week. It was an enormous sum back then, and about four times what I was earning. I accepted and had moved to Winnipeg before I realized that the job was actually selling magazines door to door. At first I was horrified, but I soon found that I could make plenty of money. I also quickly learned that direct selling was my strong point. I loved to improvise and soon was heading a team of salespeople criss-crossing Canada. I had always loved to tell stories and invent personalities, and this job gave me the freedom to do just that. I would pretend to be an Irish colleen at one house. At the next I might be a lilting-voiced Scots girl or a well-bred English lady. Once, I pretended to be a sweet little Scot at one house, and a couple of doors up, I switched over to an Irish brogue. It so happened that the woman who heard me as a Scot was now visiting the second house and heard my brogue. We shared a big laugh, and then I sold two more subscriptions.

THREE

EARLY MARRIAGE

A minister: "God made the flowers."
David: "Who made the weeds?"

WHEN I MOVED TO Winnipeg in the early 1950s, I missed my family and my friends. Then I met Lorne, and he was very supportive of me at a time when I needed support. We just hit it off. Lorne was very kind, the strong, silent type, tall, good looking, and he adored me. This was at a time when people didn't travel nearly as much as they do today, and none of my family made the trip west for our wedding. I didn't want a civil ceremony, and we were allowed to say our vows at St. Mark's Anglican Church in suburban St. Vital. It was just Lorne, me, two friends and the minister. I wore a street-length blue chiffon dress with a matching tiara, while Lorne looked distinguished in his dark suit.

I started to become a better person, and to really appreciate Lorne's fine qualities. I then began caring for him more, and loving him more fully. However, at first,

I was a headache for him. I lay around all day, ate chocolates and read romance magazines. I would drop things throughout our place, and Lorne would come home and clean up after me, then cook dinner. Mornings, he made me breakfast in bed before he headed off for work. I was demanding, selfish, arrogant and ran that poor young man ragged, but he kept bringing me flowers and candy and putting up with my nonsense. Lorne's father said I just needed a good, swift kick, but Lorne didn't believe him.

Lorne was a cabbie, and I started driving a cab when I was pregnant with David. No one wanted to hire you to work in an office if you were pregnant, so driving a cab seemed like the job for me. There was equal pay for equal work in a cab, and I liked meeting people. I wore baggy shirts, and customers didn't know I was pregnant.

Lorne was born on a farm in Crystal City, Manitoba, and grew up in Snowflake, Manitoba. He pitched for a ball team and we would go out to tournaments all the time. Lorne's a solid six-foot-four and was good enough at football to try out for the Winnipeg Blue Bombers a couple of times. He played semi-pro football, and we frequently used to have the football team out at our place. A lot of the same guys played for the ball team, and there were always parties going on. We took our kids everywhere with us, because that was the lifestyle. We used to pack up the kids every weekend and we'd go out to these ball games, sitting in the hot sun for hours. We'd get out in these open prairie fields where there wasn't a tree for shade; you'd move around the car to get out of the sun.

Finally one time we went to a tournament in the area where Lorne had grown up. To me, Crystal City should have been a city, all glass and shining and wonderful. As we drove into this dusty little place, I was so disappointed and said, "This is where you were born?" Lorne's family was originally from Denmark, and he belongs to the only Milgaard clan in the entire North American continent. It was a name people remembered, for better or for worse.

I really wasn't a very good mother back then. I was a spoiled brat when I married my husband and I expected to be waited on. I was moody. If Lorne wanted to go out and play ball or do something I didn't want him to do, I would pretend to be ill so that he would stay home and give me attention.

❧

David was born in July 1952 and he was a beautiful child. He was quickly followed by Chris and Susan, and in May 1961, Maureen. We moved nineteen times in eleven years of marriage, always trying to get ahead moneywise, but in retrospect, I know it was hard on all of us.

When David was a toddler, he was just an absolute doll with his beautiful blond curls. He walked and talked early and was on the go all the time. I used to tie him to his bed to keep him out of trouble. We'd tie a cord around his ankle and tie it to a bar in the crib. It wasn't that he was bad, but that he was just always exploring; he'd get up even in the middle of the night and do things. One night, I woke up and found the two-year-old in the kitchen, trying to feed the family cat, Snowflake. He had pulled everything out of the cupboard and had added water to it. Another time, he put Snowflake in the washing machine. It wasn't his intention to hurt the cat. David loved his own bath and just wanted to give the cat one. Luckily, Snowflake survived the ordeal and looked just beautiful.

Our second boy, Chris, was a bouncy child. But when David was two and Chris a little over one and I was pregnant with Susan, Chris began having massive convulsions. To stop the convulsions, doctors performed a surgery that opened up a hole in his skull. After that, Chris had to be held literally all of the time for months.

Even in quiet times, David was a handful, and the months when Chris was ill were anything but a quiet time. A friend of mine offered to take David to stay at her mother's farm until things settled down. Psychiatrists would later say that David felt abandoned, but the truth was that he had a great time on the farm. He really enjoyed himself out there and was cheerful when he came back several months later.

David always thought for himself. One day the minister was walking by and David was pulling up some flowers from the garden. The minister said, "You can't pull out flowers. You can only pull out weeds. God made the flowers." David looked up at him and said, innocently, "Who made the weeds?" David wasn't being sarcastic. The minister had no answer for him.

David was always impulsive and outgoing and hated not being accepted. He would show off to impress other kids. He had trouble at school, not because he couldn't understand the subject matter but because he was a quick learner and felt the need for more excitement. He was never destructive or vindictive, but if a kid was walking down the aisle, bingo, David's foot would go out. Other times, he would head off with his little wagon and, when he came back, he would have collected all of the milk bottles from down the street. He was just a very busy little kid.

As David grew older, his pranks weren't always so cute. When he was around grade seven, he and some other kids in the Winnipeg suburb of St. Boniface where we lived broke into a grain store. He also skipped classes a lot. We took him to a doctor, who put him on phenobarbital, and that helped, but David didn't like taking medication, and the troubles couldn't be eliminated so easily.

It's odd how seemingly small, insignificant events can profoundly change your life. One day, I went for lunch with some people Lorne had met through his work. The woman was a salesperson, selling sewing machines, and I bragged that I could sell anything.

"If you give me a sewing machine, I'll go out and sell it," I said boldly.

She accepted the challenge and set up an appointment for me with a professional seamstress who she expected would be a hard sell. However, I ended up selling the seamstress the professional model, the most expensive machine in the line. All I did was say, "You know everything about the machine. I'm not going to tell you a thing about it. Just give it a go." That's how I ended up going to work for Elna selling sewing machines.

I was at a party with the saleswoman's family when I felt a migraine headache coming on. Periodically, I suffered from migraines, and they were so bad I would have to lie in a darkened room. If anyone made a sound or even touched the bed I would be in agony. I asked the hostess if she had any painkillers. She told me she didn't have any medicine because she was a Christian Scientist. "What's that?" I asked, unable to believe she didn't have anything for pain somewhere in her medicine cabinet.

The hostess explained that God was their medicine and they relied wholly on spiritual means for healing, just as Jesus did. Instead of medicine, she said a prayer for me, and amazingly enough, my headaches vanished. At the time, I thought perhaps I had been mistaken, that I was not really going to have a migraine after all. Even so, a seed had been planted.

At that time, we had three young kids, and we were constantly swamped with medical bills. I would come down with one virus or another, and there always seemed to be someone in the family who was sick. Here was this hostess with these perfect two kids and no medical bills, and apparently no financial problems either. I wondered why they could do it and not us. I asked her some questions and she gave me a copy of *Science and Health with Key to the Scriptures*, by Mary Baker Eddy, who had established the Christian Science church in New England in the second half of the nineteenth century.

Christian Scientists believe that prayer is the most effective medicine and the true path to healing. When I went to my first Christian Science meeting in Winnipeg, I thought their claims were far-fetched, but I was impressed with how rich the people seemed. Several of the women wore mink coats and the parking lot was filled with fine cars. When I saw all of this, I thought, "If this is Christian Science, I want some of this." I was really materially minded.

On a less superficial level, I was also intrigued by the people's sense of inner calm. The service itself wasn't too impressive. Christian Science doesn't have ministers in the usual sense. The church's ordained pastor is not a person but two books. At a Sunday service, two people stood up and read, one from the Bible and the other from *Science and Health*. I had to fight to stay awake through it. I guess I really missed the choir and the fiery sermon that I was used to. Next, I went to a Wednesday service, and it was better. At one point, people in the audience got up and spoke, making all sorts of weird claims. However, when I spoke with them after the service, they didn't seem at all weird. Some of them were respected, educated people in the community. There was nothing flaky about them. A door was starting to open for me, but Christian Science is a discipline and I was not a very disciplined person.

I attended Anglican Sunday school every week when I was a child in Peterborough, and I sang in the choir. However, my faith left me when the minister, his wife and their baby all died of polio. The minister had been young and attractive and looked just like Frank Sinatra. I had idolized him. If God can take these people away, I thought, what kind of person was He? But it wasn't so easy to kick religion out of my life, I found. When I was working in the hospital in Peterborough with the nuns, I saw something that demonstrated to me the power of faith. The nun who ran the hospital, Sister Theophanie, was stricken with cancer. When the doctor operated, he saw how extensive the cancer was and just closed her up without doing anything. Her arms were just skin and bone, literally, but she refused to allow any amputation. More important, Sister Theophanie refused to make peace and lie down to die. Instead, she got her Mother Superior's permission to travel to the religious shrine at Sainte-Anne-de-Beaupré, near Quebec City. She returned full of health and strength, a far cry from the cadaverous condition she had left in.

One day I saw Sister Theophanie typing and was amazed. Her arms still had no muscle on them. Like the bumblebee that shouldn't be able to fly, she shouldn't have been able to type. I can't explain it. Neither could her doctor, who had given her only weeks to live. She survived more than a decade, and her doctor had no scientific explanation for it. While I found this curious, my faith had faded away by the time I was married. I just felt that I didn't want anything to do with God.

Now, however, as I started to read *Science and Health*, I became excited. I liked the idea of a God of Love who had the tender qualities of both a father and a mother. I had been taught as a child about a God of vengeance, hellfire and damnation, and I had been a miserable sinner in my books and always would be one. The God

I grew up with was an avenging father, a bit like my dad when he had too much to drink. Now I was being taught that I wasn't so bad. I was made in God's image and likeness. As an Anglican, I was born into sin; in Christian Science I was born in love. I was made in God's likeness, perfect and spiritual. I lapped up the thought of being good, and I also was attracted to the positive picture of the world it was painting.

Mrs. Eddy wrote that because God was totally good, sickness was an illusion produced by human belief, and that the only true reality was the spiritual one. She believed in actions, not just talk, and insisted that believers head out into the world and show the truths that Jesus taught. I had always been a doer, so this sense of action also appealed to me. To join the Mother Church in Boston, I had to be free of alcohol, tobacco and drugs for at least a year, which was quite a feat for me back in the early 1960s. I also had to get over my habit of blaming others for anything that went wrong in my life. It was tough not to be able to blame my mother or father or siblings or anyone else.

I was smoking two packs of cigarettes a day when I first came in contact with Christian Science. One night I ran out and I asked Lorne to pick some up at a bar. While he was out he bumped into a friend and was gone for a long time. When he got home, I was angry. I really thought I needed the nicotine. Suddenly I felt as if I was outside my body, looking down on myself, and what I saw was a screaming fishwife. I thought, "Look at that crazy woman. She has made a god out of a cigarette."

Then I heard the words from the Bible: "Thou shalt have no other gods before Me." When Lorne threw the cigarettes at me, I didn't want them any more, and I haven't smoked since.

Lorne didn't believe in Christian Science, but he respected it and defended me. I think the kids found it easier than adults to accept the simple principles of Christian Science because they weren't tainted by beliefs about germs and illnesses and medicine. I told them that God knows no imperfection and that illness was an illusion. One day David caught his hand in a car door and ran to me screaming. I reminded him of the truths he was learning in Sunday school and I wrapped something around his hand. There was no sign of damage later that day.

Not long after I discovered Christian Science, our fourth child was born. Maureen had an accident in the bath when she was a baby, and was scalded. Her little body was covered with blisters. I wrapped her in a blanket as Lorne ran to call a doctor. I asked him to let me phone a Christian Science practitioner instead. The practitioner said God had a plan for everyone. Minutes after the call, Maureen stopped screaming and I put her to bed. Poor Lorne was worried that his negative thoughts might hurt things and offered to leave the house. I laid little Maureen in the crib and she went right to sleep. I kept going in and checking on her. When she woke up, she was fine. No blisters!

At first, my mother wanted to talk me out of Christian Science. She even contacted an Anglican minister to "save" me from it. She didn't know it was a religion based on Jesus' teachings and the Bible and thought it was some sort of a cult. However, when she saw how my life and outlook were changing, she left well enough alone.

The changes took a while, but I gradually understood how selfish I had been and how I had put myself first and my husband, kids and others next. I also realized how I often had exaggerated things, which violated the Christian Science teachings of honesty. Mrs. Eddy said, "Honesty is spiritual power. Dishonesty is human weakness which forfeits divine help."

I was impressed with the Bible as a history book, with its marvellous examples of how good triumphs. One of the stories I identified with was the story of David and his battle with Goliath, which taught patience, perseverance and optimism. Soon, I would be living that story.

My involvement with Christian Science wasn't the only change in our lives in the early 1960s. In 1964 Lorne's brother, Calvin, found a well-paying job at a potash mine in Esterhazy, Saskatchewan. Although I was doing well at Elna selling sewing machines, Lorne had been running a restaurant in Winnipeg and it simply wasn't working financially. So, we packed up everything and went to the tiny farming community of Langenburg, near Esterhazy. Lorne got a job in the potash mine, and shortly after that we bought a lovely little house with a big backyard for $6,000, on a rent-to-own plan at $50 a month.

Lorne's job wasn't the only reason we moved out of Winnipeg. At twelve, David was a handful, and was always into something. Our doctor and a guidance counsellor felt he needed to be out in the country where he could run and get rid of his extra energy. The move promised the fresh start we badly needed.

But David was a lot like me, restless and eager to get out in the world. One night in 1965, he and a friend took a truck for a joyride. They didn't damage it, but the owner pressed charges and the case went to court.

We felt we couldn't cope with David. We thought perhaps he could be placed in some kind of a school. We tried to get him into a Winnipeg boys' school with some discipline and structure; we felt that it was pretty loose at the school he attended in Langenburg. We were told that if he was made a ward of the court, we could get him into the Winnipeg school, so we reluctantly agreed. It was a decision both Lorne and I would regret for many years.

It turned out that they weren't able to get him into that school, and because they had nowhere to put him, they placed him in the psychiatric centre in Yorkton. It was a disaster, a totally unsuitable environment for a young man. He learned lots of bad habits from the kids he met while he was in government care. It was very sad the way things turned out for David in Yorkton, even though the centre tried to rectify it by transferring him, after three months, to a foster home and letting him go to the Yorkton high school. We hoped that would be more challenging for him, but he soon got into more trouble, shoplifting. He didn't finish high school, leaving midway through grade nine.

FOUR

A SON LIKE ME

"This has got to be resolved. It's a terrible crime."
David on the murder of Gail Miller

DAVID DID HIS BEST to explain to me the events of
January 31, 1969. However, it would not be until years
after the crime, after countless hours of digging, that I
would have a full picture of the events of that horrible
morning. It was true that David was in Saskatoon the
day that Gail Miller was murdered, and this unfortunate
timing would come back to haunt him. He was out on
a road trip with his new-found friends, Ron Wilson and
Nichol John. Ron had long, greasy hair and an untrust-
worthy air. Nichol was very pretty, with a clear complex-
ion and dark attractive eyes. The three met in a park in
Regina and were rambling across western Canada, in
search of drugs and fun. David had some extra time
while he waited for his vendor's licence to come through,
which would allow him to sell magazines in B.C., and
he wanted to hook up with an old girlfriend north of
Calgary. On the way, they went to Saskatoon to see

David's friend Albert Cadrain and perhaps persuade him to join the trip. Most important, they hoped Albert, whom they called Shorty, could come up with some money for marijuana. Shorty was a simple-minded boy whom many young people, including David, took advantage of. I thought he was a gentle, harmless boy, although that opinion would change.

David and Ron stole a battery from a car, placed it in Ron's beat-up car, and the three of them crowded into the front seat and headed out of Regina shortly after midnight on January 31, 1969. They took their time, arriving in Saskatoon early the next morning. None of them knew Saskatoon well, and David was familiar with only a few landmarks around Shorty's house, in a working-class residential neighbourhood. Not surprisingly, they were soon lost, and ended up asking for directions at a motel on the outskirts of the city shortly after seven. Even for Saskatchewan, it was a bitterly cold morning, −42°F, with lots of snow and little visibility. They had been driving around looking for a church David thought he would recognize near the Cadrains' house. They were going down a back alley when they saw a car that was stuck, and David prevailed upon Ron, who was driving, to stop and help the people. It was a vehicle owned by a man named Walter Danchuk. In trying to get to the Danchuks', the boys themselves got stuck. David and his friends waited in the Danchuk home for a tow truck to arrive.

Around 9 a.m., they finally made it to Shorty's house at 334 Avenue O, a tiny white box of a bungalow. David and his friends spent the rest of the day at Shorty's house while the car was being fixed and then headed off to Edmonton. They had no idea of the drama that was taking place all around them.

At eight-thirty that morning, the partially frozen body of Gail Miller had been found about a block from Shorty's home. Shorty's modest home looked far too small to have a basement apartment, but it did. Living in the basement were a young couple from the Battleford area, Linda and Larry Fisher. Larry had been out all night, and Linda suspected he was cheating on her. He missed work that morning, which was out of character. Curiously, Linda could not find their kitchen paring knife. When Larry finally returned home that morning, Linda had already heard news of the Miller murder on the radio and exploded, "My paring knife is missing. You're probably the one who's out stabbing that girl." Linda didn't really think it was true, and had just wanted to upset him, but she found his reaction chilling. "He looked at me like a guilty person who'd just been caught," Linda later recalled. "The colour drained from his face and he looked shocked and scared."

Years later, I would learn plenty more about that morning, including what Shorty's little sister, Rita, saw in her home. The elementary-school student didn't often play in the basement by the Fisher apartment, but the day of the murder Rita went to the downstairs bedroom. There, she found a pile of bloody clothes. She told friends at school that she was scared to sleep down there, but they wouldn't make a connection between the little girl's strange story and the death of Gail Miller. Rita liked to be dramatic about things, and nobody paid much attention to her latest story.

David didn't bump into Larry and Linda Fisher that day. Had they met, Linda immediately would have noticed how different David was from her husband. David was tall, slim, left-handed and a shaggy-haired hippie, while Fisher was short, powerfully built, right-handed, part-native and conservative looking. They weren't just different physically. David arrived places when the spirit moved him, while Larry was almost always early, and might be considered a workaholic. David moved with the breezes, while Larry Fisher liked things done in a patterned, methodical way. On the surface, Fisher was the type of married working man police could relate to, while my David was a strange outsider and the type of young man who gave police officers the shivers, especially if they had daughters.

I was forced to become an expert on the murder through years of effort. I now know that, within three days of Gail Miller's murder, the police were clearly frustrated. This wasn't Detroit or Toronto, and the Saskatoon police weren't used to dealing with murderers of any kind, let alone the type of sick predator who had killed Gail Miller. They offered a $2,000 reward to anyone providing information leading to the arrest and conviction of the killer, and clearly they sensed something frightening was being played out on the streets of their city. On February 4, 1969, the *Regina Leader-Post* headlined a story "Killer Possible Rapist." The story began, "Police are investigating the possibility that the person who slashed a twenty-year-old nurses' aide to death Friday may be the same person who attacked three women here last fall." It was a pretty obvious story, since it seemed impossible not to wonder about a link between Gail Miller's killer and the serial rapist who had been preying on the city's women. The news report was terse and left out a lot of things that must have been troubling for police. It did not mention that the rapist was showing a preference for women in white uniforms, like nursing aide Gail Miller, or that he sometimes rode the bus with his victims.

I would learn, much later, that police officers scoured Shorty's neighbourhood, and on February 5, 1969, an officer talked with Larry Fisher as he waited for the bus to take him to work. He was standing at the same bus stop where Gail Miller had waited for her bus to work. The police report notes, "Works at Masonery Contractors at the Education Bldg U. of Sask. Wearing yellow hard hat. States last Friday he caught bus at 6.30 a.m. at Ave. O. and 20th Street. He states there was no one else around at that time and he had no information to offer." The officer didn't speak to Linda, so he didn't learn that, when Larry Fisher said he went to work the morning of the murder, he was lying.

No fingerprints, footprints or eye witnesses pointed police towards the killer. What they did have were plenty of potential suspects, and enormous pressure to catch the killer. A police report from February 9 notes that a burly taxi driver had been driving the night of the slaying. Later, he talked to his girlfriend about Gail

Miller's murder, asking, "What if I did it?" spooking her enough to call police. There were also suspicions about a French-Canadian man in his early twenties, with long hair and sideburns. A February 10 police report states that he was excitable and "he may even be a sex pervert." That report also notes that he tried to get a lawyer's daughter "to obtain a book for him written by Marcus Seraid which apparently is on the subject of sexual perversion." Obviously, the report's author had never heard of the Marquis de Sade.

For a short time, there were concerns about an old boyfriend of Gail Miller's who had a punch-up with another young man who'd showed an interest in her. Also watched by police were an apparently mentally ill man who lived close to Miller and a heavy drinker who bragged to an old girlfriend that he would soon make the front pages of newspapers. An oddball who drank heavily raised suspicions when he told a bar waitress, "I'd like to kill you and then I would forever have the vision of your face on my mind." Police noted that a fifteen-year-old Cree boy originally from the Standing Buffalo Reserve near Fort Qu'Appelle went missing from his residence in Saskatoon, allegedly to attend native games back on the reserve. Then there was a call about a strange character who would smirk and sit beside women on the bus, even when there were other open seats. Another man actually tried to confess to committing the murder and then fled to Vancouver. In the end, despite the long list of suspects, police were frustrated and empty-handed.

David's life changed forever when Shorty Cadrain was arrested that winter in Regina for vagrancy. Shorty told the police he was in Saskatoon with David and his other friends the day of the murder. He said none of them had anything to do with the murder, but after he got back to Saskatoon, Shorty's active imagination was shifting into high gear, and he told his brother Dennis that he had seen blood on David's pants. Soon, Shorty was telling a wild story and David was under investigation.

I had no way of knowing at the time about the pressures that were being applied to David's motley carload of friends. I now know that in May 1969, Saskatoon police went to Regina on orders from the chief of police to pick up David's friends Ron Wilson and Nichol John for interrogation in Saskatoon.

Investigators ripped apart Ron Wilson's car and found nothing. At first, Ron and Nichol were no help, as they told similar stories that painted themselves and David as innocent. Gail Miller's bloodstained clothes were thrown in front of Nichol to jar her memory. Still she couldn't remember anything unusual. A bloody knife was shown to her. Still no memories for police. Horrific photos of Gail Miller lying dead in the snow didn't seem to help either. Although no charges were laid against Nichol, she was locked up overnight, alone in an unfinished, empty wing of the jail.

Sometime late that night, Nichol snapped and began sobbing hysterically. They had to bring in a female matron to calm her. The next morning, police drove her to the scene of the murder, then took her back to the station to talk with Ron Wilson, who was being interrogated. Something changed dramatically. Nichol couldn't handle another night in the lockup. When she was questioned again, she began saying the things police so badly wanted to hear. Nichol was given her freedom and, she hoped, some peace.

As Nichol now told the story, she had witnessed David pull a knife on Gail Miller and kill her that horrible morning. Her story didn't make sense, though, since Gail Miller was found with her dress down around her waist and her coat still on. There were stab cuts in the coat but none in the dress. For Nichol's story to be true, David would have had to undress Gail Miller, stab her, put her coat back on and then stab her some more. That's not even close to what Nichol described, but police didn't seem to mind. David would also have had to have raped her outdoors at 42 degrees below zero. There was almost no time for David to have committed such a crime, nor any motive. Nichol's story also didn't explain the other rapes in the neighbourhood, where women were attacked in the same fashion as Gail Miller in October, November and December 1968. Her story did, however, satisfy the police.

I now know that Nichol wasn't the only one pressured to implicate David. Ron Wilson later called his lengthy interrogation by police a "sweat session," while Shorty Cadrain described his questioning as "hell and mental torture." Years later, Shorty would recall, "I was questioned for ten to twelve hours. I felt that they were accusing me of the murder. When they finally brought me home late that night I was mentally drained and shaking." That questioning was repeated some fifteen to twenty times, Shorty said; "I remember two detectives in particular . . . working me over. They worked like a tag team; one would be the bad guy and the other would act like he was my friend. The bad guy would scream at me, then the other would offer me coffee and cigarettes. Then they would switch roles.

"They asked me the same questions repeatedly, time after time after time, until I was exhausted and couldn't take it anymore. This went on for months, continuing through the preliminary hearing. They put me through hell and mental torture. It finally reached the point where I couldn't stand the constant pressure, threats and bullying anymore."

This treatment left Shorty spitting up blood from stomach ulcers. He also became even more paranoid than usual. He later said, "At one point I had told the detectives about David Milgaard bragging about being in the Mafia. After they finally finished with all of the questioning and interrogation, police advised me that I was the star witness and said I'd better find some place to hide because they didn't want the Mafia to kill me. Those detectives pushed me over the edge and I cracked."

FIVE

ON TRIAL

"They're lying, Mom, they're absolutely lying."
David watches his friends testify against him in court

ON HIS FIRST DAY behind bars in Saskatoon, David had a chat with a taxi driver who shared his cell. David told the cabbie he was innocent. This was the first of countless times in custody that David would avow his innocence. David turned seventeen in jail in the summer of 1969, waiting for his case to be heard by the courts. We were assigned a lawyer from legal aid, Calvin Tallis, who had a good reputation but seemed very official and very distant. Money was tight for us, and I considered camping in a tent to save money as I moved to Saskatoon to be near my son. I ended up taking a room at the Y, although later my friends Jim and Jackie Groat took me in, for which I was very grateful. I applied for a job working nights at a Chinese restaurant. The owner looked at my hands and said that it looked as if I had had a soft, pampered life. "These hands can work hard," I told him, and he hired me.

I got up early so that I could go to the jail cell and take David some comic books and a milkshake. I worked until two or three in the morning, waitressing and washing dishes. Once, the Crown prosecutor, Thomas David Roberts (Bobs) Caldwell, came in for a meal, and I was sure I could see him smirking at me. I don't really remember him physically, just his presence. He struck me as arrogant and full of the power he held over us. There was something scary about him, and he seemed to be trying to be flowery, like he was playing the role of a big-city prosecutor.

My visits with David in jail were only five or ten minutes each, and always under the eyes of police officers. I didn't know that they were filing reports to the police chief on whatever we said or did. Reports I later obtained showed that I was already trying to play detective. One police note stated, "From 6:00 p.m., to 6:20 p.m., June 2nd, 1969, Cst. Little and I stood guard over David Milgaard in the interview room, next to the Sergeant's Lunch Room, while Milgaard's mother visited him. During the course of conversation Mrs. Milgaard asked David, 'Shorty's' last name and address, so that she might interview him in connection with the case. She also intimated that she was going to interview Wilson and Nichol John regarding the case. Mrs. Milgaard was advised by me that before she attempts to interview any Police witnesses, she either speak to the Chief of Police, or her son's lawyer or the Agent for the Attorney General, regarding the matter."

A report from June 13 noted, "Mrs. Milgaard brought spare ribs, rice, and a glass of milk, (in plastic container), plus five sticks of Denteen chewing gum. There was no conversation relating to Occurrence # 641/69." It seemed odd and cold that the horrible murder of a young woman could be reduced in the legal system to "Occurrence #641/69."

Another report, from a morning meeting that day, read, "Milgaard was handcuffed to Cst. B. Sears, separated by a length of chain and I was the only other person present in this room, which was locked during this visit. Mrs. Milgaard brought one brownie square, one banana and one quarter container of milk. Milgaard ate the banana and brownie square and drank one paper cup of milk. Mrs. Milgaard took the remainder of the milk with her when she left. She also brought three pocket novels which David was permitted to take to his cell with him. David Milgaard indicated he had not been given his stationery in order that he may write letters. Staff Sgt. Kalthoff was advised of this situation. The conversation between Mrs. Milgaard and David consisted mainly of the clothing he should wear when he appeared in court next Monday. She also indicated she would be visiting him again at 2:00 p.m. and sometime later in the evening this date. She also left a clean shirt for David which he was permitted to take to his cell."

And this is a report from June 16: "Mrs. Milgaard gave Dave a small book dealing with bible study lessons. During conversation Mrs. Milgaard relayed a message from Mr. Tallis to the effect that Dave should watch his conduct as this could be used in court. She also inquired as to his sleeping habits and warned him about disturbing others during night while he slept all day."

The courthouse in Saskatoon was imposing, with pillars in the front. I had never been in a courthouse before, and I found it intimidating when the preliminary hearing began. In an attempt to make sense of things, I kept a notebook throughout the proceedings. The August 18, 1969, entry included the quote, "Wherefore the law was our schoolmaster TO BRING US unto Christ, that we might be justified by faith," Galatians 3:24. Describing the court proceedings, I wrote, "Start with . . . identification officer told about arrival at scene position of body pictures of body, arrangement of clothing all horrible — (couldn't be David) Girl's mother sat through it all — Couldn't help thinking of her . . . Didn't like watching or looking or listening about photographs."

A police officer testified that Gail Miller's wounds were from two types of blades, single- and double-edged. Perhaps I was grasping at straws, but I found this hopeful, writing, "Tremendous feeling elation. David couldn't use 2 knives. Lorne says didn't prove anything. Both David and I jubilant."

David was clearly unsettled about life in jail. His life was now regimented, his freedom a thing of the past. That Wednesday, I wrote in my notebook, "David upset at aft visit. Had experience with police officers. Gave cigarette to other prisoners. Wasn't supposed to. Took his cigs away from him . . . Talked to him. He apologized after in Eve. had cigs with him and all was fine."

The next day, I went shopping. "Interesting thing happened at IGA. Owner asked where I was from.

When I said Langenburg he commented, 'Oh you have a real bad boy from there.' He was completely taken aback when I replied, 'You mean my son, who was supposed to have killed that nurse. Well, he didn't. He's innocent and is not a bad boy.' Felt really sorry for him. He apologized all over the place. Said he knew people who had met David who also felt he was not guilty."

That Friday, a police officer noted that Gail Miller had wounds on the left side of her throat. A light flashed on inside my head. I wrote, "Previous witness had just mentioned throat wounds. Suddenly it came to me that in order to wound a person in the left side it would normally be done by someone holding a knife in the right hand. I could hardly wait till the adjournment to ask if Mr. Tallis was aware that David was left-handed." I passed this information on to Tallis, and he was able to introduce it, although not as dramatically as I might have liked.

On Saturday, court was out for the weekend, and I was trying to keep David amused. I wrote, "Visited 3 times took 3 pocket books. 2 or 3 comics and paper taken Fri. Found out Sat. night books had been destroyed by one of the policemen for no apparent reason."

On Sunday evening, I wrote, "Police station quite quiet. Only one man on desk. Phone keeps ringing. Very hard strident tones — gets to you quickly. Sergeant on desk is one who was first at scene of crime. Testified the other day. Very quiet polite and efficient. David wants me to sneak in deck of cards. They have made a home-made deck out of cigarette packs but he says it is getting pretty messy. Desk sergeant asks us to break it up after about 8 minutes as others waiting."

That Monday: "Took David juice and fruit. Looked odd this morning. Didn't seem to be communicating. Had one glass of juice. Took fruit upstairs. Left me after about 4 minutes to go back up." And Monday night: "Took Dave cheeseburger and milk. Arrived at station. Policeman at desk wanted to know how come I was there only 2 visits allowed per day. Told him always came 3 times. Then sergeant informed me no food allowed prisoners from 6 at night till morning. I made no comment but when Dave was brought in to the room ask det. and policemen what they knew about this and they said it was all new to them. I mentioned the food had cost a dollar and I rather hated it to go to waste so det. went to desk and they said ok for tonight but must check with deputy next day." Clearly, even for little things, the guards held all of the power now. I was the mother of an accused killer, and shouldn't expect much. We hadn't been high class before, but we had clearly dropped a couple of rungs with the charges against David.

Thursday, September 4, 1969, was a key day in the preliminary. Nichol John was on the stand as the twenty-fourth Crown witness. Calvin Tallis had prepared me for this day, saying that we were going to hear a lot of negative testimony about David from his friends, but we shouldn't worry because the court would soon find out that the so-called friends were lying. He assured us that there was nothing to their stories. Nichol was clearly a troubled young woman, and that would come across in her testimony.

She looked like a little slip of a girl as she testified, and her appearance was quite haggard. When she was on the road, she used drugs often and now, without the chemicals in her system, she looked frightened and vulnerable. She told the court that she had first met David in a park in downtown Regina and that they were soon having sex together, but she didn't really consider him her boyfriend. She testified that David broke into a grain elevator en route to Saskatoon from Regina and returned to the car with a flashlight and a hunting knife with a carved bone handle. She said there was a paring knife with a maroon handle in the car. They discussed purse snatching, she said. She said she couldn't recall seeing any blood on David's pants after the stopover at Shorty's. After they left Saskatoon, she said, David drove recklessly on the trip to Calgary, and that she found a white plastic bag with a powder pack, eyeshadow and lipstick inside. She said David tossed it out the window when she asked where it was from.

Nichol's testimony was damaging but not damning. At least she was no longer telling the story she had told police after her breakdown in the jail wing. In that story, she claimed to have witnessed David killing Gail Miller.

My hopes were dashed, however, when at the end of the hearing Mr. Justice H.J. Cummings announced that there was enough of a case against David for him to stand trial.

"What does this mean?" I asked Tallis. "You said that there was nothing, that there was no way."

"Well, it's unfortunate, but we're going to have to go to trial," he replied.

I had never felt a connection with Tallis, and I certainly wasn't doing so now. I never questioned how we got Tallis from legal aid. I only knew that he was the one that was assigned to the case, and he was the expert. However, he reassured us that it was no big deal that the judge ruled that there was enough evidence for a trail. The point of the preliminary was simply to get a look at the Crown's case, Tallis said. Now that he had seen it, Tallis said he was absolutely certain that we had nothing to fear.

I tried to reassure David, but there wasn't time, as they whisked him away from the courtroom. Later, in the holding cells, I knew I had to look strong for him and said, "Look, we're going to beat this. It's just going to take a little longer than we expected to get you out."

In my heart I wondered what purpose God had in this. Perhaps, I decided, that purpose was for David to see how much trouble he could get in just because of the people he hung around with. Perhaps the trial would straighten him out and he'd start picking his friends better.

We placed our trust in Tallis, and didn't mind when no motion was made to move the trial anywhere else, even though Gail Miller's murder received massive publicity in Saskatoon. People there clearly wanted a conviction, to put their minds at ease that the killer was no longer in their midst. Today, I know that a change of venue could have and probably should have been sought.

Tallis told us to buy David a suit for the trial. Just attending the trial pinched us financially, but I scraped together pennies from waitressing and managed to pay $75 for a deep green suit at Simpsons-Sears. David looked so good in it that I felt a little better.

~

The trial began on Monday, January 19, 1970. I spent the morning getting things to take to David. I bought him a milkshake and I bought a coffee pot so that we could make coffee during the breaks. We didn't have the money to buy coffee by the cup.

When I thought logically about the case, my nerves calmed down for a little while. The Crown based everything on a far-fetched theory that David was an impulse rapist who asked a woman he had never seen before for directions, didn't like her answer, and so he raped and murdered her in – 42-degree weather. There had never been any suggestion that David was a rapist before this, and the theory seemed too absurd to be a real threat to his liberty.

The courtroom was so crowded when the trial began that observers lined the walls and the back of the room. Some spectators even sat on the floor. Lorne glanced over at Gail Miller's family as the trial opened but I don't think that I did. It was just a blur to me.

One of the keys to the case against David was his friend Nichol John. She again looked haggard and drawn as she told the jury in a soft voice that she, David and Ronald Dale Wilson arrived in Saskatoon on the morning of January 31 at six-thirty, and that they stopped the car after seeing a woman on the side of the street. David supposedly asked her for directions to the Pleasant Hill district. Nichol said the woman told them she didn't know, and they drove on for about half a block, and that their car got stuck on ice. It took about five minutes to free it, then they changed directions so that they were now driving towards the woman. Nichol said their car became stuck again in another alley, behind a funeral home. Then, she said, David and Ron Wilson left the car for a couple minutes.

Interestingly, the police had interviewed hundreds of people who had been in the area that morning, and not one of them reported seeing a stuck car, but we wouldn't know this for years. Tallis also didn't know this, since it was not disclosed to him by the Crown, even though it is the Crown's duty to disclose all information that would tend to establish the innocence of the accused.

Nichol said she saw a knife in David's right hand. That again struck me as odd, since David is left-handed. When David and Ron returned to the car, Nichol said, they decided to go for help.

Crown prosecutor Bobs Caldwell wanted to hear more from her. "Now, Miss John, I put it to you that this is something you absolutely would never forget, if you saw that happen."

Nichol was Caldwell's witness, but she wasn't playing along as fully as Caldwell wanted. She wasn't describing a stabbing, as she had done in the police statement she gave after her breakdown.

"As far as I'm concerned, I don't know what happened," she replied, clearly flustered. "I don't even know whether I was on that trip or not."

"Yes! Yes!" I said to myself as I watched Nichol struggle on the witness stand. I couldn't understand why Tallis didn't get up and do something. Perhaps I had watched too much of the heroic TV lawyer Perry Mason. I expected Tallis to act like him and solve everything. But that never happened.

Nichol told court that when they left the car, Ron Wilson went to the left and David went to the right. Wilson returned first, followed by David, who looked cold. Both David and Ron changed their pants when they eventually reached Shorty Cadrain's house, putting on new ones from a suitcase.

After they left Saskatoon, Nichol said she checked the glove compartment and found a plastic cosmetics bag with a powder compact, eyeshadow and lipstick. When she asked whose it was, she said, David grabbed it and threw it out the window. She testified she hadn't seen a cosmetics bag when she checked the glove compartment earlier, as they were driving out of Regina. She said David and Ron didn't seem to be under the influence of drugs that day.

Bobs Caldwell clearly wanted more — nothing less than a graphic description of a sex slaying. Caldwell asked permission to have Nichol declared a hostile witness, which meant he would have the chance to cross-examine her.

Caldwell pulled out the statement she had signed after her all-night ordeal in the police station and read from it: "'All I can recall is of him stabbing her with a knife.'" Nichol was now so rattled she testified she couldn't recall making the statement. Caldwell pressed on, reading, "'Dave reached into one of his pockets and pulled out a knife . . . I can't remember which pocket. I don't know if Dave had a hold of this girl or not. All I recall is of him stabbing her with a knife.'"

By the time Caldwell was through, the jury heard every word of her eleven-page statement. Nichol was sobbing now, saying she couldn't recall saying those words to police. The judge was losing patience, firmly telling her, "You have shown that you are able to stop crying, so stop crying now."

Nichol stopped. It was strange for someone to be able to turn on and off the tears so quickly, like an actress. The mother in me felt sorry for her. However, as David's mother, I wanted to tell her, "Cut it out. Tell them what you can tell them. Keep going. You can keep going. Tell the truth. Tell the truth. That is all we're looking for — the truth." I kept hoping that she would be strong enough to tell them that they were wrong. I think she needed someone to urge her to be honest. If Tallis had gotten up and appealed to her sense of decency, maybe the case against David would have stopped right there. I think she was scared. I think that all this mumbo-jumbo business about her not remembering was untrue, and just a way of letting herself off the hook.

Tallis was at a severe disadvantage when it was finally his turn to question Nichol. He was not allowed to cross-examine her on the statement she gave to police damning David because she now denied its contents. He tried to get her to explain how she had made her police statement.

He wanted her to tell the jury that she had broken down at the police station under enormous pressure from police.

"But you hadn't been charged with anything?" Tallis asked.

"No, I hadn't."

Tallis pressed on. "Well, now, were you getting . . . Let's put it this way. Were you still unhappy about being kept there?"

"Yes, I was."

"And were you still anxious to get out of the place as quickly as you could?"

"Yes."

That, however, was as much as she would say. She wouldn't take it the next step and say police had pressured her to lie.

The judge said Nichol's statement implicating David should be taken not as evidence but only as a test of her credibility, but the damage was done, nonetheless. It appeared that Nichol was lying to protect a friend and a sometime lover. How could this statement not have an effect on a jury? It would have been better for us if she had stuck to her incriminating statement, because then Tallis could have questioned her on it. As it stood, the lies were left to hang in the air unchallenged. This back-door means of entering a statement was a legal first in Canada, and later became known as the Milgaard precedent.

Next, it was Shortly Cadrain's turn on the stand. To me, Shorty was a simple, mentally challenged boy whom I had tried to protect from the other kids. Now, he was the star witness for the Crown in a sensational murder trial. It was Shorty who had given police a big break in building a case against David when he told them he had seen blood on David's pants the morning of January 31. For this, Shorty collected a $2,000 reward.

"His brown coat was chewed up by acid, there was a rip on the crotch of his pants and blood on his clothes," Cadrain told the court. "I saw blood on his shirt and on his pants."

As he testified, Shorty clearly wanted to appear tough. Yet he never looked in my direction, probably because he knew I knew he was lying.

Shorty said David changed out of his bloody clothes in a living room crowded with people. He told how they started out for Edmonton but took the wrong road and ended up on the highway to Calgary. After getting back from their trip, Shorty said he was picked up in Regina for vagrancy and served a week in jail.

Shorty acted strangely when Tallis asked him about why there was blood on David's pants, saying, "I can't tell you why . . . because it's not nice to say." But the court didn't hear Shorty at his strangest, as we would in reinvestigating the case. And the jury unfortunately never heard that Shorty was diagnosed as a paranoid schizophrenic. They just heard Shorty describing David as a crazyman.

Jurors would never hear that Shorty's address, 334 Avenue O South, was also the home of serial rapist Larry Fisher. The court would never even hear the name Larry Fisher. Jurors would not hear how little Rita Cadrain had found bloody clothes in the basement by Larry Fisher's apartment. There would be nothing from Linda Fisher about how strangely her husband reacted when she accused him of the murder.

When David's other friend from that trip, Ron Wilson, took the stand, he also turned on David. To me, Ron looked like an ex-convict who didn't want to go back into custody. He told the court he heard David say "I fixed her" while getting back into the car.

"He's lying, Mom, he's absolutely lying," David told me during a break.

David had looked horror-stricken as he watched his so-called friends turn on him, one by one. His face was ashen at times, and at other times, he seemed so angry that I thought he would jump up and say something. When we went out of the courtroom on breaks, he would say, "How could they do this? How could they do this? It's all lies. None of that happened." These were his friends and they were lying about him. And it wasn't just one lie. It was lie after lie after lie.

Police investigator Joseph Penkala told court that a bloodstained knife was found in the snow under where Gail Miller's body had been. Her right breast was exposed, her panties and girdle were around her ankles, and her right boot was missing. Her hair was mussed and matted with snow and her fists were clenched. Penkala concluded there had been a struggle there, as the snow was trampled and bloodstained.

Court heard that the contents of Miller's purse were strewn from her body to Shorty Cadrain's house. Her wallet and a bloodstained toque were found near Shorty's house, where David had visited that day. Unfortunately, court never heard that this trail also led to Larry Fisher.

The attack on Gail Miller was so furious that the paring knife had apparently snapped inside her body. Dr. Harry E. Emson, chief pathologist at St. Paul's Hospital, said Gail Miller's wounds were consistent with a right-handed killer. Gail Miller had been stabbed twelve times, and there were also about fifteen incisions and cutting wounds at the front of her neck. There was no conclusive evidence of forced intercourse, Dr. Emson said, but Gail could have been raped while she was dead or unconscious. For some reason, the contents of her vagina were not kept by police.

I couldn't stop myself from looking at the Millers as I heard this. I felt so sorry for them. Photos of Gail's bloody body were passed around for the jury to see. I had seen them before. Now I saw them again in my memory and felt sick to my stomach. They were gruesome. Gail's fists were clenched and there was snow in them. She looked as if she had fought and yet there she was, lying in the snow. I knew that if it had been my daughter, I would have had to look at the pictures, but it would have been horrible.

It came as a complete surprise when the Crown introduced two witnesses who hadn't testified at the preliminary. The witnesses, George Lapchuk and Craig Melnyk, told of a bizarre confession made by David, supposedly during a party in a room at the Regina Park Lane Motel in May 1969. They said David re-enacted the murder after seeing it on the television news. According to Lapchuk and Melnyk, David joked that he raped her and stabbed her fourteen times, then re-enacted the crime, stabbing a pillow repeatedly. No one asked them whether David was joking or sarcastic.

I knew this was damning testimony. I looked at the jurors' faces and knew that they believed it. The ironic part was I could easily imagine how David might have jokingly re-enacted the incident just to stop his friends from asking him about being questioned by police. I badly wanted to stand up and say, "Hey, my son would have said that just to get them off his back, never, ever dreaming that it could be said in a courtroom about him."

The credibility of Lapchuk and Melnyk should have been suspect, since they both had serious criminal charges pending against them. Nine days after testifying for the Crown against David, Melnyk received a six-month sentence for armed robbery, the lightest sentence in memory handed out for that crime in Regina. Lapchuk had a criminal record for forgery and conspiring to take David's identification to pass cheques.

So many other parts of the Crown theory were far-fetched. Gail Miller was last seen alive between 6:30 and 6:45 a.m., and David was seen at seven by one witness, leaving a very narrow time frame for him to commit such a crime. I would learn much later about a six-inch knife that the jury wasn't shown. Police found it in the snow on February 28, 1969. Its blade was identical in size to the entry sites on Gail Miller's body, and it hadn't been in the snow long, since there was very little rust on it. The knife's location made it highly probable that Gail Miller was on Avenue O, not on Avenue N, as the Crown had argued. However, the discovery of the knife was not disclosed to our lawyers. If he had been told, Tallis could have used it to attack the testimony of Nichol John and Ron Wilson. We would later hear that this second knife somehow went missing from a police officer's locker.

After sitting in silence for more than a week, hearing people he thought were his friends telling lie after lie, David badly wanted to testify. Tallis recommended, however, that David not testify, so that Tallis could have the advantage of being the last to address the jury. He said that was very important, and Lorne and I recommended that David follow Tallis's advice. The defence called no witnesses, as if to say the Crown's case wasn't worthy of a response. We would agonize over this for decades, but the case against David seemed confusing, and Tallis, the respected lawyer, was the expert.

Mr. Justice A.H. Bence did everything he could to help David. He reminded the jury of eleven men and one woman that David came to them an innocent man and that he did not have to prove anything. The onus was on the Crown to prove beyond a reasonable doubt that he was guilty. I couldn't help but feel a little better as he urged them to consider the credibility of Nichol John, Ron Wilson, George Lapchuk and Craig Melynk. The judge pointed out that during the trial Ron Wilson had said David was away from the car for fifteen minutes, whereas in the preliminary hearing he had said just five minutes.

The judge noted that surprise witnesses Lapchuk and Melnyk testified that David confessed to the murder. However, the judge said that even if the jury decided David said this, they must also decide if David, who was high on drugs at the time of the Regina motel-room party, was telling the truth himself. The judge clearly also had his doubts about Nichol. He asked the jury to ponder the character of a girl who would leave on a trip with two boys she hardly knew and take drugs along the way. The judge added that Wilson, Lapchuk and Melnyk all had criminal records and were admitted drug users.

As the jury deliberated, I was allowed to go back into the cell area with David. We played cards, and the two police officers who were guarding David joked and laughed with us. We were full of hope, sure that he would be freed. The judge's two-hour charge to the jury had been wonderful and we were sure they'd come back with a not-guilty verdict.

After eleven hours, we got word that the jury had reached their decision. Oddly, it was January 31, 1970, a year to the day that Gail Miller was murdered. The guards seemed to sense David would be found not guilty too, because when they took him back to the courtroom the stiffness they had displayed before was gone. Like them, we expected to hear that our family's ordeal was over and that life could return to normal.

David looked handsome as he entered the court for the final time, in his green suit with a gold shirt and tie. He half-smiled at the jury when they entered the courtroom, but for the first time, he clearly looked afraid.

When the jury foreman said "Guilty," David turned to the jury and gave them a weak smile. He later said that he didn't hear the word, but got the verdict from the horror and pain he saw on the faces of his family. I heard a deep, agonizing groan from Lorne, who had always seemed so strong and suddenly looked so weak. I could feel him slump beside me, as if he suddenly dropped from six-foot-four to four-foot-six. David looked at him with disbelief. He was so used to turning to us for help and now we couldn't do a thing.

I felt I was encased in a block of ice. I was numb. I know that I heard the words but I couldn't believe them. I was so cold, so stiff. This couldn't be happening. David was innocent. This is Canada. I was so scared. Lorne squeezed my hand and said, "Don't cry," but the tears poured out as I watched them take David away. David looked so afraid, so young, so vulnerable. He was just seventeen and he was going to prison where we couldn't help him. I tried to wipe back the tears but they wouldn't stop. The last thing David saw before he left the courtroom was Lorne gathering me in his arms as I sobbed uncontrollably.

Gail's father came over to us. He was crying too as he took Lorne's hand and said, "I'm sorry." I would often wonder what he meant by that. Were the Millers as surprised as we were by the verdict? Did they also believe David was innocent? Did they also get the clear message that the judge wanted David acquitted? Or was Mr. Miller simply being a nice man, saying he wished the whole horrible mess hadn't happened? This moment would haunt us for years.

Things blurred even more after that. I remember being in the car and driving back to Langenburg, trying somehow to make sense of what had happened. How were we going to tell Chris, Susan and Maureen? The car radio broadcast the news of David's conviction, so we shut it off. I'd bought a tape of Elvis's latest recording to take home as a treat for the kids. I can't tell you the name of it now but I do remember the flip side. It started out, "Oh Lord, you gave me a mountain. You gave me a mountain to climb." My tears started all over again.

Chris and Susan had already heard the news on the radio by the time we got home, and they were just shattered. Little Maureen still had to be told. How do you tell a seven-year-old child that people have lied about her big brother and that he is going away to prison for a long time? In the eyes of the law, her big brother was now a convicted sex killer, facing the maximum sentence of life in Canada's toughest prisons. Thank God the law had been changed a few years before so that he didn't face the death penalty.

In the days that followed, I watched our family falling apart. Susan, our oldest daughter, was suddenly always on her own. Her best friend thought David was guilty, and so she could no longer be a friend for Susan. Susan, just fourteen, was now doing her very best to replace me, to take over as mother of our family. David's guilty sentence marked the end of her childhood.

Chris, who was fifteen, also tried to help. He had always been very quiet and studious, and now came home with signs of being in scuffles and fights. Most of his friends stood by him, but he was still in a couple of major fights defending his brother's reputation.

No one suffered more than little Maureen. More than once, she was brought home by a teacher after being encircled by children in the schoolyard and taunted, "Your brother is a killer! Your brother is a killer!" She was held, knee-dropped and shoved into a fence by grade-five students. She was pushed down the stairs and screamed at that she was a killer like her brother. She was often told that her family was no good and neither was she. Her grubby, tear-stained face told it all and broke my heart. It wasn't going to be just David who would be suffering. It would be all of us.

Lorne was never one to complain about his problems, and he didn't say a word about what he faced at work. I could only imagine. I did know how uncomfortable it felt to walk into the grocery store and instantly have conversation cease. I'd walk down the street and someone coming towards me would deliberately cross to the other side in mid-block to avoid talking to me. In a small town like Langenburg, something like David's conviction meant instant notoriety, and suddenly we were known as the sex killer's family. Suddenly, in the eyes of many, the name Milgaard meant "murderer."

Lorne's career at International Minerals effectively ended. He had been moving up in the company, but now he was no longer the fair-haired boy. Suddenly there was a stigma attached to his name. Lorne found most people at work reasonably supportive, but it took only a few to cause real pain. He felt the sting of being ostracized in town and became involved in some scuffles and near fights. He was able to hold his temper, despite nasty remarks. Only his great size and strength kept the altercations from getting out of hand.

I would wonder, at times, about Tallis. I think that he was so sure that David was guilty that he didn't feel badly when he was put away. He couldn't have had much confidence in David, or he would have put him on the stand. Tallis was the police association lawyer, and I have often wondered whether his affiliation with the police department had coloured his perception and maybe kept him from digging as deeply as he might have. I would try to comfort myself with the words in *Science and Health with Key to the Scriptures* by Mary Baker Eddy, "Step by step will those who trust Him find that 'God is our refuge and strength, a very present help in trouble.'" I started to take those steps to put aside self-will and wholly rely on God. God knows, I needed a refuge.

Some good people stood by us, like the Kitch family, who took our children and looked after them when we were in Saskatoon for the trial. However, it was soon very evident that we would have to move away. Chris and Lorne stayed on so Chris could finish the school year, and I took Susan and Maureen to Winnipeg. There was no Christian Science church in Langenburg, and I needed the strength of the company of other Christian Scientists. The move to Winnipeg wasn't just for our comfort but also for David. No one else was going to follow up on his story, and in tiny Langenburg I wasn't going to be able to make the kind of money it would take to finance an investigation.

In Winnipeg I worked three jobs at once, waitressing, handling a hospital switchboard and selling jewellery through fashion parties. Then I got a job selling InchMaster, an exercise machine, travelling Manitoba and northern Ontario, promoting it in homes and on TV. There was also work doing promotional programs for a newspaper and a photography studio. Meanwhile, Lorne found a good job running a quarry.

I eventually applied for a job as manager of a little marina shop. It was just what I needed, or so I thought. When I didn't get it, I talked to God about that. He was making a big mistake, I told Him. I could have done the job very well. The location and pay were right. How could somebody else get it? I went on and on. Then in the message at church that week, there was a citation, "Thy will be done." It got through to me. I told God I would be willing to do whatever He had planned for me. I ended up with a far better job, as ticket director and fund director for the Royal Winnipeg Ballet. What had happened? God suddenly got it right? No. It had been necessary for me to let go of my self-will. Looking back over my life, I can see the purpose of each job that I have had. It has been like a golden thread, as each position prepared me for something in the future that I would need. For instance, through my job with the ballet, I learned how to work with volunteers, which would be invaluable in the fight for David's freedom.

During this period, I spent every extra waking moment

in an effort to get David out of prison. People often ask me why, if I've always believed my son innocent, I didn't start from the very first to fight for him. I can only tell them that we did. It's just that no one was aware of it. There was so much for us to learn. None of us had any legal training. We still also thought that he would get out on parole and we could clear his name once he was freed. We still had that Canadian trust in the system.

Meanwhile, although we had no way of knowing it, the serial rapist from Shorty Cadrain's neighbourhood seemed to be striking again. On February 21, 1970 — three weeks after David's conviction — another woman had been attacked in the same neighbourhood as Gail Miller. She worked at the same hospital as Gail and was assaulted in the same way, except for one huge difference: she did not die. A detective with the Saskatoon force remarked to her, "This is just like Gail Miller," but they kept things quiet, and the public was not alarmed.

Obviously, David had an alibi this time. He was in jail, awaiting shipment to prison, as Federal Penitentiary Service prisoner number 289699.

SIX

PRISONER #289699

"He said that had it not been for his parents' support and encouragement, he would have taken his own life some time ago."
Prison report on David shortly after he was locked in maximum-security Saskatchewan Penitentiary in Prince Albert

THE SENTENCE WAS LIFE imprisonment, and that could literally mean the rest of David's life. David was admitted to Saskatchewan Penitentiary on March 2, 1970, a convicted sex murderer in the eyes of the law, and he badly wanted me to provide him with comic books.

A week later, on March 9, a prison report perceptively stated, "This inmate is a quiet, soft-spoken individual who impresses as being a person who is extremely depressed but hides the depression behind a smile. He is holding back a great deal of emotion and on one hand seems anxious to express it and yet is almost afraid to do so. He repeatedly insists on his innocence and is convinced that the appeal courts will verify that this is so. He mentioned that he suffered a great deal from the hostility and hatred that he felt in the courtroom throughout the trial. He said that had it not been for his parents' support and encouragement, he would have taken his own life some time ago. When asked about his plans following his appeal, he was somewhat confused and refused to believe that he would still be in the institution after his appeal had been heard. He is terrified that he may lose his appeal and have to face a lifetime in prison and at this time is convincing himself that suicide is the only answer. Milgaard is still very young and very emotionally immature and will require a great deal of support and encouragement from the staff of this institution if he is to survive this sentence. During the initial interview he did not in any way give the impression that he was manipulative or that he was trying to create [an] 'innocent' picture."

On March 13, a case management worker noted, "Very difficult to believe that this boy could be guilty of this offence. Insists on his innocence and is equally insistent that his appeal will finally prove this. Defenceless, immature, young man, incapable of facing a life sentence at this time. Deeply depressed, very emotional. If his appeal fails Milgaard may well become a case for the psychiatrist."

That final sentence of the March 13 note would take on a haunting quality as time passed. David wasn't crazy going into prison, but that environment was capable of destroying his mind, as it had destroyed so many others. Soon, he was in need of medication. David's prison file notes him saying, on June 12, 1970, "I am becoming very tense because of my coming appeal." The report continues, "He appears tense and agitated. Complains of sleep disturbance. Suggest Valium 5 mg T.I.D."

I will never forget my first visit to the Saskatchewan Penitentiary, as much as I might like to. It was a half day's drive from Langenburg, and the northern Saskatchewan roads at times seemed impassable because of blowing snow. However, David was expecting me and I felt that I had to be there. The stone prison was so huge I couldn't help but feel very small as I approached it. It was both sprawling and tall, like a fortress, with gun towers and armed guards patrolling the grounds. Behind its doors were some of the worst people in the country, and it was so awful to think that David was trapped there. Once inside, I was faced with staff who demanded documents with a tone of authority that frightened me.

How can I explain how it feels to visit a loved one when you can't touch him or hold him? When you are just inches apart, but separated by glass, having to speak into a phone or into a hole in the glass? We pressed our hands against the glass, as if we were touching. My arms just ached to hold him and comfort him, but visits without the glass barriers were something we would have to earn. It is so degrading, so dehumanizing. I drove home the same day after that first visit, since we didn't have the funds for me to stay overnight.

Later, we would let the children come too, but that wasn't easy. Susan and Maureen sometimes could not bear to go because of the glass barrier and the fact that David looked so caged. Many times, it was David who didn't want the visits, but you can't stop visiting. Life trapped inside glass and bars and concrete was David's reality now, and David needed us, even though it was painful for all of us.

That first Mother's Day with David in prison was just heart-wrenching. It was the first time that we had celebrated such a holiday without everyone around. Later we would face the same for Christmas and New Year's and all of the big holidays when the family would get together. In my thoughts there was always an empty chair at the table now. There wasn't much we could do for his birthdays. We could put money in his account and that was basically it. I hated looking for cards to send him. It was so hard to give anything meaningful to someone in prison. I decided to make him cards instead, with lots of pictures of the family, so that he would open it up and see his loved ones.

The drama of the Saskatchewan Court of Appeal ruling on his case didn't compare to the tension of the trial. A letter came in the mail to our home, the envelope marked with the official seal. I took a deep breath, tore it open, and read that the high court had rejected David's appeal on January 31, 1971, two years to the day of Gail Miller's murder, and a year to the day of his conviction. I called Calvin Tallis to ask if David already knew, and he said that he did. That was it. It was an enormously significant event, but somehow it just didn't feel that way. We felt so distant from the appeal process.

That June, David staged a hunger strike, saying, "I will not speak, nor shall I eat. I am silently, non-violently protesting." He saw everything as pointless. He couldn't go anywhere. They took him to the hospital and force-fed him through tubes. Once more David was reminded how powerless he was. On August 4, 1971, a prison psychiatric report noted, "This frightened young inmate is currently very concerned about the outcome of his appeal to the Supreme Court of Canada. The Court of Saskatchewan have already dismissed it. He claims his innocence vehemently and does not appear to me to be the criminal type. He has no criminal record whatsoever . . .

"More recently he is very upset because $554.00 worth of leather making tools have been stolen from his cell and he worked a long time to get them. He also is in the process of making a bag for his young sister's birthday. He does not want daytime sedation which is fortunate but would like some Mandrax at bedtime so he can get some sleep. He is very alert and wide-eyed and keyed up today."

Within a couple weeks, David felt he had taken all he could handle. On August 17, staff discovered him lying face down on his bunk, with several self-inflicted slashes to both forearms. He had tried to take his life after failing to get a transfer to Stony Mountain Penitentiary, about a twenty-minute drive from our new home in Winnipeg. David felt so terribly alone and isolated in northern Saskatchewan.

When I saw him afterwards, we didn't talk about the suicide attempt. I just hugged him and said, "Never, never do that again. We are going to help you."

That fall, though, he tried yet again to kill himself, this time by swallowing wires, in the hopes they would tear open his bowels. He required emergency surgery, and recovered enough to hear, on November 15, that his appeal to the Supreme Court of Canada had been rejected. That decision also came to me in the mail. I had only to rip open the envelope and read that our hopes were dashed.

We had no way of knowing then that, as David's final legal appeals were being played out, police had arrested another man for that string of rapes in Gail Miller's old neighbourhood. One rape bore a particularly stark similarity to Gail's attack. It was in the same neighbourhood, and the victim's coat was removed and a knife was used. We were never told this, nor the fact that the attack took place three months before Gail Miller's murder, when David was not in Saskatoon. Two months before Miller's murder, a rapist in the same neighbourhood, also using a knife, also forced his victim to remove her coat. Again, David was not in Saskatoon that day, and again, we were not told. These weren't the only victims of the serial rapist who lived in Gail Miller's neighbourhood. Just like whoever killed Gail Miller, this attacker seemed to be right-handed and, like Miller's murderer, he attacked near bus stops and liked to haul his victims into alleys. He appeared to have an enormous hatred for medical workers. Ironically, the same rapist had attacked women in our new hometown of Winnipeg. This rapist was Larry Fisher, the former tenant of the basement apartment in Shorty Cadrain's home. The murder trail hadn't just led to David. It had also led to Larry Fisher.

Fisher was caught, literally with his pants down, on September 19, 1970, trying to flee an attack on a woman in Fort Garry, a suburb of Winnipeg. At first he said nothing to police. When he was roughed up by jail guards, Fort Garry police officer Lorne Huff was enraged. Police hate it when their prisoners appear in court covered in bruises and welts, since it makes it look as if someone tried to beat a confession out of them. Huff threatened to charge the guards if there were any more bruises on Fisher, and Fisher seemed to soften, apparently moved that someone was sticking up for him. When they were alone, Huff noted that Fisher had a newborn daughter. How would Fisher feel if someone sexually assaulted her some day? Fisher cracked. Out of the blue, he confessed to a string of brutal sex attacks in Saskatoon, some in Gail Miller's neighbourhood.

The Saskatoon police were called, and Huff found their reaction to be odd. They should have been pleased that they were being spoon-fed a major arrest. Instead, they seemed aloof. They made a point of not socializing with the Winnipeg officers, even when they were offered a free steak dinner. They seemed in an enormous hurry to get Fisher out of the way. One of the Saskatoon officers, Eddie Karst, had also handled the Gail Miller investigation, so he must have known her file was replete with the mention of Larry Fisher's victims.

Fisher's confessions were dynamite news, the type of information that might set David free, except that no one, including our lawyer and Fisher's victims, was told about it.

For reasons that were never explained, Fisher's case was quietly handled in Regina, rather than Saskatoon, where Fisher and his victims lived. The media was not alerted, even people who would certainly have liked to know that the serial rapist was now caught. In Saskatchewan, garage break-ins sometimes make the newspapers, and surely there would have been great public interest in Larry Fisher's crimes. Years later, when I learned of Fisher's arrest, I wondered, "What would police usually do if they caught a serial rapist? They'd tell everyone and bathe in the glory." The order for Fisher to be tried in Regina and not Saskatoon was made at the level of deputy chief, so even most rank-and-file officers were kept in the dark about Fisher, although rumours were soon circulating in the force.

If David's case had been reopened then, with this fresh evidence, precious little would have been lost of his life. It would have been embarrassing for the Crown and police, but not much more. Instead, it would be decades before even Fisher's victims knew he was behind bars. They would go to bed each night, fearful that the man with the knife who raped them was still on the streets, while my son died a little each day in prison. By the time that Fisher's victims learned of his capture, he was almost free again.

I later learned that Crown Attorney Serge Kujawa signed Justice Department files out on David and Fisher at exactly the same time that fall. Kujawa had handled David's appeals and knew his case intimately. He also handled Fisher's prosecution. How could he be blind to similarities between Gail Miller's murder and Fisher's rapes? Most of Fisher's victims were roughly her age. Fisher liked to use clothing to cover the faces of his victims so that they could not scream out for help, which would explain why Gail Miller's sweater was found inside out. Whoever killed Gail Miller, and attacked the other women in her neighbourhood, sought to debase, degrade and control his victims. Gail Miller was the victim of what some would call a punishment rapist, and punishment rapists follow a pattern. Larry Fisher was a punishment rapist, the least common category of rapist. Despite all of this, is it possible that somehow Kujawa couldn't see any connections between Fisher and whoever killed Gail Miller?

And so, as David was attempting suicide in prison, Larry Fisher was quietly shuffled off to the same prison, after pleading guilty to two rapes in Fort Garry, robbery and possession of a dangerous weapon. Although Fisher's victims never got the peace of mind of knowing he was off the streets, the police and Crown were spared the embarrassment of people wondering whether they had convicted the wrong man for Gail Miller's murder.

Inside the brick and stone walls of Saskatchewan Penitentiary, the moccasin line, or prison rumour mill, said that David was innocent. I don't know how they came to this conclusion, but they did, and I am so grateful. He was protected by some of the lifers, who told convicts who wanted to prey on him that he was innocent and to leave him alone. Normally, skinners — convicted sex criminals — don't last long, but David was treated differently. Years later, I would feel a jolt when David introduced me to some of the lifers who protected him. A few had fearsome Mohawk haircuts, and many were tattooed and huge. I had to learn from David that you can't judge people from their exteriors. I thought I already knew that, but David reinforced it for me. Through David, I also marvelled that some of the most horrific-looking lifers were capable of writing absolutely beautiful, sensitive poetry.

The prison moccasin line also said that David was going to take a fall and Calvin Tallis was going to get a judgeship. "David, that's wrong," I said. "You don't have to believe it. That's movie talk. That doesn't really happen." However, David did take a fall and Tallis did get a judgeship. We weren't the only ones who knew something wasn't right. There was a man on the parole board who later said he was just hounded by a remark David made to him around this time. David had said that the prisoners in Saskatchewan Penitentiary knew he wasn't a sex killer: "I'm fine. With the other prisoners, they know I'm not guilty."

My son was getting a fairer hearing from prisoners than from the justice system.

SEVEN

FAR FROM HOME

"I did not want to die in prison.
I felt I was dying a little bit there every day."
David, in maximum-security Dorchester Penitentiary

THE REAL TROUBLE BEGAN in March 1972, when David was transferred to the ancient penitentiary in the village of Dorchester, New Brunswick, outside Moncton. He was a skinner there, a sex killer, which made him a target for other prisoners. Also, he was a good-looking, slender nineteen-year-old, which made him appealing to prison perverts. He was so far from home now, stuck on the other side of the country, in a stone fortress built back in 1880. It was hard enough to visit the Prince Albert jail, but Dorchester was horrible. I was able to make it to Dorchester three times, once with Maureen and Lorne.

I looked to the Bible for strength, and I found it in the story of Joseph. He was also thrown in prison for something he didn't do and came out of it a great leader. I also found some comfort in the story of David and Goliath.

When David went out for the battle, he said, "The battle is the Lord's." To me, that meant that I was not fighting alone. Sometimes I read the Twenty-third Psalm, which said, "I shall walk through the valley of the shadow of death." David was in the shadow of death in that prison. I know God doesn't give us more than we can handle, but sometimes I would still say, "Enough's enough, already."

That was never more true than the day we got a letter from a doctor telling us that David had been gang raped and that the doctor worried this would keep happening if he wasn't moved. I didn't tell David about the letter. I simply couldn't. I thought it would kill him if he knew that I knew. From then on, if I saw David and he had bruises, it was especially hard on me, as my imagination ran wild. David knew how things worked in prison, and he wasn't about to make life worse by ratting on other prisoners. Once, when he required medical treatment for a shoulder injury, David simply told authorities, "I fell down." Another time, he hurt his wrist and explained simply, "I fell up the stairs." Sometimes he hurt his hands just punching at the walls to get out. He was stuck in protective custody for a month after some kind of ugly trouble with another inmate. He would never tell me the details.

Not all of the prisoners were unfriendly, however. One of the inmates he met in Dorchester was Junior, the nickname for Donald Marshall, a Micmac Indian who served eleven years for a murder he did not commit. Like David, Junior was convicted after witnesses lied under police pressure. They were both outsiders and easy marks for the justice system. David had been a hippie, while Junior was aboriginal, and both of them had previous brushes with the law. Neither had enough money to hire private investigators to verify their stories.

David had many trips to solitary confinement, also known as "the hole" and "disassociation." For someone like David, who hated to be alone, this was particularly rough. Some guards would entertain themselves by throwing tear gas into the solitary-confinement cells, and David quickly learned to place his head over the toilet and put a towel over it to minimize the burning to his face and make breathing easier. Still, he suffered skin problems from the gas, which still bothered him years later.

Not surprisingly, as time passed in prison, David's mental health declined. A psychiatric report from Dorchester dated May 11, 1972, noted, "This inmate was seen by Dr. Michael Wright two weeks ago when the diagnosis of schizoid personality was made. He was due for review by Dr. Wright this week but in his absence, Milgaard was seen by me. He readily admitted that much of his previous behaviour had been consciously manipulative. He continues to assert that he should not have been convicted and should not be in this institution. Despite his apparently negative attitude and his disassociative denial of what must be regarded as proven facts, he evidently appears to be making a reasonable adjustment to his present environment."

Our family now had no money for extras, and we couldn't afford to take real holidays. If we did go somewhere, it was to see David in prison. Maureen thought that her big brother lived in a castle, and she would always get angry at the end of a visit when they wouldn't let her stay or let David leave the castle and come home with her where he belonged. David himself appeared very childlike in prison, and wanted to play on teeter-totters and swings, although, with effort, he could be persuaded to play cribbage. Visits were always booked in advance, and we knew David would prepare himself for them and make a point of not letting us see just how awful his life was now. Christmas and birthdays were particularly hard. We could be with him only for a short time, and we were always watching the clock. However well they went, visits always ended sadly, with David having to stay in his prison and watch us return home.

David's mood brightened when he was told in March 1972 that he could expect a transfer to Stony Mountain, outside Winnipeg, in a year. That would put him just a twenty-minute drive from our home, rather than on the other side of the country. David waited the year, and when nothing happened, he gave up on waiting. In prison, you don't know what's going to happen from one day to the next, or one moment to the next, as things can go from numbing boredom to stark terror within a heartbeat. Prisoners lose their sense of time, existing only from moment to moment. "I did not want to die in prison," David told me. "I felt I was dying a little bit there every day."

In 1973, David overheard some other prisoners planning an escape.

"I'm going to go with you," David said.

"No, you won't," said one of the prisoners, who was a particularly "heavy dude" — prison talk for someone dangerous.

"No, I want to go."

David felt so alone and so far from home that he wasn't going to pass up an opportunity, even if the prisoners planning the breakout were a rough group. David had just failed in another suicide attempt, and he wanted out of Dorchester dead or alive.

The prisoners plotting the escape could see David wasn't about to be scared off, so they let him join in. They left dummies in their beds to mislead guards, then overpowered and tied up a guard and scaled a stone wall to freedom. They hid out in the farmhouse of an elderly couple, who recognized them from a news bulletin. They tied up the couple, but didn't hurt them, then they fled in the couple's old pickup truck.

I learned of the escape on a Saturday night when everyone was in bed. I had just come home from demonstrating jewellery at a home party, and was tired, since I was holding down three jobs. A small column in the newspaper caught my eye. It told how three convicts had escaped from Dorchester and were being hunted down with dogs. The prisoners were still on the run, and David's name leapt out at me. I felt so isolated. I immediately phoned the institution, but staff would say nothing except that I'd have to call back on Monday. I didn't tell the rest of the family. I didn't want them having the same nightmares I had, of David running with packs of dogs on his heels.

My nightmares weren't far from reality. The escaping prisoners didn't get far before the pickup broke down. They fled into the woods, where the tracking dogs found them. David froze in terror as the dogs growled and snapped at him.

Many years later, David joked as he recounted the experience, and I couldn't stop laughing, except when David got to the part where the dogs caught them. David told us the guards just stood there and let the dogs chew on them. He said that afterwards, when they got back to the prison, the guards beat him. He said he had been beaten before, but never, ever, with such brutality.

When I learned of David's capture, I knew none of this, only that he was being transferred again, this time back to Prince Albert, Saskatchewan.

When David was shipped back in 1974, the new warden at Saskatchewan Penitentiary was Jim O'Sullivan. He proved himself to be a decent man, something you can't take for granted in the prison system. O'Sullivan actually listened to us when we spoke, treating us as people and not as numbers or as a case study he had read about in a book. And he took the time to get through to David, who was becoming more and more withdrawn. He promised David that if he kept his nose clean for a year and took some courses, he would transfer him to Stony Mountain, where we would be able to visit him regularly. O'Sullivan had a reputation for being true to his word, so David did what he asked. In August 1976, when the year was up, David was transferred to Manitoba, just as O'Sullivan had promised.

David had now been in prison more than eight years.

Stony Mountain Penitentiary is a harsh, bleak place, built in 1874 on a hill outside Winnipeg. It was inside these stone walls where chained native leaders Poundmaker and Big Bear were sent after the Riel Rebellion of 1885. It took only a few years for the health of both leaders to be broken. Both men died shortly after their release. There had been countless other sad stories at Stony since, but for us, Stony held out promise. It was wonderful to be able to see David often, and he was able to continue with his studies. His parole officer told us how pleased they were with his progress.

However, there remained a massive stumbling block. David could not be considered rehabilitated and ready for parole until he showed remorse. But how could he show remorse for something he didn't do? He found the very mention of Gail Miller's murder repulsive. One of the parole officers sat down with David and me and suggested that he admit to being guilty, whether he was or not, because it would make things so much easier for him to get out on parole. Yet no matter how much David hated prison, he wouldn't consider that. He told me bluntly that he would not bargain with his innocence. I was proud of him, but also afraid.

The warden at Stony Mountain was nothing like O'Sullivan. O'Sullivan didn't see the need to act like a tough guy and bully people. The Stony Mountain warden was a little Napoleon. Once I went to his office on what seemed like a simple matter. David had been allowed to play music in Prince Albert on an eight-track cassette player. At Stony Mountain, the rule was that prisoners were allowed only standard cassette players. We didn't have the money to get one, and didn't really want it anyway, since all of David's music was on the eight-track format. I started asking at the lower ranks of the prison if David could keep his eight-track player, and the answer was continually no, with no reason given, as I worked my way up to the warden's office. I felt quite intimidated when I told him my story about the tapes.

"Mrs. Milgaard, do you see this piece of paper?"

"Yes," I replied, feeling like a schoolchild.

"Do you know that if I write my name on this piece of paper, David will go back to New Brunswick? Is that what you want?"

"No."

"Then don't let's hear anything more about a cassette player. Is that clear? Good day, madam."

I felt I had been kicked in the stomach. At the first washroom, I was physically sick. I felt so hopeless. I couldn't do anything. I knew that if I fought back, I was only going to hurt my son. I was a second-class citizen.

My heart ached for other second-class citizens. I watched young mothers struggle through the snow and cold biting winds as they carried their little ones in their arms. Some had a couple of toddlers trudging along with them. Sometimes, they would not be dressed very warmly for the unforgiving Manitoba winds, and they had to walk well over a block to get in to see their loved ones. They walked by many empty parking stalls that were set aside for the prison staff. I tried to be objective.

The staff came to work every day. The prisoners' families came maybe once or twice a week. It was right that the staff have parking spaces near the prison. But what about at night, and on the weekends, when there was reduced staff? Through the system, I tried to get permission for the families to have the use of these empty parking spaces. My request was turned down with no reason given. That was the worst part of it all: they didn't have to give a reason. They could do whatever they wanted.

Once, after David started the Justice Group, which brought in inspiring speakers to talk to the prisoners, one of the group's coordinators told me about an evening when a number of them had struggled through a blizzard and the cold. They got inside the prison doors only to be turned back. Their meeting was cancelled by the guard at the door. Out of caring and concern, these people were coming up to spend a few hours of fellowship with the prison members. They even had a guest speaker with them, and they were all turned away with no reason given. A member of the John Howard Society told me of an incident where a guard told her, "A good prisoner is a depressed prisoner and we try to keep them as depressed as possible." The saddest part of it all was that the guard didn't even realize there was anything wrong with what he was saying.

David lived vicariously through us. He would ask us to describe everyday experiences in great detail, so that he could picture them and feel them. He focused particularly on Maureen. Maureen turned sixteen in 1976, the year David was transferred to Stony Mountain, and that birthday probably meant more to David than to Maureen. Sixteen was the age at which David was locked up, the age when his carefree life suddenly died. Now, everything Maureen experienced from the age of sixteen onwards was of massive interest to her brother. What was a movie like? A first kiss? A pizza? If Maureen went to the beach, David needed to know details about the water, the sky, the people, the smells, the sounds. Everything. In David's prison world, there were no bright colours. There were no breezes, no sunsets, no birdsongs. Often, to get a feeling that he was not trapped in a box, David would hold something reflective between the bars, so that he could see down the length of the prison range. From his jail cell, David was teaching us something. We learned to look more deeply at things we might have otherwise ignored, like a beautiful sky and butterflies and the feel of sand and grass and dew beneath our feet and rain on our backs. We learned to better appreciate life, which meant appreciating God.

We were learning from David, but it wasn't easy. Lorne would try to be strong when he visited, but once he got out to his car, he would slump over the steering wheel and sob for his lost son. It would often take a half-hour for Lorne to regain his composure enough to drive home.

My father died while David was in Stony Mountain. David hadn't known him that well, but he knew how much I loved him. It hit David that people weren't going to stay the same while he waited in prison for his release. Life — and death — were going on without him. David now grew even closer to Grandma Milgaard, and they were close to begin with. They loved to talk about how, when David was finally free, they were going to have a special dinner together. Just the two of them. They shared such a sense of closeness. They never told the rest of us any details of their dinner plans, as it was something special for the two of them. David always prayed for that day. We all did. Grandma Milgaard found it so tough and difficult to visit him in prison, but she was a strong person and rose above that. When she became sick, David was allowed an escorted three-hour pass in August 1976 to visit her. She hung on until May 1977. We had hoped David would get parole that year, but finally David realized they would never have their special dinner. It was so very hard on him when she died and he was still alone behind bars.

I have always loved David, but there were several days when I didn't like him too much. He was thinking only of himself, I felt. One day, I got really mad, saying, "You've got a mother! You've got a father! You've got a family that cares about you! Look around you! These people here have nothing!" He really looked shocked, and to his credit, he started looking around and reaching out to other people. I think that's when he started to grow away from the hardness and the activities that go on in prison. He learned how to fix sewing machines in the prison sewing shop. He finished high school and began university liberal arts studies. He also started to take an active role on the prison's advisory committee, letting prisoners know they still had some rights. He was growing into someone concerned and dedicated and compassionate.

∾

On November 1, 1977, David's application for parole to attend the University of Manitoba was turned down. His parole report stated, "Parents experiencing marital problems. May separate in near future . . . grandmother passed away May 1977. She was a strong, stable support to Milgaard. One of the few family members who had a realistic grasp of David's situation . . . Incarceration has been debilitating. Surprisingly, subject is not institutionalized. In fact, behaviour record indicative of a lack of adjustment to this milieu. From a warehousing perspective, this is dysfunctional [behaviour problem to staff]. From a perspective of re-entry into the community this is functional. That is, institutions are not viewed as home to Milgaard nor are they safe or secure. Therefore, motivation to return to community is high.

"There is no question Milgaard's family are concerned and supportive. They firmly believe in his innocence and have indicated, in numerous correspondence, their willingness to do anything to effect a TA [temporary absence] program or release. Mrs. Milgaard, in particular, has elicited the support of a number of influential community members.

"This writer questions how constructive this familial support is. First, if subject is guilty, familial belief in his innocence provides a firm block to subject ever admitting to or working through intrapsychic aspects of offence. Second, although support is strong, it is at times overpowering, dominant, inhibits independence, stress producing, high expectations and demands on David to obtain release — demands often unrealistic."

This was so ironic. Now the experts of the system were blaming us for both David's imprisonment and his stress. A November 10, 1977, report from Stony Mountain stated that David seemed to be stagnating: "Milgaard seems to be in a constant depressed state since his parole board hearing on Nov. 1/77. He feels that all hope is lost. He wants to give up on his scholastic studies as well as everything else. Feel he is just seeking attention."

Two days later, Chris and Kathy married in tiny Kipling, Saskatchewan. Kathy was quiet but fun loving, and, like Chris, she enjoyed camping and fishing. It was a beautiful service, and I was so happy for them, but at the same time, there was the painful knowledge that David wasn't there as he should have been. I tried to remember every detail so I could tell him later, but of course it could never be the same. We had been through the same combination of joy and pain two years before, when Susan married Miles at the Portage La Prairie air force base, where he served as an air traffic controller.

The parole board was right about one thing: Lorne and I were experiencing marital problems. In 1976, Lorne told me he had fallen in love with someone else, a young widow. Lorne had been a faithful and support-ive husband, and I was devastated. I asked the children not to judge him, and we managed to remain friends.

I don't know how much of our marriage breakup can

be blamed on the stress of the imprisonment. There are many things that can make a marriage work or fail, and it's tough to give neat, easy answers. I do know that circumstances made it hard. Many times the other kids wanted to talk about something with me, but I held back because I really didn't need anything more to deal with. Maybe it was the same with Lorne. There were so many secrets now.

Lorne pleaded with David not to try another escape now, since I couldn't deal with the extra stress. "I've put your mother through a great deal and she doesn't deserve any of it," Lorne told David during a visit to prison. "I've been so unfair to her and she has had so many trials and tribulations. You just can't do this to her. I want you to promise me that you won't try to escape."

However, I sent poor David a different message. "David, it doesn't matter to me what you have done or what you will do in the future," I told him. "You have my love regardless of anything. And if you feel at any time that you have to do what you have to do, there isn't anything that would make me stop loving you or caring about you."

I moved into an apartment with Maureen, who was then sixteen. For her, the separation had been a hard blow. Her dad had not just left her mother for another woman. He had left her. She was angry. She was sure that Lorne and I would have stayed together if not for the distraction and stress of David's imprisonment. She said her dad would never have looked at another woman if I had remained the type of person I had been before.

I had been forced to change to become more forceful and independent. As a result, when this young widow, who seemed so helpless, came into his life, he once again felt needed.

Maureen often cried privately, when no one could see her hurting. There were tears for the pain Lorne and I were suffering. There were tears for the physical pain she had suffered herself, and the memories of washing blood off her face after a beating by classmates. As she grew older, Maureen often felt that she had no social life to speak of, as it seemed that often when other teenagers were going to parties or socials or the beach, she was going to the penitentiary.

The children had all lost the mother they remembered. The more I focused on David, the less time I had for them. Even though they knew I still loved them, I often felt that I was a failure to my three other children. I knew they avoided coming to me with their problems, because they realized I had so much on my plate already. I wondered whether they would understand how I agonized over the decisions that I was making and that I didn't love them any less because of what I was being forced to do.

Meanwhile, we seemed to have reached a dead end in David's case. It didn't matter who I called or wrote to or went to see. There seemed to be nothing anyone could do. Most people were polite, but their attitude was, "Sure, lady, you believe him, but you're his mother."

Then, in 1979, David had a fresh hope for freedom. He heard of a truth drug, sodium pentothal, and desperately wanted to take it to demonstrate his innocence. A prison psychiatrist wrote on January 22: "In discussing the offence Mr. Milgaard repeatedly asked to be given the 'truth drug' in spite of it being pointed out to him that such a test could never conclusively demonstrate his innocence although it might suggest his guilt (it is unlikely to do more than suggest because even if Milgaard did give an account of the offence while under the influence of the drug he might argue afterwards that he was doing so from memory of the facts as they were brought out at the time of his trial). His strong insistence that such a test be performed is interesting and possibly hopeful in view of his repeated and very firm assertion that he remembers clearly all his actions on the day of the offence, the killing of the nurse not being one of them. If he did not in fact commit the offence then it is natural that he would seek any method to try to demonstrate that fact. If he is in fact guilty of the murder then his insistence on the truth drug might be just one more example of his bravado in trying to buck the system but it might on the other hand be an attempt to come to terms with his guilt in a more gentle way than would be the case if he were to reveal his guilt in full consciousness after all these years of protesting his innocence. I believe this latter to be quite likely but I think that it would be better to wait and see whether he will be able to discuss the offence openly."

David took the truth drug, and the results pointed to his innocence. They had taped the session, but we were told that the tape quality was very poor. Finally, mysteriously, the doctor couldn't find the tape. We were told it had somehow gone missing — just like the knife that vanished from the Saskatoon police officer's locker, and the material extracted from Gail Miller's vagina. We were also told the truth drug wasn't really conclusive anyway and didn't prove anything. It was a terrible blow for David, who desperately needed to cling to some hope.

In 1979, David was yet again turned down for parole. However much he hated prison, he refused to lie and say that he repented the murder. The worst thing about the whole nightmare, he said, was when people looked at him and he could see in their eyes that they considered him guilty.

We had come a long way in the decade that David had spent behind bars. I was doing well financially now and had enough money to afford piano lessons and flying. I also took courses at the University of Winnipeg and the University of Manitoba in micro-economics, property management and other things. I was upgrading myself, making myself stronger for the fight to free David. I borrowed some money and invested it by myself, and by 1980, I owned eight rental houses and had assets of $250,000. Through it all, we still had some faith in the system. We believed that David would be paroled, and that once he was with us where he belonged, we could fight to clear his name.

EIGHT

STEALING FREEDOM

*"I shall continue to seek good in others
and do good as I see it."*
David, after escaping again from prison in 1980

ON AUGUST 20, 1980, two days before David was
to get out on a pass to attend a barbecue party for Chris's
twenty-seventh birthday, he and I met with prison
authorities. Once again, they told us that David could
not be considered rehabilitated in their eyes until he
showed remorse. In addition, the prison officials said
they didn't think David could function on the streets,
since he had been in custody for so long. It was so ironic
and so heartbreaking. They told us about a long-range
plan for David to get into a halfway house, but it would
mean that he wouldn't get a taste of freedom until four
years or so down the road. He had spent eleven birthdays as a prisoner, and the prospect of at least another
four was too much to imagine. David left that parole
meeting quietly planning to escape.

We had been planning the family barbecue for

weeks. We were living then at Quail Ridge, a townhome property in St. James in the west end of Winnipeg that I managed, and it had a lovely country club and tennis courts. Susan was playing racquetball with David's guard when Maureen and David disappeared together. Lorne and I were busy preparing the food and didn't think much about it until the guard came back after finishing his game to ask us where David was. The search began in earnest, and we discovered Maureen's car was gone. The guard and Susan drove around the area, thinking perhaps Maureen and David had gone off joyriding. It seemed an eternity, and finally the guard reported David missing. The phone rang, and it was Maureen, and she was sobbing. She told us that David had forced her out of the car, took whatever money she had, and left her.

It wouldn't be until much later that we learned the truth: Maureen helped David escape, then guarded this secret to protect us. We then learned that after he and Maureen left Quail Ridge, David wanted to drive, but Maureen pointed out that he hadn't been behind the wheel of a car in more than a decade. Instead, she drove to a drugstore to get bleach for his hair and dyed it for him. As he left, David said to Maureen, "Just tell Mom and Dad I have to go. I can't go back."

Wednesday nights are my Christian Science church nights, which David knows. One Wednesday night shortly after this, I returned to my car after church and found a red rose on the seat. There was no note. Nothing but the rose, and I knew it must be from David. I looked around but there was no sign of him anywhere. I knew he must badly need money, and I knew he knew I would be in church again on Sunday. So, the next Sunday, I left an envelope with money inside on the front seat when I went in to church. I could hardly wait for the service to end, and when it was finally over, I rushed to the car, and sure enough, the envelope was gone. Shortly afterwards, I got a letter from Toronto, written in green felt marker, with no return address on the envelope:

Dear Mom,

Where to start and what to say . . . I am happy but truly wonder what direction I am to . . . or should have . . . I have a job starting Wednesday, it is part-time 4 hrs, 6 days a week but a start.

I have met a few people and somehow realize I must practice a better regimen of self discipline in the sense that so far I've been doing or living in a very hedonistic sort of fashion. Freedom is beautiful and Toronto a place that has a strong pulse, if you like; compared to Winnipeg's nite life.

I keep asking myself what is my direction, what do I want from life now and I only come up with to enjoy it. Maybe that will refine itself somehow, I hope so.

Tell father for me that I hope he understands my leaving and that I care for him and hope he knows that . . .

I wish I could come home. 11 years wanting only that and then putting myself in a position where I can't have what I want most.

I love every one and miss you all.

If I could understand why life has been as it has for me where I am to go in it, where I've come from, I would be content, but it all makes no sense . . . I shall continue to seek good in others and do good as I see it.

I love you,
David.

A little while later, my brother phoned from Toronto and said, "The package that you sent has arrived."

Of course, I hadn't sent him a package. His code was easy to follow. "Oh, that's great. I'll get back in touch with you," I replied.

I called back from a phone booth and talked with David. He had hitchhiked to Toronto. There he changed his name to Ward McAdam, got a job in telephone sales, and was soon making $200 a week selling Grolier encyclopedias. He had fallen in love with a girl named Rhonda whom he met on Yonge Street. He wanted to see me, but on one condition — I couldn't talk to him about turning himself in. I decided to go. I drove around and around, knowing that I was being followed. Then I took a shopping bag with a different raincoat and a wig in it and went into a washroom in Eaton's in downtown Winnipeg, put on my disguise and slipped out through another door.

I took a cab to the airport and flew to Toronto under my maiden name, Baxter. I was terrified that I'd meet someone I knew. I was also scared because I knew I was doing something wrong, that I should be turning David in. But I couldn't erase the memory of his voice when he told me on the phone, "If you come here, don't come with the intention of talking me out of it."

When I saw David in Toronto, the bleach in his hair had gone funny. It was patchy and looked awful, but he also looked so free. It's hard to explain, but he just looked free. There was a vibrancy about him that I hadn't seen for years. That look had almost died when he was in prison. There was no way I could shut that door on him.

I knew it was ridiculous. It wasn't rational at all, but nothing seemed real since he had been arrested. There was also something unreal about seeing David's picture published in newspapers as a dangerous murderer on the loose. The photo they used of him showed a scary-looking man, with a few days' growth of beard and unruly, long hair. He was wearing a hockey sweater but truly looked like a thug. If I didn't know him, I would have been scared of him too.

Despite the publicity, David wasn't looking over his shoulder, and would stroll down busy Yonge Street, soaking up the sounds and smells and rhythms of the city's main street. He was determined to savour every moment of freedom. David and I thought that if he could stay out for a while and show that he could function, he would prove the prison authorities wrong. He would show them he could survive outside prison as a productive, peaceful person. It was crazy, but that thought offered us some comfort.

We had a wonderful time in Toronto. We took long walks together. We must have looked pretty funny: I was disguised in my red wig and David had his orange-coloured hair. We attended church together and had a beautiful Thanksgiving dinner in a restaurant. In prison, we couldn't even send him candies, although I could buy him chips from a vending machine. Now I could act like David's mother again. I went shopping for clothes for him. We found him a furnished apartment in a house, and I bought him a comforter for his bed, and some clothes, including a parka. They were all the mothering things we had both missed so badly.

Soon it was time for me to leave, and it was with a heavy heart that I headed home. David later wrote to me, "My success and sense of self-pride was diminished only by the fact that I could not share it [freedom] truly with those that I love, my family."

Meanwhile, in Toronto, a new man at David's work needed a place to stay, and David took him in after telling him, "No drugs. I can't stand any heat." The man caught on that David must be hiding something from the police. When the young man left and quickly got into trouble with the police, he told them he knew someone they wanted. He picked David out of the mug shots and they got him to arrange a meeting with David.

The man David helped told him that he wanted to meet him to thank him for all of his help, and they arranged a get-together near the corner of Queen Street West and Roncesvalles Avenue, in the Parkdale district. When David arrived, he saw two big men who looked like police. As he walked by them, one of them said, "David?"

"Excuse me," David replied, breaking into a run. Unknown to him, he was running directly into a buildup of police in a parking lot. They yelled for him to stop, and he did, raising his hands above his head. There was a single blast from a double-barrelled shotgun anyway, and David was down on the pavement, bleeding. "Call the police!" shouted a bystander, only to be told, "We are the police." The pellets had lodged in his spine, and David feared he had lost the use of his legs forever, as well as his taste of freedom, which had now ended after seventy-seven days.

As in the last escape, I found out news about David from the newspapers. I blamed myself for not turning him in, while Maureen faulted herself because she had helped him escape in the first place. Strange as it seems, it wasn't until years later that I even knew she had helped David. There were so many secrets now, as we didn't want to add to each other's burden.

Few questions were asked about the shooting, since David was believed to be a wanton killer and had no public sympathy. Besides our family and a few close friends, who really cared? Police said they thought David was armed when they shot him. Witnesses interviewed by the press said police could have easily reached out and tripped him, but the officer shot him instead. David was unarmed and looked "out-and-out terrified," in the words of one witness. Other bystanders said they never heard the police identify themselves as police officers, and no one said anything about David actually having a weapon.

I flew back to Toronto to comfort him. There was a police officer outside his room at St. Joseph's Hospital, and David was handcuffed to the bed. I sat on his bed, rubbed his feet, and told David that I loved him. He looked so frail, so helpless, so pale. He later explained that he had to escape, despite the risks. "I was dying a little bit . . . something inside me, every day. I stole my freedom."

I blamed myself that he could no longer walk, and kept thinking, "I should have turned him in. I knew where he was. Then he wouldn't have been shot."

That was a turning point for me. I stopped placing hope in appeals or parole or politicians or any part of the system that had already failed us so badly. I prayed to God for a sense of direction and I got it. The thought came that I should place a reward for the real killer. When I returned to Winnipeg, I called a family conference. "I've got $10,000 and an RRSP," I said. "I can cash it, but then there won't be any money for anything else if I put it into a reward. We'll have to go public. It means everything you went through as the brother of a murderer or sister of a murderer will all start up again. You've all made new families. I know how hard it was on you before. Are you prepared to go through it again?"

We had talked about it already a lot on the telephone, so I wasn't surprised when everyone said, "Yes, no question."

We were setting out to set David free, and that probably meant we would have to find the real killer ourselves.

NINE

GUMSHOE MOM

"We want him home again. Please help us."
Line from family reward posters

IN DECEMBER 1980, we offered a $10,000 reward for anyone with information that freed David, and papered the city of Saskatoon with posters that declared David was innocent. "Somewhere out there is someone who can help us prove it!" the posters read. "The Christmas season is one of joy and love and hope, a time for sharing and caring. Our last Christmas as a family was when David was sixteen years of age. Now, he is twenty-eight. We want him home again. Please help us."

Our son Chris didn't hesitate a second in supporting our plan to make the case public, even though he lived in Regina and was basically a shy person. I can only imagine what it was like for him to go about life in Saskatchewan with the rare last name of Milgaard as we called attention to the fact that his big brother was a convicted sex killer. Oddly, Chris felt somehow guilty about David being in prison, as though he didn't have the right to be free as long as his older brother was imprisoned.

Plenty of people responded to the posters, and we kept busy following up leads. The best tip, however, and one we never got a chance to follow up, was given to police a few months before the reward was offered. In August 1980, a shy, soft-spoken woman walked up to the front desk of the Saskatoon police station and said she thought she knew the identity of the real killer. She knew from news reports that David had escaped from prison and that he had always claimed he was innocent. The woman was Linda Fisher, now the ex-wife of the serial rapist who had lived in the basement of Shorty Cadrain's house. She had long since broken up with Larry. Linda outlined her suspicions about Larry to police, telling of the missing paring knife and Larry's strange reaction when she accused him of the murder. She noted how out of character it was for Larry to miss work, as he did that morning. There were also disturbing similarities between his other rapes and Gail Miller's murder: Larry attacked women either getting on or off the bus; most of his victims wore medical uniforms, just like his mother, a hospital cleaner. But no one from the police got back to Linda, and her report was quietly filed away.

I cut back on my work and religious activities to devote all my time to David. Our brief flirtation with being well off was rapidly coming to an end.

It was during this time that I met Peter and Cathy Carlyle-Gordge. Peter was a British-born journalist who was the Winnipeg correspondent for *Maclean's* magazine.

The *Winnipeg Free Press* had just carried a story about our fight to free David, and Peter and Cathy, a hospital publicist, contacted me, eager to help. Like Linda Fisher, they were interested not in the $10,000 reward but in seeing justice done. Peter and Cathy had just completed fighting for years to win a new trial for Katie Harper, a Winnipeg woman who they thought was wrongly convicted of murder. They remortgaged their house to help support that fight. They made it clear they were working not for me but for the truth, and I welcomed their intelligence and zeal.

"There's got to be a purpose," Cathy told me. "Right now, you're in the middle of it and you can't see."

Peter and Cathy weren't glory seekers after a quick story. In fact, Peter urged me to help him keep a low profile so that he could do his job better. "If you're being interviewed, don't mention me. It will be much easier," he cautioned me.

We decided to make a video re-enacting the Crown's murder theory. I drove the car, pretending I was David, and my daughter-in-law, Kathy, was Gail Miller, walking from her boarding house to the bus stop. Chris filmed the event with a rented video camera, and we timed it all with a borrowed stopwatch. Chris was a little uncomfortable with the camera, and I felt uneasy watching Kathy retrace the final steps of Gail Miller, but it was still exciting to be actively doing something to help David at long last. It seemed the right thing to do and we shared such a sense of togetherness. By the time I did my U-turn to circle back for Kathy, as the Crown said

David had done, Kathy was already at the bus stop. We tried this several times, always with the same result. The Crown's theory simply didn't hold up. I had always known in my heart that David was innocent. Now I also knew in my head.

I bought and read transcripts of David's trial and unsuccessful appeal, which weren't cheap. They cost thirty cents a page for twelve hundred pages, and we needed four copies of each. We pored over them, looking for cracks in the Crown's case, which weren't too hard to find even for someone like myself not trained in the law. Susan and her husband, Miles, spent hours reading them. The Crown witness statements were inconsistent, and it was increasingly clear that David's friends had been intimidated into taking the stand against him.

We made several attempts to contact Ron Wilson, Nichol John and other Crown witnesses, with no success. The Saskatoon police were always aware of what we were doing, and interfered, making the long drive to Regina to sternly tell witnesses not to talk to us. It was as though the police were above us on a hill, pushing us downwards whenever we tried to move ahead. However, their efforts also gave us hope. If their case was so strong, why were they worried? What were they hiding? Were they shielding someone powerful?

We spent many weekends in Saskatchewan, following up leads and interviewing people. We'd find someone and they'd disappear, and then we'd find someone else, and they'd disappear too. Then, in late January 1981, we finally got what appeared to be a major break. After poring through *Henderson's* city directories and calling old neighbours and anyone else we could think of, Peter Carlyle-Gordge and I tracked down Ron Wilson. Ron was uncomfortable to hear from us, cagey and eager to put the whole ugly incident out of his mind. I had never really trusted him, and that opinion did not change when he suggested there might be a dark side to David that I didn't know about. He told us he was nervous when David had escaped from Dorchester a decade before. The unspoken message was that David was a dangerous man. He thought I had come for revenge, not justice, and we got no information to advance our case. I secretly taped Wilson with a recorder hidden in my purse, and the family would sit around for hours analyzing what he said.

We were told in an anonymous note that the night before Gail Miller was murdered a male psychiatric patient escaped from the North Battleford Provincial Hospital, a couple of hours' drive from Saskatoon. The fugitive appeared the day of the murder at an isolated farm, covered in blood, and muttering something about killing a rabbit. The news came to us from someone who wrote, "I am withholding my name because of family connections. Also I am not after a reward. I just feel I would like to help you, if possible. God be with you. A concerned person."

The whole story might mean nothing, but the lame-sounding story of killing a rabbit gave me hope. On February 15, 1981, I phoned one of his relatives. "Could I come and talk to them about something?"

My Saskatoon friend Jackie Groat and I, with a tape recorder safely hidden in my purse, set out.

The relative confirmed that the event had happened as it was described, but they believed the man's story of the rabbit, and so the family had simply cleaned him up and taken him back to the institution. He looked like a promising suspect, and on March 22, Jackie and I drove up to the North Battleford facility.

On went the tape recorder as the patient told us he had escaped twenty-five times from the hospital. It seemed unbelievable, but he explained that it was really easy. Sometimes he just walked along with the golfers who played on a course nearby. At one point during an escape, he managed to join the Armed Forces for a couple of weeks before they found out he was a fugitive from a mental institution.

I started to question him about the time he had been on the farm when he said he had killed the rabbit. It was as if he was transformed. The friendly, laughing person became very stiff and agitated, saying over and over, "It wasn't me. It wasn't me. I didn't do it." Jackie and I were quite frightened and beat a hasty retreat.

As we drove away we were so excited. This was it. The big break we had been waiting for. My heart was singing. I dropped Jackie off and headed to see our lawyer, Gary Young, quickly telling him the story. He phoned the psychiatric hospital and they confirmed that the man had escaped some twenty-five times, but that he wasn't at large the day Gail Miller was killed. Hospital records showed the patient received medication that day.

"He's lying," I told Gary.

"Mrs. Milgaard, we certainly would not lie about something like that," the hospital administrator said.

The patient's relatives had said he had escaped on the day the nurse was killed. How was I to know that another nurse had been found in a shallow grave under a bridge near Saskatoon, and that was the time frame they were talking about? Might we have accidentally stumbled onto *that* nurse's killer?

Of course, we still desperately wanted to talk with Nichol John. If she cooperated, we could immediately explode the Crown's case against David. We kept phoning anyone who might know her whereabouts, and we were finally steered towards an apartment building in Regina. She was in her late twenties now, and cautiously kept the door chained as she answered her door.

"I'm Joyce Milgaard and I know you won't be glad to see me, but I know what you must have gone through and I'd like to talk."

She slammed the door in my face, then opened it again, keeping the chain fastened.

"How did you find me? How dare you come here."

Her words were tough, but she looked horrified. Soon we were both crying, but she still wouldn't unchain the door. I apologized for intruding, and said she must have felt horrible pressure from the police.

"Why doesn't he just stop escaping and he'd get out sooner?" Nichol demanded.

She let slip that she was still in contact with Ron

Wilson. Like Ron, she was scared of David now. They feared David must truly hate them now, after so long in prison.

"He says he didn't do it," I said. "You and Ron both know that. It may be upsetting to you to have some unpleasant memories dredged up, but think of him. He's been in prison for twelve years and you must be able to remember what happened. Think about him."

"I know something happened," Nichol said. "I know that I saw something but I don't know what I saw. You want the truth? Well, that's the truth. There's too much that I don't remember. There's too much I don't want to remember."

Nichol agreed to meet me again that night, but Cathy Carlyle-Gordge and I suspected she was giving us the slip. There were packed boxes in her apartment, and she was obviously in the middle of moving when we found her. We sat in our car in the parking lot, our eyes trained on the door. True to our suspicions, Nichol moved out that night, bag and baggage. Cathy and I followed the truck that carried her belongings, finding out her new address.

I still had to speak to her. Perhaps the phone would be better than knocking on her door, but we didn't have her number, which was unlisted. Susan entered her apartment block, hid her coat in a laundry room, then knocked on Nichol's door. Susan pretended she had just moved into an apartment down the hall and needed to contact her movers. Would Nichol mind if she called them from her place? Could she give the movers Nichol's number if they needed to reach her?

"That would be fine," Nichol said.

Susan phoned back to a number where I was waiting.

"Atlas Movers," I answered and took down the new number.

A little later, I phoned Nichol at her new number. I said again that I wanted to see her.

She refused again, clearly upset that I had found her.

"I'm not going to leave you alone," I said as she hung up.

Not surprisingly, Nichol quickly moved again.

She was changing names as well as addresses. A friend of Susan's gave us what we thought was her new name, and Susan called the home, saying she worked for Apex Marketing.

"The reason I asked for you is we usually talk to a housewife," Susan said. "What it is, is I'm doing a survey for a client, a consumer magazine." It would only take two minutes, Susan said, and she wasn't selling anything. Did she subscribe to a daily newspaper? A monthly magazine? Did she have any children? Their ages? What magazines did they read? Was she the sole wage earner?

"Do you take *Time* magazine or have you ever taken it?"

"No," she said.

"That's it," Susan said, then she zeroed in on what she had really been seeking all along. "Then all I want to know is your first name and your husband's first name."

"Nichol and Bill."

Jackpot. It *was* her. Now I could make my approach again. I had a recorder on my phone when I phoned

Nichol. It was immediately clear she still had no intention of talking with me, and she moved again.

We were again able to locate her, this time in a tiny community outside Saskatoon. Cathy Carlyle-Gordge knocked on the door, knowing that if the next few minutes went well, David would be well on his way to freedom.

"Hi, I'm just looking for Nichol John," Cathy said when the door opened.

Cathy was struck by how small the woman at the door was. Cathy's five-foot-three-and-a-half, and felt considerably taller than Nichol.

"I'm here on behalf of Joyce Milgaard, and you've got nothing to be afraid of," Cathy continued.

Nichol was wide-eyed in terror now. Cathy thought she looked like a rabbit caught in the headlights of a truck.

"You've got to go," Nichol said. "You've got to go." Nichol was shaking uncontrollably now as she blurted, "I don't remember anything. I don't remember anything. I've got children! I've got children!"

Cathy knew witnesses had been spooked by police, but until she saw the horror in Nichol's eyes, she had no idea how badly they were frightened.

Later we received a threatening letter from Nichol's lawyer, warning us that she might sue us. We kept writing and pleading with her. Eventually, Nichol agreed to a meeting in Regina but said she could remember nothing on any critical point. She couldn't even recall making her police statement, she said.

Perhaps she had a mental block, I suggested to her, somewhat delicately. Would she consider being hypnotized?

Lorne and me on our wedding day.

(JOYCE MILGAARD)

Quiet times with David, Susan and Chris, September 1955.

(JOYCE MILGAARD)

Chris, 5 months, and David, 17 months,
sharing the bath, October 1955.

(JOYCE MILGAARD)

David, Susan and Chris — all smiles and all dressed up.

(JOYCE MILGAARD)

Christmas Day 1962, with my parents and baby Maureen, David, Susan and Chris.

(JOYCE MILGAARD)

Above: *David with Pappa Milgaard.*

(JOYCE MILGAARD)

Left: *Myself and David, age 3, with his beautiful blond curls.*

(JOYCE MILGAARD)

*Teenaged David
in his hippie days.*

(JOYCE MILGAARD)

*Gail Miller
in a community
college yearbook
photograph.*

Visiting David at Stony Mountain Penitentiary, with Susan and Lorne.

(JOYCE MILGAARD)

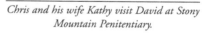

Chris and his wife Kathy visit David at Stony Mountain Penitentiary.

(JOYCE MILGAARD)

David and me at Kingston Penitentiary, 1980.

(JOYCE MILGAARD)

David in Kingston Penitentiary, age 32.

(JOYCE MILGAARD)

David and Emily Dapkus, soul mates.

(SUSAN MILGAARD)

David and me with Paul Henderson, super sleuth.

(PAUL HENDERSON)

Rev. Jim McCloskey,
whose privately-funded Centurion Ministries aided David's cause.

(KRYSTIA GRANBERG/P.T.S. PHOTO SERVICES)

Confronting Kim Campbell, former minister of justice, to whom I repeatedly appealed.

(CBC)

Prime Minister Brian Mulroney stops to listen to me in Winnipeg, 1991, as I plead for a speedy review of David's case.

(FRED CHARTRAND/CP)

I would pay for the hypnotist and truth serum and her lawyer could be present. She said she'd consider it, then quickly moved again, this time to be with her family in Kelowna, B.C. In correspondence with her lawyer, I tried to ease her mind that we didn't plan to take any action against her, legal or otherwise. Her lawyer demanded — and got — $1,400 from me for setting up a meeting with a hypnotist, but the meeting never took place. A year later, when I asked her lawyer if he would return the $1,400 so I could at least earn interest from it, he replied that he was still working on the matter.

Meanwhile, Ron Wilson had taken off to Calgary, and we had no clue where we might find Shorty Cadrain. Shorty's family said he hadn't been home in Saskatoon for three months, although his name was still listed there for billing with the hydro department. The police continued to spook our witnesses, which didn't help.

On February 1, 1981, we got a break when we tracked down the Danchuks, the couple who had invited David, Ron Wilson and Nichol John into their home early the morning of Gail Miller's murder. They lived just a couple of blocks from the site where her body had been found. David had used their phone to call a tow truck, and they had chatted briefly that morning while waiting for the truck to arrive. Wally and Sandra Danchuk were extremely important since they could help establish the almost impossibly tight time frame when David was actually free and alone to commit the crime. Wally Danchuk had been promoted and transferred to Camrose, Alberta, and when we reached them on the phone, they were initially wary.

"Sandra, my name is Joyce Milgaard," I said. "You testified in a trial many years ago for my son David. Is it convenient for you to speak to me for a minute on the telephone?"

"Sure."

"You may have heard that I am hoping to reopen the trial for David because we never really believed that he was guilty. We've had a little bit of fresh insight and fresh information . . . Do you remember that morning?"

"Yes, I do."

"Was he normal? You didn't feel that he was kooky or mental?"

"I always stated that nothing was abnormal or unusual about him," she said. "There was nothing to lead us to suspect that anything was wrong."

She recalled how David had praised their home, and also clearly recalled the car he had ridden in to Saskatoon: "It was a convertible and there weren't many convertibles."

"And you still remember about David's clothing, that you didn't see any blood?" I asked.

"No, definitely, I didn't see anything to incriminate him."

"If it [blood] had been there, with the lighting the way it was, you certainly would have seen it if it had been?"

"Yes."

"And actually with such a vicious crime as this was, it's almost certain that the killer would have had to have a lot of blood on him . . . It certainly doesn't figure at all."

I asked whether David had seemed scared or upset. "No, definitely not."

Her husband, Wally, was on the line now, and I explained my concerns and why I felt I had to do my own investigation for David. "He tried to escape twice and I believe they're going to throw away the key this time."

It didn't take long in the conversation to get the feeling that the Danchuks were a nice, well-grounded family, the opposite of the witnesses who had testified against David. Wally had trouble pinpointing the exact time when David showed up at their door that morning. David had been seen between seven and seven-thirty at the Travaleer Motel, so it had to be later than that. According to the Crown, Gail Miller was murdered around this time, although her body wasn't found until about eight-thirty.

I told the Danchuks how we had re-enacted the Crown's case to see if their version of the timing of events was plausible. "We've just sort of tested out the Crown's theory of her walking down the street and we did it with cars and everything. Basically now, there's just no way it could have happened the way they said it happened because of the time element and all of the things that happened to that poor girl."

The Danchuks hadn't followed the case after they moved from Saskatoon. They seemed interested in listening to me.

"This doesn't make sense for David to get out and offer to help you start your car if he had just murdered a girl a few blocks away," I continued. "You'd think he would really want to get out of that neighbourhood fast."

"He was nice to us," Wally recalled. "I can remember him being in the house. He talked, he was polite."

That was significant, since they had seen him just minutes after the murder, according to the Crown. They also noted how calm Nichol seemed that morning. Would she be that way if she had just seen David knife a woman to death? Especially if she was still in the company of a murderer-rapist? She certainly seemed emotional enough during the trial.

"Can I ask you a question?" Wally asked. "Why has it taken so long to bring this back up again?"

I was often asked that. Each time I answered, it was painful, and I always felt guilty we hadn't been able to do more, although I knew in my heart we had tried. "We kept trying to appeal and we couldn't," I replied. "You go along with the system."

That day, February 1, 1981, was memorable for another reason. I made contact by phone with Shorty Cadrain's mother, who had moved across town in Saskatoon. We were both a little tense and wary. There was a pleading tone to my voice as I asked if she would mind talking for a moment. A minute of their time for David's freedom didn't seem like too much to ask.

She replied that they were expected across town, adding that Shorty wasn't in town anyway and couldn't be reached by phone.

"Maybe I could write to Shorty," I offered.

"No, we have to wait until he writes to us, because he's moving around a lot, following a camp, cooking. He's way, way, way, way up north. We have to wait. There's no place to contact him. He can't be reached by phone. He's cooking for prospectors and things like that."

"Would you mind if I drop by?" I asked, trying to ignore her not-so-subtle hints to leave her alone.

"Well, you see, we have a full schedule," she said, noting that her plans included banking and shopping. "I wouldn't want to have to try to squeeze in anything else tomorrow. It's just too full."

As a mother, I could understand her urge to protect her son. However, I couldn't just go away. I also had a son to look out for.

On March 21, I contacted Shorty's family again. I didn't enjoy the rejection or the games, but we hadn't been able to find anything about Shorty through a tracing agency. I had learned about tracing agencies through my work in property management. We would hire them if someone had skipped out without paying their bill, and they would track them down by using their driver's licence or change-of-address form.

"Have you heard anything from Shorty at all?"

"Oh, we don't call him."

"Is he back in town yet?"

"He comes and goes."

"I would still very much like to talk to him, even if it's on the phone. I understand that he's married now."

"I don't like to answer all kinds of questions."

Then her tone turned ominous. She said that Shorty told her that a lot of things were not brought out in trial. Dangerous things. Things I wouldn't want to hear. "He [Shorty] asked Nicky in for a coffee and she screamed blue murder and he couldn't understand why and now he knows," she said. "And he feels sure that the other two saw what happened."

Then Shorty's mother asked me why David didn't testify at his trial. I explained that his lawyer had advised him not to. We had some leads that looked promising, I said, and Ron Wilson and Nichol John were changing their stories. We needed to know everything.

"How come you didn't do this before?" she asked. "How come you waited all of this time?"

It was the second time I had been asked that this day, and the question got no easier to answer. If anything, it got tougher. "We kept trying to appeal and do the ordinary steps, and we always thought that he'd get parole."

Mrs. Cadrain said that Shorty told her only bad things would come from a new trial. "If this is going to be rehashed, no good is going to come out of it," Shorty had said. Then she added, "He feels that David is guilty and he feels very sorry for him."

She described Shorty as a friend for the unfortunates of society, and that he considered David a loner who needed a friend. I pressed her to at least set up a telephone conversation between Shorty and me.

"He doesn't give his phone number to anybody and he's been doing that for quite a while because when he wants to rest, he doesn't want that darn phone ringing all the time."

"Would he answer a letter if I sent a letter?"

"Well, you'd have to send it over here to my address. I'm not antagonistic. I'm not blaming you for doing what you're doing."

"Albert may have some very vital information, and as you know I'm offering a $10,000 reward."

"He would tell the truth no matter what."

I saw no point in noting that Shorty had already collected $2,000 for helping put his friend behind bars. I wasn't trying to win arguments. I was trying to get David out of prison.

It would take us two years to find Shorty. Peter and Cathy Carlyle-Gordge were still helping. Peter demonstrated an impressive skill for getting people to talk, even when he didn't particularly like them. He told Shorty's brother Dennis that he was working on a book on famous western Canadian murder cases, like serial killer Clifford Olson of Vancouver and Katie Harper of Winnipeg, who accused her second husband of killing her first husband, only to be convicted of the crime herself. Peter said he would like to interview Shorty about Gail Miller's killing. Dennis said he wasn't a writer but that he had once thought of doing a book himself on the murder.

Dennis noted that he was the one who told Shorty about Gail Miller's murder. Through that night, Shorty thought about it, then went to police the next day. By the time he left the house to talk with police, Shorty was vividly describing how David's clothes were soaked in blood. His eagerness to cooperate with police almost backfired. "They spent months trying to blame it on him [Shorty]," Dennis recalled. "He's a little bit, like, mentally unstable. The police, they did it to him."

Dennis was in full flight now. He seemed to enjoy the

drama of the situation, saying, "Milgaard is such a good talker. You read about [killer Charles] Manson, how he had a power on people. Milgaard was the same way. He could walk into a place where he never knew a soul and five minutes later, he'd be eating everybody's food and screwing all the women. I saw him do it. I met him. I knew him. He stayed at our place. One time he stayed about three weeks."

"Did he seem violent towards you?" Peter asked.

"Oh, I wouldn't say that he seemed violent. I'd say that he had a really high opinion of himself with women and if he couldn't get a woman to come across for him, that would really hurt his ego."

Dennis said he had never spoken with police about his memories of the morning Gail Miller was murdered. "I remember the morning just like it was yesterday," he said. "It was so cold. It was forty below. It was so foggy."

After Shorty gave his statement to police, they wouldn't let him go. "They came just about every day for three months, eh, interrogating him there for eight or ten hours a day, just checking his story out. My brother was just telling what he saw and being a good citizen, eh? He had to go to the psychiatric ward after, a couple of years after. They screwed him up."

Dennis clearly cared about his brother, but warned Peter, "You have to watch what he says. I wouldn't take everything he says as gospel." Dennis noted that no one else saw the blood on David that Shorty claimed to have seen.

Dennis continued that he also knew Larry Fisher. "Yeah, he lived in our basement. He wasn't living there at the time. I think he had lived there before. He was quite a guy too."

Dennis seemed a little proud of his brother, and the fact that he played a role in such a big murder case, saying, "They had nothing until he went. It was hard on Albert." The $2,000 reward for his role in convicting his friend didn't bring him much joy. "He gave it to my dad. My dad needed some money on the farm or something and my brother didn't want it. Some people might have said he did it for the goddamn money, but he didn't care about money. They fucked his life right up. He couldn't handle it, you know. It wasn't only the cops."

Dennis then started to describe Shorty's suspicions that David was part of the Mafia. Saskatchewan wasn't exactly a hotbed for the Mafia, and even if it was, I doubt they had too many sixteen-year-old kingpins. "He'd certainly be game for it," Dennis said.

Dennis added that it didn't mean much to him that other witnesses couldn't recall blood on David the morning of the murder. "To me, I would say they were threatened by Milgaard."

He was happy to put Peter in contact with Shorty, who lived in a small town outside Saskatoon. Finally, Peter was able to meet up with Shorty on February 18, 1983, and it didn't take much to get Shorty talking of his many suspicions. After leaving Saskatoon the day of the murder, David had broken off an aerial from the car, and tossed a powder compact out the window as far as he could throw, Shorty recalled. And when they got to Calgary and Edmonton, David always felt compelled to read the newspaper. Shorty had wanted to go with David to a library, but David didn't want him. Something about that struck Shorty as suspicious. Then there was the blood on David, Shorty said. He said at first he thought it was from a virgin.

Shorty then described his treatment by the Saskatoon police. "They worked me over, boy. They questioned me and showed me pictures. Oh, man, it was freaky." Freaky was the same word he used for Nichol John. "I'll tell you, she was one freaky girl. I never met a freaky broad like that in my life."

As for David, Shorty saw evil and deception behind my son's smile. "Yeah, he's one scary guy. He thought I was going to lie for him in court too. Well, he was sitting in the box there and I remember the police telling me, 'Don't look at him.' I looked at him anyway. You know what he did? He looked at me and he put on a real baby-face smile. You know, as if to say, 'My buddy, my pal. You'll free me, eh.' I never listened to any face, face you know. Gestures and all."

Shorty vividly recalled David's expression when he finally caught on that his friend's testimony might land him in prison. "You should have seen the horror on his face when he seen I wasn't gonna try to save him. You should have seen the horror in his eyes."

Shorty imitated David when he showed up at Shorty's house the morning of the murder. He said David told him, "I need clothes." Shorty's voice was rising and falling now, full of drama. "All I had on was a pair of gotchies," Shorty recalled, while he thought David had on grey pants. "It seems to me there was some holes on them from battery acid or something. He had blood on them. But I looked at that girl [Nichol John] and I says, 'You poor virgin. You sure got it last night.' That's what I thought when I looked her over. I was surprised that a virgin would be chasing after me after he popped her."

In the end, it was clear our big break wasn't going to come from Shorty.

Our detective work took a bizarre twist when a businessman who had worked with David at Maclean Hunter offered to pay our legal bills. The only condition was that we had to drop our lawyer, Gary Young, and hire high-profile Regina lawyer Tony Merchant. The reasoning, we were told, was that Tony Merchant, the son-in-law of federal Liberal cabinet minister Otto Lang, brought with him much-needed political connections. We were very happy with Gary Young, but the offer seemed generous and the money was badly needed. Besides, perhaps a political insider might pull some strings, and there was clearly a political dimension to David's predicament. It wasn't until a few years later that we learned that the businessman, whom we considered so generous, had actually applied to collect reward money for urging David to turn himself in to police back in 1969. Was he now suddenly feeling guilty? Or was he trying to trick us?

Merchant wasn't one to feed us false hope. He said it would take something dramatic to reopen the case, like a key witness coming forward and admitting to lying on the stand. Merchant was impressed with our efforts and our sacrifice, but he said the case we were building was too difficult to understand; all the facts we were gathering about the impossibility of the Crown's theory of timing made sense to us, but were too hard for anyone else to follow.

Merchant got in touch with Calvin Tallis, who was now an Appeals Court judge, to see whether he could offer any help. Tallis wrote back that he thought it significant that Gail Miller was stabbed through her overcoat but not through her dress. The logical assumption is that she had no dress on when she was stabbed. Exactly where this left us, however, was puzzling. If the killer dressed Miller after stabbing her, it seemed to make the Crown's theory that David killed her out in the open in the extreme cold even more implausible. For the Crown's theory to be true, David undressed her, raped her, stabbed her and redressed her all in frigid temperatures and without being seen, near a bus stop in a residential area when people were heading to work, in an almost impossibly tight time frame of about fifteen minutes.

I didn't know at first that Merchant was also the lawyer for Colin Thatcher, the former Saskatchewan cabinet minister who was convicted in 1984 of murdering his wife, JoAnne. However, my uneasy feeling about Merchant wouldn't die. Obviously, powerful people were working against David. Why else would the Saskatoon police keep telling witnesses to stay away from us? Why would they care so much, so long after the murder?

We heard that Colin Thatcher and Gail Miller had gone out for a while, then had broken up. Did Tony

Merchant know this? Merchant was a friend of Thatcher's, as well as his lawyer. What if he thought that his friend had killed Gail Miller? I began to suspect that Colin Thatcher was the killer. We heard that the day after Miller's murder, Thatcher's family sent him away to college in the States. We also knew that Thatcher had a terrible temper, and whoever killed Gail Miller was extremely violent. I had always suspected that someone powerful might be involved, and in Saskatchewan few people are higher up than the Thatcher family. Colin Thatcher was the millionaire son of a former premier and a cabinet minister himself. The media frequently referred to him as a Canadian version of J.R. Ewing, the devious oil tycoon from the hit television series *Dallas*. Like the fictitious J.R., Colin Thatcher grew up learning to wield power and control things, and wasn't used to taking no for an answer.

TEN

STIFLED

*"I believe in her so much that I think
her way will be the only way."*
David, writing about me

DAVID ARRIVED IN KINGSTON Penitentiary on
crutches. He was defiant, and at first refused medical
attention, preferring instead to be locked in solitary
confinement as he gradually regained the use of his legs.
It was a bad choice, as he was in a lot of pain once the
painkillers from hospital wore off. He self-medicated
himself by dipping into a pail filled with prison hooch,
which earned him ten days in solitary confinement.
That didn't faze him, as he wrote Lorne:

> I think I can handle it! Both the 10 and the lost
> pail.
> I got to thinking about the home front and
> how you might be feeling these days . . . I will
> never be the way I was 12 years ago. Yet some-
> how I remain the same. My 77 days of fresh air

opened my eyes to a lot of things. A person can do what he wants with his life but he had to *do it*, it won't get done for him. Within this framework of resolve I'm trying to formulate a game-plan. Considering what I am and what I truly want are very important here. Then of course the fact that I'm where I'm at right now in this dump, at this point I must work to establish or reestablish upon my return to Stony my credibility — no small task. The game then becomes who can do the bureaucratic shuffle the best and you & I both know the government can. As a convicted murderer and prior to last November one of Canada's most wanted men out of it I don't think it will happen, my conditional release in the next 3 years for sure and it wasn't that different before August.

We come to our ace in the hole, Mom, and her effort. I believe in her so much that I think her way will be the only way. Dad, I believe in you too and I don't know why I ask how you feel, I'm only reaching I guess.

Then, David reminded his father that Mother's Day was coming up and asked him to send me flowers.

For the next couple years, David shuffled between Kingston Penitentiary and nearby Millhaven, in Bath. He was trying to behave better behind bars and become a more positive person, but it wasn't easy. In an undated letter, he wrote me, "I work in a shop now and am trying to get a six month stretch without trouble. I know you think with a reward as important as my freedom, it would or should be something I breeze through, yet, Mom, it is hard not to try making prison easy by goofing off if you can get a handle on where I'm coming from."

David exercised and wrote poetry and enjoyed weekly visits with Christian Scientist friends of mine, Barb and Phil Lever. That human contact made a huge difference, and his thoughts turned more positive. This came out in a letter he wrote me on June 14, 1981: "I ran seven miles last night and pushed myself. It felt good, Mom. Those bullets have got nothing on me now (smile). Looking back to my crutches and my feelings that I wouldn't be able to walk or run, well, I feel I've come a long way. I have also developed a healthy respect for the people that tried to kill me."

In that letter, David wrote that he was virtually assured of getting transferred from Millhaven to nearby Collins Bay, where long-term education opportunities were better. He had plenty of time to think of how he had suffered at the hands of his old friends. "I would like to know why they did it though," David wrote. "I don't hate them and wouldn't harm them, but one day I'd like them to admit they lied."

To this end, David wrote to Ron Wilson:

> I have always wondered what it was that made you and Nichol go against me as you did. All our early statements are the truth, we had no reason to lie or make up stories because we never murdered anyone . . .

I want you to go to a lawyer of your choice and put this thing right. You can do so without getting yourself in trouble. You will also probably end up with the $10,000, still up for grabs . . .

Think back to early morning Saskatoon, the boulivarded road that we really came in on . . . remember an old lady we saw probably headed for a bus, we turned around in the intersection and cruised by . . . I am not sure if we stopped or not . . . we then kept on until we had some soup at a garage before we crossed a bridge and went downtown and then on to Cadrain's. We never killed anyone, I never killed anyone. It is all in your mind just like it is mine; I want you to tell it like it was.

It was while David was in Millhaven Penitentiary that we received this unforgettable letter from K.W. Howland of the National Parole Board, which said, in part:

I can still recall very distinctly a conversation which I had with you regarding why you were not experiencing any conflict or difficulty with other inmates given the circumstances of the offence for which you were convicted. At that time, you stated that while you had been convicted, inmates knew that you were not guilty and therefore, you did not receive any 'hassle' from them. I have never forgotten that statement. I was pointedly reminded of your own assertion of innocence by the publicity which surrounded the reward offered by your family a few months ago in an attempt to obtain information which would assist in exonerating you. I saw your mother interviewed on a Regina television program and I was interested to hear her say that some information had been obtained which they were pursuing and she hoped that additional information would be provided . . .

My assessment of your situation, David, is a personal one and as you know, not representative of the National Parole Board . . .

I look forward to obtaining a much more thorough understanding of your situation so that I will be in a better position to comment more knowledgeably about it with you. It is evident to me that you have not given up on yourself and neither has your family and all of your efforts must be directed towards convincing others to believe in you as well as to support you in reaching the goals which you have established for yourself.

I hope that the transfer to Stony Mountain Institution occurs soon and that you will keep me informed of developments in your situation.

On June 22, 1981, David wrote me from his cell in Millhaven, obviously depressed:

Dear Mom,

Where to begin . . . Well I am feeling pretty down lately, my days are all the same and they just go on and on. I feel that bad to have to write you — I couldn't think of anyone else to lay it on Mom and reach to.

My daily diet of people and things in general are starving me mentally . . .

I love you very much . . .

Maureen had moved to Kingston to stay near David, supporting herself by working at cheap hotels. She grew up knowing there would be no money to send her to college, and didn't question this. Her move to Ontario meant she could see David in prison about three times a week. Often, these visits were extremely frustrating for her. Sometimes David was fasting. Other times he would walk into walls. Sometimes he would scribble Maureen notes on toilet paper. Often, she left her visit feeling totally helpless.

However, there were also good times, when Maureen knew her sacrifice was worthwhile and helping David. On September 18, 1981, in a letter to his dad, David described a visit with Maureen:

It has been awhile since I've written and with Maureen out this way a lot of my "to dos" are behind schedule.

Things transfer wise look like they are either going to take forever to get me back west or I won't get back at all. Believe me I've looked at the whole thing and the only way I figure to see any action on the parts of the bureaucrats involved would require some serious political clout . . . What doesn't these days.

Maureen and I are having a great time! I expect that if we have any more fun they will lock the both of us up. [We] have the cottage of Barbara Lever a friend of Mom's (someone she met while down this way to visit me before) . . .

Still working at becoming physically healthy, weights and running. Mentally, I finished the U course from Winnipeg and believe I did fairly well. I should receive my final exam mark back shortly. I'm to start a new course from the U of Waterloo but I don't know if I really want to do the work. I might as well. It will give me something over the winter to do. There just doesn't seem to be a end to this whole smozzal, I hope Mom and Anthony Merchant can pull the rabbit from the hat.

Take care of yourself, Dad, because when things do get together I want for us to do a little hunting and fishing where nothing and no-one can get at us.

"I hate reality, or at least my reality for now," David wrote me on April 1, 1982. "When I put my act together as I'm doing this last little while, it is so much more apparent to me — the sadness, the madness and the overwhelming worthlessness of this place."

David was constantly undergoing psychological testing. After all, in the eyes of the law he was a crazed sex killer who would not own up to his crime. Reports in August 1982, while he was at Millhaven, noted that David tended to live in the future rather than in the present. The report concluded that he badly needed approval, which made me shudder. What place is there where one gets less approval than a penitentiary? Who gets less approval than a convicted sex killer? The report also said that David had difficulty expressing negative emotions. Could this be more ironic, since he was falsely convicted of murder?

During this harsh time, one of the toughest comments for me to cope with came from within my own church. One of our members said, "I probably shouldn't say to this to you, Joyce, but I have heard other members say that if you were really a good Christian Scientist, your son David would not still be in prison." That hurt so badly. I went home and reread the Bible lesson from that morning. It was the story about the fiery furnace. I read about the Hebrews being bound and put in the fire and the king suddenly seeing another person walking around being free and he was the son of God. It suddenly came to me. The reason the Hebrew boys were in that fire was so that the king could see Christ. I was in the fire so that the power of the Christ could be seen. It wasn't my fault.

The joy I felt for this clear thought washed away any bitterness I had felt. Experience taught me that when we put ourself under God's law, it supersedes all other laws.

I was also drawing strength from wonderful letters

from people all across the country who wrote that they were praying for us. There were schoolchildren, seniors, professionals, mothers and lonely women who had crushes on David. I was told to expect some hate mail, but it didn't come. I didn't feel so alone anymore. I loved answering the letters.

ELEVEN

UNLIKELY HERO

"I didn't understand the whole thing myself."
Crown prosecutor Bobs Caldwell describes the forensic
evidence that helped convict David

A STRANGE THING HAPPENED during a parole hearing in the 1980s. A member of the board blew up at us. Looking furious enough to leap over the table in our direction, he screamed about the way that Gail Miller's body looked and the horrific pain frozen on her face.

"How could we take a chance of letting that happen again?" he shouted.

"I've seen the pictures of that girl."

"How did he see the pictures of her?" we wondered. We soon discovered, through our contacts in the system, that every time David was up for parole, Crown prosecutor Bobs Caldwell found out who was going to be sitting on the hearing and sent them a big brown envelope with the pictures of Miller's body. They were just absolutely gruesome photographs, accompanied by a letter describing what a monster David was and why he should never be allowed to walk free. Caldwell never did this in any of his other cases.

Later, we would get to see the letters Caldwell sent. In them, he invoked the authority of his position and claimed to have particular insights into David's mind, as in this June 14, 1972, letter:

> In preparing this case, I had the privilege of reading Milgaard's entire psychiatric history, which, as it happened, was very well documented since his early youth. He had been in constant trouble since kindergarten days, and the file even contains predictions by social workers who had examined Milgaard that he would one day kill somebody.
>
> Having been intimately involved in this case from the time of the killing until the final disposition of the matter in the Supreme Court of Canada, I, of necessity, came to know a great deal about the personality of the accused, Milgaard. While I no longer have his psychiatric history available to me, it was an extremely lengthy record of continual trouble with educational institutions, persons attempting to help him, et cetera. Albert Cadrain, whose evidence was very important in trial, knew Milgaard previous to this episode, and told the police and myself of episodes in Calgary wherein Milgaard had young girls in his living quarters to whom he would supply

heroin to the point at which these girls completely lost their senses. One of these episodes involved Milgaard inviting Cadrain to have sexual intercourse with a girl in this state whom Milgaard had in a bathtub filled with water. This was only one example of the almost unbelievable life style of Milgaard before this offence, which I came to know as a result of preparing for the prosecution of this trial.

The offence, of course, is of the utmost gravity, and was unprovoked, senseless and brutal in the extreme, resulting in a violent and horrible death to this girl, who was a stranger to the accused . . . He has a sociopathic personality, and in my view there is not just a possibility, but rather a certainty, that he will return to crime on his release, since he is unqualified for any other occupation.

While dealing with this point, it is ironic to note that the only occupation which Milgaard held with any degree of success in past was that of a door-to-door salesman of magazine subscriptions, etcetera, which is a circumstance which should be of great comfort to the housewives of the nation if he is eventually allowed to return to his trade.

This letter also noted David's failed bid to escape from Dorchester Penitentiary, and played openly on fear: "I would also hope that Milgaard's escape from an institution in Eastern Canada . . . would be taken into account by the Parole Service and the Parole Board as evidence of a lack of reformation or rehabilitation on his part. Milgaard is an extremely dangerous and unpredictable person, and I for one would not care to be in the position of allowing him to be released from custody on any terms whatsoever during his lifetime, since I feel that responsibility would bear heavily on the person making such a decision when Milgaard seized upon the first opportunity to rape and/or kill a female person."

We learned more about Bobs Caldwell around this time, when Peter Carlyle-Gordge interviewed him. As before, Peter introduced himself as a writer working on a book on sensational murders in western Canada, and Caldwell was eager to have the biggest case in his career included. Caldwell was middle-aged, balding and robust, giving the impression that he had once been a competitive athlete.

Peter thought that Caldwell fit the profile of a zealous American prosecutor, hell-bent on getting the bad guys. He seemed to see the world in right-wing, black-and-white terms, and gave the impression that he honestly believed David was nothing less than a Canadian version of American cult killer Charles Manson.

Caldwell gave Peter access to his files on the case, and in them, Peter saw the name Larry Fisher. A police report noted that Fisher rode the same bus as Gail Miller and that he told police he was at work the day of the murder. The files also showed that there had been a series of sexual assaults in the neighbourhood, in an alley

behind a funeral home. Those attacks began before Gail
Miller's murder and continued afterwards.

In their interview, Peter and Caldwell first discussed
Nichol John's often-changing story and how it worked
against David. "I interviewed her," Caldwell said. "She
was very reluctant with the interview. She didn't get
along with me. She ran out of my office once in tears."

Caldwell proudly reminded Peter that the case was a
legal milestone, because Caldwell was able to read into
the evidence the statement Nichol had made to police
against David, even though she denied this version in
court. It made the standard law text, *Martin's Criminal
Code*, with a brand-new amendment on adverse
witnesses. Caldwell made no apologies for indirectly
entering Nichol's police statement. It didn't trouble him
that she gave it to investigators when she was under
considerable pressure, or that she would no longer
support it. "Finally, they [the investigators] got them to
come out with what we think is the accurate story,"
Caldwell said.

"Do you believe that she saw that?"

"Yes, I do. I mean, I wasn't there. I wasn't in the investigation," Caldwell said. "There was the usual divergence
on details, you know. You get that on all cases . . . The
final versions that they came out with I felt to be the
truth. One thing, these people are frightened of that guy.
That's another thing that's not to be overlooked."

This fear explained Nichol's nervous state during the
trial, Caldwell said. "She was very defensive and very
uptight all of the time," he said. "It's very tough to

incriminate somebody like that when he's sitting there and you're terrified of the guy. And these guys were very much afraid of Milgaard."

Nichol's fear of David explained why she travelled with him to Alberta, even after the gruesome murder, Caldwell said, and also accounted for holes in her memory. "It's a terrifying thing because they're still afraid of that guy. And I wouldn't be surprised if . . . [it was] similar to hysterical amnesia — the mind finds it so terrible that you just forget it."

He noted that there were forty-five Crown witnesses and forty-one exhibits, and that witnesses Lapchuk and Melnyk came right out of the blue, at the last minute, as a true godsend for the Crown. "We had no idea of them," he said.

Lapchuk and Melnyk surfaced literally on the eve of the trial with their story of David's motel-room confession. Caldwell said nothing about how or why they came forward. No mention was made that they had charges pending against them at the time, or of the light treatment they received from the Crown's office after they gave their testimony. "I didn't know what to do," Caldwell said. "I didn't know whether I could call that evidence. That was a spooky thing." Caldwell praised Lapchuk and Melnyk for hanging in under a determined cross-examination from Tallis. "Is that ever eerie evidence," Caldwell said. "When do you ever get a murder re-enacted? . . . Only the person who did it could have known what he did there. You know, . . . saying, 'I stabbed her X number of times and then she died,' and then to look up and laugh, holy, that is just . . . Holy suffering. That couldn't have been invented by them in my opinion, that had to be done by the guy who did it."

Caldwell made it clear that he was nothing if not prepared for the trial. Three weeks before it began, he was in the jury room every day, spreading out documents in isolation and focusing his strategy. If he hadn't gotten a satisfactory verdict of guilty, he would have considered quitting his job, Caldwell said. "So much rode on it and there had been so much effort by everybody, the police and the civilians and pathologists and everyone, our office, everyone. Secondly, it was such a horrible thing in the beginning. Third, the whole attention of the community is on . . . And if you believe that this is the guy and you've got the evidence, it would be a very severe disappointment if you couldn't bring it home . . . I think it would just really be very, very diffcult to come back from that when we all felt that this was the guy and all this effort's been made . . . I think I would have felt then that the system's not operating the way that it should.

"The hero of the thing, other than policemen, was Albert Cadrain," Caldwell continued.

"If he hadn't gone to police. . . ?" Peter asked.

"Without him, clearly, I think the thing never would have come off. He hung in there under Tallis's extremely skilled attacks . . . I just couldn't say enough good about the guy."

Caldwell tried to downplay the fact that he had a well-staffed, professional team in front of the jury. "I didn't want to look overstaffed in the case. When you're prosecuting, you get this thing, 'My learned friend has all the resources of the state at his command — the army, the air force and the navy' — and that can go against you . . . I had three full-time support staff . . . I had all kinds of help, but it wasn't obvious." In fact, the jury saw Milgaard with two counsel, and just one for the Crown. The Crown looked like the little guys, even though David was a legal aid case.

The forensics had been complicated and hard to understand, and the Crown was excited when some pants were recovered, but it turned out they must have been washed because there were no traces of blood on them. "I didn't understand the whole thing myself," Caldwell said of the forensics. However, he said he did understand enough to know that Wilson couldn't have been a source for the seminal fluid in the snow, while Milgaard was a possibility, and "there was no suggestion of anybody else being around."

Caldwell said that the entire incident and subsequent emotional courtroom battle probably began when David unsuccessfully asked a woman for directions. Within minutes, that escalated into a brutal rape and murder that cold January morning. That might sound odd and improbable, he said, but, "if you see this guy's character, he wasn't going to take that answer from anybody. They were asking for Peace Hill and the real name of the area was Pleasant Hill and this girl said in effect, 'I don't know where it is' or whatever, and he called her 'stupid bitch' . . . I'm not sure that it began as a purse snatching. I think it was just one of his forays. Hey, here's a chance to do this. It's no wonder that poor old Nichol John and Wilson were afraid of him."

Oddly enough, through the entire drama, Caldwell and David never once spoke with each other, even though they sat only six feet apart in the courtroom. Perhaps that's why it was so easy for Caldwell to demonize him. "He was a very innocent looking, baby-faced guy," Caldwell said. "When you consider that his occupation was door-to-door magazine sales . . . And there were reported incidents of women taking him into their houses and everything and giving him lunch because he looks undernourished. That just makes my blood run cold. Holy smokes." Caldwell noted that David had refused psychiatric treatment in Penetanguishene, and was discharged quickly from another psychiatric facility because he bluntly insisted that he was innocent. "That is not really great evidence of being rehabilitated, I would say."

Caldwell concluded, "As far as prosecuting a murder, that's the worst that I've been involved in. That's not to say that I've been involved in that many, but I sure don't want to see another one like that again."

At least Caldwell and I agreed on one thing.

TWELVE

A LITTLE SAD

*"If David is innocent, as he fervently claims,
of his conviction, he has done remarkably well
for a young teenager who has spent his youth
and young adult life in prison."*
A reverend writes in support of
David's parole application

DAVID LIKED TO SEND me flowers for Mother's Day and leatherwork from his therapy classes. He drew lovely cards and wrote poetry in them. One Mother's Day, he planned to give me a grapefruit he had grown from a seed. Somehow, this contravened a prison regulation, and so David had someone in the prison take a photo of him with the grapefruit and he mailed the picture to me. Neither of us was easily deterred.

David's mood was optimistic just before Mother's Day 1983, when he again applied for day parole. David had impressed Rev. Nelson Trafford, who supported his bid and wrote:

I first met David last November and at that time he was very depressed and frustrated. He has always maintained his innocence, and therefore his frustrations were trying to struggle in an orderly way to be free of injustice. Part of his method of relating to some sense of freedom was to 'act out' against authority. This in turn only put him into more isolation with its added frustrations.

For the past several months, however, David has begun to work in a more positive approach to his release. This is due in a great way to his new attitude towards freedom, which must also include self-discipline. He has maintained regular work hours at his place of employment. He is seeing Barbara Lever from the Christian Science organization on a weekly basis. These visits take place in the chapel area, and are quite productive especially in the area of personal support and interaction with a woman. He handles these times very well. I find him personally very cooperative, polite and sensitive to people and things around him. He exhibits much less anger and offers good philosophy for his future and how he sees freedom with new values.

His poetry shows a gentle and creative spirit with a joyful expression of the world around him. It is not morbid.

David and I have talked often and I have watched him come from depression to new expression. From an unkempt appearance to clean and well groomed. The pained expression has given way to a pleasant and warm smiling face which includes his eyes.

If David is innocent, as he fervently claims, of his conviction, he has done remarkably well for a young teenager who has spent his youth and young adult life in prison. If he is guilty of his crime he has served a substantial period and his conduct of late, the past few months, give every indication of a thinking and maturing young man, who I feel needs a break.

But again, David did not get a break. His application for day parole was rejected, with the panel concluding, "He has not demonstrated that he is not a continuing risk to society." In rejecting his application, the panel wrote, "Milgaard comes across as an intelligent and bright individual but has only recently accepted his sentence. He continues to feel that he is innocent of the crime for which he has been convicted and his mother is actively pursuing evidence and a hearing to prove Milgaard's innocence. While he understands that the NPB [National Parole Board] must start with the finding of the Courts, he has only recently accepted that the parole decision is premised on the finding of guilt.

". . . Milgaard seemed to be dominated and greatly influenced by his mother. 'His plans' were clearly the work product of his mother. At times during the interview, his facial expression showed disagreement with some of the thoughts espoused by his mother. She created unduly high expectations for his parole hearing notwithstanding the recommendations of the Court."

It was around this time that David's baby sister, Maureen, was married. It was a beautiful ceremony with bridesmaids, flowers and everything else except David. It was tough for him to miss the event; Maureen was special to him. Underlying the joy of this family occasion was the sad knowledge, once again, that David should have been there too.

Not surprisingly, he again fell into a depression, and his letter-writing dropped off. We finally heard from him early in the new year, when he wrote,

> I realise I have been a long time in getting to you with how things have been for me and I've no real honest excuse except to say that the ruts, the rough times aren't something you need to know about all the time or just the sort of thing to make you feel all that happy. I figured you'd be up in the air with all the good feelings that come from Christmas and then the up of the wedding too. All you needed was me to start crying on your shoulder . . .
>
> How is Dad and tell me all of Christmas and what's what with everyone. Think you could sneak down here for my T.A.? Fried mushrooms, mincemeat pie (hot of course) and ice cream and rhubarb pie too, so far we have that much planned.

I love you very much and I know that this
year is one that will make me realize how lousy
a place this is as I get closer to my freedom and
all of you. I really feel what doing time is all
about. Sorry if this was a little sad, Mom, but
I'm coming out of it all right and I'll make it.

In the late fall of 1985, there were hopes that the CBC
investigative program, *the fifth estate*, would air a piece
on David's case. Our attempts at interesting the media
finally appeared to be bearing fruit. An investigation by
the fifth estate would be a huge coup, since programs are
seen coast to coast and are often rebroadcast. They have
a reputation for being thorough, and we knew that the
deeper they dug, the more convinced they would be of
David's innocence. David sounded a bit wary, but also
hopeful, when he wrote me, on November 29, saying he
hoped he could also somehow use the program to help
his fellow prisoners:

I feel blue and want to share my thoughts with
you . . .
    I got your letter when I arrived — your timing
or God's is great . . . it was funny how I felt being
back — the only way to say it is cared for —
back on to the same range just downstairs
instead of and after all the sh+t (like my effort to
disguise my swear word) (smile) anyway . . . all
my friends, mom, care and when I think of
upcoming 5th estate presentation I have to hold

that high and fight for all prisoners because they
are people and not garbage — they need love
and compassion not walls surrounding them, all
together, just so they get worse.

By now David had spent half of his life behind bars for
a crime he did not commit. He clung desperately to his
last year of freedom, when he was just sixteen. It was as
if he couldn't allow himself to grow beyond that year.
Psychiatrist Stanley Yaren did his best to treat David
during the mid-1980s, and eventually concluded that
health professionals, including himself, had made a
mistake when they diagnosed David as having a personality disorder. Even at David's worst, however, Yaren
wrote, he was not violent. "He has *not*, however, exhib-
ited any propensity towards violent or aggressive behaviour while in a psychotic state." Treatment with lithium
carbonate was working very well, preventing the return
of psychotic episodes, Yaren concluded in a February 6,
1986, report. "During his non-psychotic state Milgaard
relates in a reasonable, sensible manner. He is polite,
personable and exhibits no problematic behaviour."

Yaren noted that David was still maintaining his
innocence and was frustrated at the slow pace it was
taking to prove it. "It does however appear that he has
attracted the attention of interested individuals including the media who are willing to present his side of the
story . . . In my opinion, in his treated state Milgaard
represents no significant risk to the community and
should be released on Parole. He of course should be

required to continue psychiatric treatment upon release. He is in agreement with this and has considerable insight into the nature of his illness and the requirement for continued treatment."

THIRTEEN

WHITE KNIGHT LAWYER

*"I'm sure glad you love me large
or I'd be a goner for sure."*
David, writing to me in 1986

BY 1986, I WAS WEARY of false leads and worried
that time and money were running out. It had been six
years since we held the family meeting at which we
decided to pour every available penny into proving
David's innocence, and he was still locked behind bars,
with no release date in sight. Leads had grown cold, and
we had the awful feeling we were getting nowhere. We
still had our suspicions about former Saskatchewan cabinet minister Colin Thatcher, but we hadn't been able to
prove anything. Even if someone surfaced to crack open
the case, we no longer had the $10,000 we had promised
in our reward posters way back in December 1980.

It was then that Peter Carlyle-Gordge came up with
what was probably the best of his many bright ideas. He
suggested I call Hersh Wolch, a Winnipeg criminal lawyer
and a former Crown attorney who now had a defence

practice at Wolch, Pinx, Tapper, Scurfield. They had met when Peter was working on the Katie Harper case, and Hersh's spirit and intelligence had impressed Peter.

I took my trial transcripts to Hersh and asked him how much he would charge to read them and give us an opinion. We needed to be told bluntly whether we were banging our heads against a cement wall or whether there was something else we could do. I gave Hersh my last $2,000 as a retainer. He never did read the transcripts, but he did something even better. He gave them to David Asper, a smallish young lawyer with soft features and an air of boyish vitality. Asper was eager and inexperienced, having graduated from law school a few months before.

"Have a look at it," Hersh said.

David Asper read the transcripts and started to get hooked. He liked the challenge and the opportunity to do some good. He also had patience of biblical proportions, which he would need to work with me. But first, Asper needed to be convinced about my son.

"Did you do it?" Asper asked David bluntly when they first met in prison.

"No."

David Asper hit my son with all the tough questions he could think of, and my son's answers only made Asper more concerned that a gross injustice had been committed. My son also impressed him as a person. He was then taking university courses, and running his Justice Group, to the annoyance of prison officials. The group met every second Thursday night, and David attempted to bring in speakers who could act as positive role models for convicts. He was convinced that prisoners needed positive guidance, not punishment. Shining rays of light into prisons couldn't help but cleanse them, David reasoned. David also had a foster child in India, whom he hoped to see some day, and he dreamed of someday having a son of his own. He planned to name his boy Jeb. David had worked himself into great physical shape, with his running and weight training, and had almost completely lost his limp from the shotgun blast in Toronto. Considering he had spent half of his life behind bars, David was doing well. David Asper was impressed.

Asper rented a video camera and headed off to Saskatoon, where he re-enacted the Crown's version of the crime. It simply didn't make sense to him. Nichol John couldn't have seen what she told police. The timing was impossible. It also meant that, on the coldest day of the year, Gail Miller chose to take a meandering route to the bus stop.

While in Saskatoon, David Asper visited the courthouse where my son had been convicted and discovered that, sixteen years after the trial, all of the exhibits were still warehoused. They were delivered to him in two large cardboard boxes, and Asper examined them in a jury deliberating room — ironically the same room where my son's fate was decided sixteen years before. Asper hung Gail Miller's bloodstained dress and coat on hooks on the wall, and spread other exhibits, such as her underclothes and the awful photos of her body, on a table. For a green lawyer, whose roughest work to date dealt with robberies and thefts, it was a chilling experience. Before leaving, he put the court staff on informed notice that the exhibits should be preserved because they might be the subject of an ongoing investigation of the case. It was a blessing the exhibits were still around at all. In ordinary cases, exhibits are destroyed after all of the appeals are completed, but these exhibits sat in a shopping cart, with a note, "Not to be destroyed without the expressed written permission of T.D.R. Caldwell." What a twist of fate.

Soon, I was seeing young David Asper as my knight in shining armour. His father, Izzy Asper, was head of Global Television and former head of the Manitoba Liberal party, and David sincerely wanted to establish himself as his own person. He was full of idealism and a deep belief that people needed to be protected from the bullying tactics of a sometimes overreaching state. He spent countless hours reviewing transcripts of the trial and the preliminary hearing, and soon became an expert on minute details of the case. Most important, he revitalized our struggle. He not only believed in my son David's innocence, he convinced all the others in Hersh's law firm as well.

We badly wanted to gather new evidence, and an odd stroke of luck led us to Deborah Hall, who as a teenager had attended the Regina motel party. It was there that George Lapchuk and Craig Melnyk supposedly had heard David confess to the murder. Deborah had given a statement to Saskatoon police that totally contradicted their tale, but it was never passed on to our defence team, leaving us vulnerable to the last-minute, damning testimony of Lapchuk and Melnyk. In her police report,

Hall was misspelled "Hull" and then her file was apparently misplaced.

When my daughter Susan told her friend Regina radio reporter Chris O'Brien the story of searching for Deborah, he realized she was talking about his barber. Deborah was now a thirty-four-year-old single mother, and she immediately impressed us as someone with a brain and a conscience. When she spoke with us on November 23, 1986, she told us that the testimony of Lapchuk and Melnyk was nothing more than lies. She found it incredible that police and a jury actually took them seriously when they said that David bragged of raping and stabbing Gail Miller. "I don't remember any conversation like that," she told us. "It would have freaked me right out."

Deborah remembered that night of the party well. It was in a tiny motel room, so a dramatic incident like a murder-rape confession would have been hard to miss. Deborah recalled seeing a news report on Miller's murder on the television in the room, but couldn't hear what was being said because everyone was talking. David had already told his friends that he had been questioned about the murder, and at some point during the broadcast, Melnyk said to David, "You did it, didn't you?" David fluffed up a pillow and sarcastically replied, "Oh, yeah, right."

That was it for the alleged confession. There had been no crazed re-enactment of the killing, just a childish, sarcastic comment.

It wasn't as if Deborah hadn't noticed David that

night. It was impossible not to notice him. David had peeled off his clothes and invited her into bed, which she declined. "Needless to say, he was joking around a lot," Hall recalled. David then bounced into bed with his girlfriend of the moment, Ute Frank, giggling and laughing.

There were plenty of drugs in the room, and Hall took some THC, or synthetic marijuana, which heightened her senses. She was contemptuous and a little fearful of Lapchuk, and recalled a strong sense of relief when he finally left. She scoffed at Lapchuk's trial testimony that he had driven her home, saying she considered him repulsive and dangerous and would never have climbed alone into his car. Besides, she lived just four blocks away, so it wasn't much of a walk. "He was just a sleeze. I never trusted that guy."

As we told her details of Lapchuk and Melnyk's testimony, she kept saying things like, "Lie, that is definitely a lie," and, "I can't believe that. Boy, did they ever twist things." It was clear she wasn't now acting out of any great love for David. She bluntly told us that she lost respect for David after he ripped off someone for drug money that night, and how she disliked the way he treated her friend Ute. "He lowered her that night. She was so emotionally unstable with men."

The next few years took a toll on everyone. I was putting in eighteen-hour-days for David now, and there were many times that I just wanted to pack it in. Sometimes, I would be working away in the basement and then simply drop my head into my hands and sob, "I can't take it anymore." I know how hard it was on my kids to see me like this. Prayer helped me through these dark patches, and I would awake at five in the morning, so that I could fill my head with thoughts of good, and know that God was working with me, before the telephone started to ring and the battle heated up again. David Asper once jokingly moaned, "I'd just like to lock myself in a dark room and come out when it's all over."

Out of my wages, I tried to pay as much as I could, but my travelling back and forth looking for witnesses and evidence was costing me a fortune. Hersh and David Asper were losing track of what our case had cost their firm.

We had been turned down by legal aid in Saskatchewan and Manitoba, and our finances dipped to the point where the only thing I had left of any value was a mink coat, which I had bought in the mid-1980s, at the height of my success as a property manager. One day I wore it into Hersh's office and asked, "Do you want it?" He didn't. Hersh and David Asper's generosity was rare, but I felt determined to eventually pay them their money, one way or another. After about three years, we began working on a contingency plan with them, in the hope that someday there might be some settlement from the government.

The length of the struggle took a horrible toll on David. Once, I went to see him at Stony Mountain, and prison officials said he didn't want to see me. David had suffered forty-five days in solitary confinement. He was originally sent in for insubordination, then kept in as his behaviour got worse, not better. The warden wasn't in, so I told the assistant warden that I would sit on the front steps of the prison and call the press and make things unpleasant if he didn't allow me inside to see my son. He relented. It was the first time in the history of Stony Mountain that a woman had been allowed into the segregation area. There was a tiny peephole in the doorway of his cell, which the guards could pull open, but which David couldn't see out of. The room was absolutely stark, with no windows, and there was no mattress or any furniture of any kind, except for a toilet without a seat. Even empty, the room looked so very, very small, and with two or three steps, David could have crossed it in either direction. It seemed crowded, even when empty, and I shudder to think of the misery felt inside its tight walls. What sticks in my mind particularly strongly is how brightly lit up it was, and how the lights remained on all of the time, day and night.

David was taken out of his cell to a small adjoining room to see me. The person I saw wasn't the David I knew. His hair was ratty and dishevelled and he was shuffling like an old man. His eyes were wild and he looked so dirty.

"Is it you, Mom?" he asked. "No, it can't be. It must be a vision."

I told him it was really me, and sobbed. I told him, "God loves you and I love you and we're going to get you out of here."

When I left Stony Mountain, I immediately phoned my Christian Science teacher to help pray for David. The next day, when I went back to see him, he was clean and in his right mind. It was the most amazing thing. One of the guards said, "I don't know what you did for him, lady, but keep up the good work."

David hated life inside Stony Mountain, but appreciated how close the prison was to Winnipeg and his family. On November 24, 1986, he wrote us, "I'm sure glad you love me large or I'd be a goner for sure (SMILE)." However, David didn't always have the strength to keep on hoping. Sometimes, he wondered how long he could go on, and he would literally bang his head against a stone wall.

One day, he decided to end it all. He put sheets on the floor of his cell to soak up the blood. Then he lay down and slit his wrists. Blood soon appeared, and he waited for darkness, but noticed he didn't seem to be dying. After a while, he thought it was silly in a sick sort of way. He reached over and pulled a vein out of his wrist and cut it. Then the blood ran freely. The next thing he knew was when he came to in the prison hospital.

His arms were now scarred by about a dozen long, ugly, deep slashes. Some scars were from suicide attempts and others just the slashing that's common in prison, when prisoners choose pain over the dull feeling of being one of the living dead.

FOURTEEN

LOVE, SCIENCE AND LOVE

"I need to stop seeing people that are 'hurting.'"
David, writing from prison

BY THE SUMMER OF 1986, I thought our struggle was finally over. David Asper and Hersh Wolch were drafting an application for David to be released on a special power of mercy given to the justice minister under Section 690 of the Justice Act, and I felt that my work had been done. It was seventeen years since David was arrested, and finally it looked as if I could get on with my life.

I was in Ardenwood, a Christian Science facility in San Francisco, where I was taking religious training, when I read a story about how Jesus had asked a rich man to give up everything and follow him. The rich man couldn't do it. I must have read this story a hundred times, and each time, I thought, "Oh, you stupid man. How come you didn't follow Jesus? I would do that." I read the story again, in a beautiful San Francisco eucalyptus grove that was home to hummingbirds. I was startled to hear a voice.

As clear as a bell, it asked me, "Oh? What about the yellow tea pot?" I thought, "Oh, no, God, not the yellow tea pot." And then the voice said, "What about the corner china cabinet? The antique couch?" And all of a sudden, I realized what Jesus had really been asking that young man to give up. It wasn't money. It was his life. I thought, "How committed are you, Joyce? How much would you give up for the Christ?"

For the next two weeks, I really prayed, and when I came back to Winnipeg, I had made up my mind that I was going to work in Christian Science and that I was going to work for God in whatever way I could. I took Maureen out for lunch and I started to explain to her that I was going to give away everything that I owned. Poor Maureen figured I was dying of some incurable disease. Why else would I give up my precious things? I kept only my mink, since I still needed to keep warm, and things that were unimportant to me. I sold every-thing that tied me down, including my house, and applied for a job at the headquarters of the Christian Science church in Boston. When I received a very polite thank-you-but-no-thank-you letter from them, I decided to take a trip around the world, starting in England. I had absolute faith that God had a purpose for me and that I was going out to see what it was.

I felt so free, and went to my hairdresser, Bev, at the Magic Mirror and said, "I want to be a blonde."

"You're joking," she replied.

"I've heard that blondes have more fun and I'm just going to go out and have more fun," I said.

So I became a blonde, and when I walked out of the shop, someone whistled at me. I couldn't remember the last time that had happened, and it struck me as a good sign as I set out on my new life.

When I arrived at Heathrow Airport in London, there was a convention of some sort under way. The woman at a lodging service at the airport told the lady in front of me in line that every place was booked up for miles around. When I got to the front of the line, I asked for the name of the nearest hotel. She gave me the name.

"Would you mind calling it for me," I asked.

She looked at me like I had just lost my marbles. Hadn't I just heard her explain to the woman in front of me that there was nothing?

"Would you just humour me?" I asked. "I'm a Canadian. I'm also a Christian Scientist, and I know that there is a room for me here. Please make the call."

She started dialling, and said something like, "I know what the situation is, but I have this lady that insists that I should call." Then she stopped. They had had a cancellation and there was a room for me. That's the way it went all of the time in England. Always, I was provided for in the most wonderful ways.

Soon after I arrived, I was on a train in the countryside, heading to Sheffield for a two-week period of class instruction in Christian Science, when I shared a compartment with a young nursing assistant named Naomi from a nearby Catholic hospital. She was feeling depressed. She worked in the stroke victims section of her hospital, and recently one of her patients had died.

"What do you think is the difference between the patients who make it and the ones who don't?" I asked.

"That's easy," Naomi answered quickly. "The ones who survive don't accept the doctors' diagnosis. No matter what the doctors say, they are determined to walk and they do."

"Well, if it really is the thought of the patient, don't you think your thoughts are also important to them?" I asked.

We talked for a long time. I didn't mention Christian Science, although I did pass on some Bible truths. I also discovered that she was learning to play tennis. Since I was just starting the game myself, we made arrangements to see each other soon.

"You know, Joyce," Naomi said, before she got off the train, "God put you on the train for me today. I'm sure of it. I feel so much better."

The train started up again, and the thought came that I should become a Christian Science nurse. I just laughed right out loud. "Forget it, God," I thought. "I don't do bedpans. I'm a property administrator. I worked hard to get there. Not me. No way."

Sometimes God just won't take no for an answer. In my case, the arguing went on for days. How did I know I wouldn't like nursing? Didn't I say I wanted to help serve the cause of Christian Science? Well, yes, I did say that, but I had in mind more running the Mother Church. But they didn't want me. But nursing? I felt that God was just adding insult to injury. However, I couldn't stop that argument with God. "Okay, God, I'll make you a deal," I thought. "I'll take the nurse's aide training course, but I'm not going to like it."

I started making the necessary inquiries, but inwardly I was thinking, "I'm a Canadian. I'm in England. There's going to be so much red tape. There's no way I'm going to be able to get into a course. They won't even have a course by the time I have to leave the country."

When I sat down next to the superintendent of nursing at a Christian Science facility in Whitehaven, I asked her, "When do you think the next nursing course would be?"

She looked at me, smiled very sweetly and said, "When would you like it to start?"

I could almost hear God chuckling and saying, "I've got you. Nurse's aide training."

Those ten weeks changed my life. I became a giver instead of a taker and it felt good. Jesus said in the Bible that it is more blessed to give than to receive, and I felt blessed. One of my very first patients wasn't able to speak clearly. An entire side of his body, including his face, sagged downwards sadly, and not surprisingly, he wasn't able to move very well. However, a week and a half later, he went home, walking and talking. I was witnessing Christian Science healing and it strengthened my own faith. I could hardly wait to tell Naomi when we met to play tennis.

"Do you remember when you told me God put you on the train for me?" I asked.

"Oh, yes, I remember."

"Didn't you know He put you on the train for me too?"

I told her how I was now taking nursing, and we both rejoiced together.

Another odd, wonderful thing happened while I was in England. I was living in a flat in Weston-super-Mare, in southern England, a restful seaside community. People come from miles around to holiday there. I loved to walk at night along its piers, looking out at the ocean. A boy of about seventeen named Mark lived in the house where I was renting a flat. I was having troubles with my camera, and Mark was an excellent photographer, and soon we struck up a friendship.

Mark's parents were divorced, and he had lived with his mother until he was sixteen, but now she was in Portugal with a new husband and Mark was in the care of his father, an investments salesman who was often on the road.

I loved the chance to mother Mark, who was a nice, polite young man who would do any parent proud. His father was a little leery of the relationship, and feared I might be a version of Mrs. Robinson from the movie *The Graduate*, a middle-aged woman who tries to seduce a student played by Dustin Hoffman. Mark's father, Geoff, decided he had better check me out and see exactly what I was up to. We shared tea and scones, then went to church together. Geoff was distinguished, with silver hair and a slim, tall build, and so very British, with button-down collars and nicely tailored suits. His eyes were gentle, with what seemed to be a constant sparkle. In what seemed like no time, we were head-over-heels in love.

This happy ending was ruined by a call from David Asper in Winnipeg. Our Section 690 appeal to Ottawa was apparently going nowhere. Asper thought it might be a good idea if I return to North America and crank up the Free David Milgaard Machine once again. I cried with Geoff at the airport, then flew back across the ocean, to split my time between nurse's training at Tenacre, a Christian Science facility in Princeton, New Jersey, and Winnipeg. Lorne and I were on good terms, and he let me set up an office in the basement of his townhouse, where I slept while in Winnipeg. Lorne's also a great cook, and would come downstairs with wonderful meals for me, so that I could devote all of my time to freeing David. Tenacre was a good place to mend a broken heart. It was originally built on ten acres of farmland, and now had expanded to hundreds of acres, where people are treated for physical and mental illnesses.

Geoff and I tried to keep in touch through the phone and letters, and in January 1987, I wrote, "You said you love me and that makes me feel very special, but you deserve more than a part-time woman in your life. You need a full-time wife, someone that can put you first and foremost in front of everything else. Someone that can make a home for you, be there on the bad days just to love you and take away the hurt that comes from a poor day in the field, someone that will believe in you and will share your dream for the future. Geoff, I would love to be that person for you but I know I cannot be, I have too much going on in my life already. I shall hold close in my heart all the wonderful times we have had together, but I do think it will be better not to see you again. Please understand."

With that, Geoff was out of my life, except for the memories. It was tough not to think about what might have been with him.

After the training course at Tenacre, I continued to divide my time between Winnipeg and my nursing jobs, which were often far from home. It was a month on, a month off for more than a year.

Then one day new hope came. A prisoner told David he had heard about a new scientific process called genetic fingerprinting. David was excited and asked me to look into it, saying, "Mom, there's this stuff DNA and they're testing it in England, and they can get lots of information, even if it's hundreds of years old."

We read a news report about a lab in England. So I called them for more information. "Well, actually, there's a Canadian fellow who has just been over here and he has been working on it," a worker told me, giving me the name of Dr. James Ferris of Vancouver. Dr. Ferris had performed some 6,000 medico-legal autopsies, including 650 for homicide cases, and testified both for the prosecution and the defence. His opinions were sought around the world, and he had worked for a royal commission in Australia probing the death of nine-week-old Azaria Chamberlain, the so-called Dingo Baby case. The prosecution argued that Azaria was murdered, while the defence said she was likely killed by a wild dingo. The baby's mother, Lindy, was first found guilty, then exonerated of the charge, and the case was made into the movie starring Meryl Streep called *A Cry in the Dark*. I phoned Dr. Ferris in Vancouver. I told him that

I was a Christian Science nursing student and that I didn't have much money and asked for an estimate of how much testing would cost.

"Don't you worry about it, Mrs. Milgaard," he said. "I'll do it for you."

Dr. Ferris struck me as a wonderful man, and my opinion of him never changed. Months passed as Dr. Ferris did his tests. I often phoned him to see whether there was any news. If my calls bothered Dr. Ferris or his wife, they didn't let on.

One day in late summer of 1988, the doctor called me to say he was terribly sorry, but the samples were simply too old for him to find anything. DNA testing was then in its infancy, and there was nothing he could prove with the process in David's case. Then he paused and said, "But you know, Mrs. Milgaard, I don't understand why you need it. You've got more than enough evidence here to prove that your son is innocent."

"I do?" I replied, more than a little stunned. "Will you tell my lawyer that? Will you put it in writing?"

"Of course I will."

Although he could not do the new DNA testing, Dr. Ferris's conclusions on the blood and semen he had analyzed went even further than we had hoped. Those samples actually eliminated David as a suspect. From his study of Gail Miller's clothing and other exhibits from the trial, Dr. Ferris was able to present a graphic description of the murder that cleared David. On September 13, 1988, he wrote to Hersh Wolch that Gail Miller may have been alive for fifteen minutes after she was stabbed, slowly bleeding to death while lying in the snow. Dr. Ferris postulated that the rape was probably prolonged, and that it wasn't likely to have taken place within the tight fifteen-minute time frame suggested by the Crown.

A study of her clothing suggested that she might have been raped elsewhere and then her body dumped in the alley, where it was found. The stab marks through her coat but not her dress or underclothing suggested the killer had at least partially redressed her after the knife attack.

Since David was on foot when the Crown said he murdered Miller, it was next to impossible for him to have done the killing in the residential neighbourhood without being seen. David had neither the means nor the time to kill her in the manner the Crown had suggested, Ferris concluded.

Ferris also had serious problems with what were presented in court as semen samples. They were discovered four days after the killing, when the crime scene had been so badly trampled that Ferris was surprised that they were even accepted in court as evidence. Even so, a study of that sample excluded David as a suspect because of his blood type. Ferris wrote, "On the basis of the evidence that I have examined, I have no reasonable doubt that serological evidence presented at the trial failed to link David Milgaard with the offence and that, in fact, could be reasonably considered to exclude him from being the perpetrator of the murder." In other words, faulty science had helped convict David. Now, eighteen years later, proper science offered the hope of setting him free.

David was already getting a different kind of freedom, through letters he wrote to Emily Dapkus, a Christian Science friend of mine from New Jersey. I had met Emily at my nursing class, and she became interested in David's case. Soon, they were a couple, separated by thousands of miles and stone walls but deeply in love. In his letters to her, David seemed so hopeful, as when he wrote,

> Some day we will share times where all we have to do together is smile at the sky.
> Lucky sky huh?
>
> Love, XOX, David.

Emily was in her early thirties and had an elfin air about her that belied her tough past. She had been a jazz musician who was heavily into the drug scene, and had also worked as a bicycle courier in downtown New York City. Emily was a loner, living in an apartment with barred windows in a terrible section of Harlem, where derelict cars littered the streets and knife fights and drug use were the norm. When I first met her, I was struck by the chip she had on her shoulder, and I thought to myself, "Well, I'm just going to love that chip right off your shoulder." Christian Science helped open her up to the beauty of life, and she and David hit it off. Their love was spiritual, almost a meeting of souls. Emily needed him just as he needed her. She could relate to where David had been and what had happened in his life. From time to time, she would visit him, but most of their communication was through letters.

"I'll be okay," David wrote me. "Tell Emily her beautiful letters help and to keep them coming. Also that I always keep an eye on her star! Dad is doing good. Prayer works, so we can both hold Dad in thought. He'll have no choice in the matter! (Smile) I love you and miss you." In an undated letter to me, he wrote, "I am doing alright and flying with God all day everyday these days. Actually he has it on auto-pilot and I just think I'm flying!"

On April 10, 1989, David wrote, still happy as a puppy, "Learn any new tricks? I just learned one from Emily that has seemed to work for me some . . . It is about feeling so serious about things . . . She said that no matter how weighted down we may feel, there is part of us that flies freely! That knows nothing of earthly chains. Just reading that for the first time made me think of the times I have felt I was flying and how nothing can touch that!"

Not long after this letter, David was knocked down to the ground again. Emily had died in hospital of cancer, and David took this new loss very, very hard. I also received news from England that Geoff had died of a heart attack.

FIFTEEN

NEW CENTURIONS

"Surely, this one must be innocent."
Roman centurion, looking at Jesus on the cross

DAVID GOT EXCITED when he read an article about a crusading minister in New Jersey who specialized in rescuing wrongfully accused prisoners from death row in the United States.

"Mom, he's down where you are," he told me. "Why don't you go and see him?"

So I went to see Rev. Jim McCloskey in the summer of 1989 in his tiny Princeton, New Jersey, office, near Tenacre. It was such a little box of an office, and there were files and charts every place, dealing with hundreds of prisoners. His outfit, Centurion Ministries, is a tiny, privately funded Christian organization that had freed eight death-row or life prisoners from wrongful convictions. One of the men was just nine days from his scheduled execution. Centurion took its name from a Roman soldier who looked up at Jesus dying on the cross and said, "Surely, this one must be innocent."

McCloskey had been a naval officer in the Vietnam War and was awarded the Bronze Star Medal for service in the Mekong delta. He returned from war to spend thirteen years in business, mostly as an executive for international management consulting firms. During that prosperous time, he drove a Lincoln Continental, wore expensive clothes and felt a deep spiritual void. At thirty-seven he started going to Presbyterian church again. Soon afterwards, he quit the business world for good, selling his ranch-style home so he could earn his master of divinity degree from Princeton Theological Seminary, not too far from Tenacre.

While at the seminary, he worked at Trenton State Penitentiary, where he met George (Chiefy) De Los Santos. De Los Santos challenged James's Christianity and goaded him to do something besides pray. James took up the challenge and became convinced that De Los Santos had been wrongly convicted of murder after a prosecution witness perjured himself to get off other charges. There was also shoddy police work and overzealous prosecutors. Sadly, De Los Santos was soon back in prison for beating his wife. Another man saved by James from death row was later arrested on rape charges. After those heartbreaking cases, James attempted to assess individuals as well as their cases. He began to ask whether the prisoner was making good use of his time behind bars, and what kind of citizen he would be, if he — or she — was ever freed.

Jim was very nice when I approached him, but unable to help me. He was swamped with cases and couldn't possibly take on another one, especially one from the faraway Canadian prairies. Since I was nearby at Tenacre anyway, I offered to help him on my days off, working in his office as a volunteer. I screened calls and letters from inmates, and when there was time, I would talk to Jim about David. My volunteer job for Centurion from the summer of 1989 to December 1990 was to write back and tell people that they didn't meet the criteria for us to take on their case. Jim had some three thousand requests a year for help, and a limited budget and staff, and cases were extremely time consuming. Writing rejection letters was very difficult, but I tried to do it in a way I knew my son David would want to hear. I knew what it was like to get a rejection letter. I told them how badly we felt, and to hang in there and that some time the truth would come out. I would draw little smiles on the letters in the hope that this might make the person feel a little better. The Centurion criteria were extremely strict. You have to be completely finished with any appeals and you can have absolutely no involvement in the crime. Even if you met those criteria, you weren't guaranteed anything. Jim simply didn't have the resources or staff to handle many cases.

Even after the Section 690 application for mercy had been filed in Ottawa by Hersh Wolch and David Asper, information kept coming in to bolster our case. In October 1989, Fernley Cooney, a former juror and part-time janitor, said his mental state during the trial may have resulted in the wrongful conviction. Cooney said he felt pressured by other jurors into agreeing to a guilty verdict, even though he believed David was innocent, and now he hoped we could win a retrial. The graphic photos of Gail Miller he was shown at the trial still haunted him, he said, almost two decades later.

I never blamed Cooney or others on the jury for the guilty verdict, since they gave a decision on the information that was presented to them. David was in prison because officials in the Saskatchewan government withheld information from our lawyers. In a sense, jurors like Cooney were also victims.

SIXTEEN

LONG, FRUSTRATING WAIT

"It's dreadful to think that you have to politically campaign."
I talk with David Asper about what it takes
to get David's case reopened

AS THE 1990S BEGAN, news reports referred to
David as Canada's longest-serving prisoner. He was now
semi-famous in Manitoba, and there were "Free David
Milgaard" bumper stickers on cars in Winnipeg. We were
finding, however, that the media and the public were a
much easier sell than the federal Justice Department, and
our frustration built as efforts to free David seemed to be
getting nowhere.

The delay mystified us. When we filed our Section 690
appeal in 1988, we had highly respected forensic expert
Dr. James Ferris and fresh witnesses. David had already
served more than twenty years, and there wasn't a scrap of
paper anywhere in the prison system that suggested he was
a danger to anyone except to himself. We had a far
stronger case than what the Crown had needed to convict

David, and yet we were ignored. I asked Hersh why nothing was happening.

"It's a big decision to say 'We screwed up.'"

"We're not asking them to say 'We screwed up.' Just open the case."

We were developing a sophisticated media strategy. We had made our point in Manitoba, thanks in large part to the persistent efforts of Dan Lett of the *Winnipeg Free Press*. However, we needed to break into the eastern Canadian media to get politicians in Ottawa to sit up and take notice. *The fifth estate* approached us again about running a piece on David. At first, it was tempting to reject them. We had a bad experience with *the fifth estate* in the mid-1980s, when they interviewed David and others involved in the case, then scrapped the project. Our first story was apparently nixed in a power struggle within the program; now, a fresh set of editors and producers truly believed in the project. We had learned some lessons from our initial brush with *the fifth estate*. During the filming, David had been told to expect journalist Eric Malling at 10 a.m., but David didn't face the cameras until 8 p.m. By the time the interview began, David was so agitated that he looked shifty and evasive. Being innocent clearly wasn't enough for television. You have to *look* innocent too. We knew that many viewers would ignore our hard-to-follow arguments and make their decision simply by looking into David's eyes as the camera zoomed in.

We decided to go ahead with the second try at *the fifth estate*. This second time through, I made sure there wasn't a long wait between David's daily shave and his interview. Too much was at stake to let a five-o'clock shadow hurt things. This time, David did wonderfully, and *the fifth estate* team boiled down the complicated case into a very watchable, powerful piece. Parts of the crime were re-enacted and documented on grainy black-and-white film, giving it a feeling of eerie realism. I found it a little amusing that this gritty cinéma-vérité was the product of actors, cotton batting and steam. The feature kicked off *the fifth estate*'s fall 1990 season and was our national media breakthough. It helped our credibility enormously.

David Asper worked with us to develop specific messages, delivered in easy-to-understand bite-sized pieces. If the message was to inspire widespread support, it would have to be repeated over and over until it hit home.

We now set our sights on the *Toronto Star*, Canada's largest newspaper; the *Globe and Mail*, which saw itself as Canada's national newspaper; and on *Morningside* and *As It Happens* on CBC Radio. We needed the story to play big in Ottawa, so that Kim Campbell, the new justice minister, and others in Parliament could read about it over their breakfast coffee. George Oakes of the *Toronto Star* had written a supportive piece and seemed to offer an in for future coverage.

I was leery about saying too much about my Christian Science beliefs. Faith is an area the press doesn't handle well, and I wanted to unify people in the fight to free David, not create divisions. I had been nervous watching *A Cry in the Dark*, the movie about the Australian family whose baby went missing. The public turned against that family because they mistrusted their strong religious beliefs. This made me very cautious. I wanted to protect Christian Science, not expose it to attack and ridicule. One of the few reporters I spoke with on this intensely personal topic was my friend Lesley Hughes of CBC Radio, who wrote a profile about me for *Chatelaine* magazine. I told her, "At the end of a long day, when I could not lift another pen to another politician, worry about another bill or call one more freshly emerging witness, I would retreat to a beach in my mind. In sleep, I was on the beach, and always, God was there as the sea; that power embraced me, washing away doubt, weariness, pettiness, vengeance. I woke feeling as fresh and pure as God's original idea of me. My mistakes were gone. But — and this was hard — so were everyone else's. Every day I had to see us all as God does, capable of truth and other great things."

Hughes was receptive to such a message, but she was the exception. So we pressed on, stressing the universal theme of a family fighting to protect its own.

We guessed that the appeal had reached the bureaucratic or even ministerial level. We needed to shine a light on David's plight, but we couldn't make the justice minister feel she was being bullied, or our efforts would backfire. We had a good feeling about Justice Minister Kim Campbell. She had appeared decisive on abortion and gun control and showed encouraging signs of independence handling her party's right wing.

"She really does her own thing," David Asper said.

"That should give us hope," I replied. "Because if she really does her own thing, surely when she reads the case against David, she's going to see."

"Well," David Asper said, "that's what we thought about the Justice Department. We see it so simply and clearly, we can't imagine why it's so difficult for the bureaucrats. And yet it is."

"But it's not just us. Anyone who looks at it."

"I know, I know. But the people who count ultimately don't see it as clearly."

No one counted more than Kim Campbell, and she was obviously an extremely busy person. Whatever report she received from her bureaucrats on David was crucial. Those bureaucrats didn't have to face public pressure like politicians do, and were long-time members of the same Justice Department that had locked up David and kept him behind bars. We didn't expect them to be sympathetic.

We needed insiders pulling for us. Luckily, Stony Mountain MP Felix Holtman believed in David's innocence. He also had a healthy western mistrust of bureaucrats, and, as a member of the Conservative caucus, he met Kim Campbell in closed-doors meetings.

I met with NDP leader Audrey McLaughlin and Justice critic Ian Waddell, and Manitoba Liberals Lloyd Axworthy and John Harvard. There was an interview on the CTV program *Canada AM*, but overall, I found the eastern media interest underwhelming. It was almost as if there was a wall between Manitoba and Ontario.

We were starting to see signs that Kim Campbell might be a tough nut to crack. She admonished us every time we gave her fresh information, saying this only delayed a decision. So we gave a Centurion Ministries report on David to every member of Parliament except her.

"It's dreadful to think that you have to politically campaign," I told David Asper.

There were some hopeful signs, though.

Peter Leo of CBC's *Sunday Morning* radio show marked the twentieth anniversary of David's conviction with a documentary that raised questions about the credibility of witnesses, time factors and forensic evidence. Actors played the roles of Nichol John and Bobs Caldwell for the radio drama.

The actor reading Caldwell's testimony said, "Now, Miss John, I put it to you that this [seeing David stab the girl] is something you absolutely would never forget if you saw that happen."

"As far as I'm concerned, I don't know what happened. I don't even know if I was on that trip or not," the Nichol character replied.

As our attempts to free him sputtered along, David fretted that it would be wrong in principle to take a parole, even if he somehow was offered one. Parole is for guilty people and he was innocent. "I don't really want a parole because it's simply something which would have me always reporting to someone for the rest of my life for something I didn't do," he said.

Behind bars, he wasn't violent, but he clearly would stand up for his rights. He argued with Stony Mountain authorities for a cell at the end of the hallway. This was a perk prisoners with seniority might expect, and it meant he would not have to listen to the opening and closing of metal doors all night long, or the laughing and talking of guards on main walkways. He eventually won the cell, but irritated prison authorities further in the process.

David's mood was brightened by the inquiry into the wrongful murder conviction of Donald Marshall, David's old acquaintance from Dorchester Penitentiary. The inquiry report concluded that the justice system had failed Marshall at every turn, and David dreamed that someday his case would have a similar report, and that he would be both free and cleared of the crime. "I certainly want to walk away a free person," David said.

SEVENTEEN

FINALLY FISHER

"You're probably the one who was out stabbing that girl."
Wife of serial rapist Larry Fisher accuses him
of the murder of Gail Miller

THE MAN CALLED THE Wolch, Pinx, Tapper, Scurfield law office in Winnipeg on February 26, 1990, and said he knew who killed Gail Miller and it wasn't David Milgaard. "Why don't you check out a guy called Larry Fisher?" the man, who identified himself as Sidney Wilson, asked Hersh Wolch. "He's serving time in Prince Albert right now for a bunch of rapes. If you can find his wife, she'll tell you that he came home on the morning of the murder covered in blood." The caller added that he believed police had already heard Linda Fisher's story.

I recalled Larry Fisher's name from the police report Peter Carlyle-Gordge had read years before in Bobs Caldwell's office and I was excited. We'd had so many suspects in the past, and we were still suspicious of Colin Thatcher. But this call seemed to be different. I told Hersh that this could be our big break.

"What do you mean?" he asked.

"I remember that name. The police interviewed him at the bus stop a few days after Gail Miller was killed. He was listed as living at the same address as Cadrain. I had originally thought the police had just put down the wrong address, made a mistake."

I called Rev. Jim McCloskey at Centurion Ministries in New Jersey to share my excitement. Although Jim hadn't officially taken on the case, he was advising me, and now I told him I wanted to dig out more information on Larry Fisher in Fisher's old hometown of North Battleford.

"You can't go out there on your own," Jim said. "You're crazy. That could be really dangerous."

"I have no choice."

"Let me see if Paul's available," he said, referring to Seattle-based private detective Paul Henderson. Paul's a Pulitzer Prize-winning investigative reporter whose stories had helped free a man who was wrongfully convicted of a series of rapes. "If he's available, could you pay his fare and his accommodation, and I'll pay for his time?"

"Sure. I've got MasterCard."

Paul was a full-time private investigator now, and had a soft spot for Centurion, cutting his fees 30 per cent for Jim. I had to borrow $4,000 from the bank to cover expenses. I also had to borrow a car.

When I first met Paul Henderson, I thought, "What does Jim McCloskey see in this guy?" There had been a mixup when he crossed the border, and it took him a while to get through Canada Customs. Then, as we drove out to the North Battleford area in a borrowed car, he kept fumbling around looking for a paper and pencil, and finally scrawled some notes with a makeup pencil. However, once I started working with Paul, I understood his gift. He has an ability to chew on things incessantly until he gets to the nitty-gritty of something extremely complicated. He can take a detailed, rambling, emotional statement and say, 'This is what you're saying," and be dead-on right. With Jim and Paul, we finally had the professional investigative edge we so sorely needed. On that first visit, my plan was to approach Fisher's mother, Marceline. She still lived in North Battleford, in the same tiny, stuccoed home where Larry grew up, and Larry's initials were scrawled outside in the sidewalk pavement. When I introduced myself to her, Marceline replied, through the locked screen door, "Go away. Go away. I'm going to call the police."

"I'm not going to harm you," I pleaded. "I just want to talk to you."

The police rushed over. They were polite but shooed me away. Paul was waiting in the car, panic-stricken since he was working in the country illegally. He was in such a rush to come north that he hadn't gotten his work papers in time.

Like Shorty's mother, Marceline was scared of me, which I understood. I think we mothers are naturally courageous when it comes to our children, and when we're backed into a corner, we simply have to fight. I was frustrated, but I couldn't hate Marceline.

I would later hear more about the tough life of this small, nervous woman, who was so full of energy, self-pity and suspicions. Marceline claimed she was raped by her husband when she was pregnant with Larry, and that she was frequently beaten by her husband until he walked out, when Larry was just three. His current problems had deep and ugly roots.

People naturally trust Paul. Strangers open up to him, perhaps because he's nonthreatening and doesn't present himself as some big media star. If anything, people seem to feel the need to help him. Paul was constantly coming up with plans and contingency plans, while never losing sight of our main goal.

Paul and I next drove together on March 9, 1990, to see Linda Fisher. Thanks to a tip from a cooperative school official, I knew Linda lived in the tiny native hamlet of Cando outside North Battleford. We wanted an insight into the mind of a serial rapist — her former husband, Larry — as well as facts on the case. The plan was to show up at her door unannounced. I worried that, as soon as I told her my name, she would bolt, as her former mother-in-law had done. We parked our car blocking their driveway, boxing her car in.

Surprisingly, Linda looked happy to see me. After I introduced myself, I quickly made it clear to Linda that the $10,000 reward money we had promised a decade before was long since gone. This seemed irrelevant to her. She lived simply enough, and impressed us as someone guided by her conscience, not greed. Linda had had a tough life, but she was a good mother and she truly cared for her children. She dressed well, and there was a sense of neatness about her and her home. She wondered why

I was coming to see her now, and not ten years ago, when she had gone to see police. I replied that this was the first I had heard about her visit to police back in August 1980, three months before we offered our reward.

Oddly, Linda said she knew no Sidney Wilson, the name of the telephone caller who had provided us with the Larry Fisher tip. We would always wonder about his true identity. Maybe he was a police officer who knew of Linda's 1980 statement, or perhaps he was an old acquaintance of the Fisher family. Whatever the case, we were grateful to him.

Linda told us Larry was born in North Battleford. His mother, Marceline, was part-Cree and a workaholic. His Irish father was capable of extreme cruelty. His father left home when Larry was just a toddler, and Larry was constantly pushed away when he tried to re-establish contact. When his father died in the late 1970s, Larry's hopes had turned to bitterness, and he refused to go to the funeral.

Larry was eighteen and Linda just sixteen when they married, and it wasn't long after that Linda was hearing troubling stories about her handsome new husband. There were complex problems between Larry and his mother. Marceline had been overprotective, not allowing him to play much with other children; she didn't want her little boy hanging around rough children. As he grew older, Larry was constantly humiliated by what he considered overtly sexual behaviour by his mother, and he developed a deep, simmering hostility towards women. He would also later claim that he was sexually abused by an aunt. Linda heard that Larry had assaulted a girl of about fourteen when he was about that age, and that he had also raped a friend of Linda's around the spring of 1968, and later assaulted their landlady.

In the spring of 1971, shortly after all David's legal appeals were exhausted, Larry Fisher was sentenced to thirteen years in prison after pleading guilty to the two knifepoint rapes in Winnipeg. He was paroled in 1980, and within two months he raped a fifty-six-year-old neighbour in North Battleford, then slashed her throat from ear to ear. Even for Larry Fisher, that attack was particularly horrific. As she lay hog-tied and bleeding on the ground, Fisher boasted that he had killed before. At that point, the Crown might have tried to lock him up indefinitely as a dangerous offender, but didn't, although he was denied parole in April 1989 because he was still considered too dangerous for the streets.

Despite his violent nature, there was a strong bond between Larry and his daughter, who was twenty-one now. When she was an infant, Fort Garry police officer Lorne Huff had asked Larry how he would feel if someone raped her someday. That's when Larry cracked and confessed to the Saskatoon rapes. Now, his daughter saw him not as a rapist or an angry man, just as a dad. Linda had also visited Larry in prison, and once asked about the morning of the Gail Miller murder.

"I just want to know one thing," Linda said. "Did you have anything to do with that nurse?"

"Nope" was Larry's reply.

Linda had once asked him how he was capable of

raping a woman in Winnipeg, saying, "Why did you do that? How could anyone do that?"

Larry tried to explain that he got a pain in his head, and when the woman left a city bus, he followed. He claimed he couldn't remember anything after that. It wasn't until the attack was all over that he finally recalled what he had done.

I felt a jolt as Linda described how Larry attacked women near bus stops in Winnipeg and Saskatoon. We were learning things about his pattern that we hadn't known. Everything was falling into place.

Our suspicions about Larry Fisher's involvement in the Miller murder increased by the second. Larry and Gail Miller usually rode the same bus to work. We looked over a map of their old neighbourhood, as Linda pointed out where someone found Larry's wallet on Avenue O, near their home. We were interested to hear that Larry was just slightly taller than five-foot-five, which was significant, since the church custodian across the street from the Miller murder scene said he saw a short person walk in front of the headlights of a car parked in the alley not far from where Gail Miller's body was discovered. David was five-ten, nearly half a foot taller than Fisher.

Linda was extremely interested in helping David. I asked her whether she would wear a recording device for a meeting with Larry in prison, but Linda said there was no way he would talk in prison; he knew the authorities recorded some conversations.

"I don't think that he would tell me anything anyway," Linda said.

I was buoyed by the thought that Larry Fisher had confessed to rapes when caught in Winnipeg. "He didn't have to confess to all of the others, but he did," I noted.

We drove with Linda to find her uncles, Roy and Clifford Pambrun, who had worked in construction with Larry at the time of the Miller murder. I felt a strong mother-to-mother bond with Linda, who had a son who was about the age David was when he was convicted. Linda directed us to her uncle Roy, who quickly told us he was useless as far as dates were concerned, but was willing to try to help. Roy was friendly enough, saying he was just in from Moose Jaw, where he had been playing broomball.

Roy recalled a strange winter scene in his backyard. Larry stood barefoot in front of a barrel with a fire burning inside it. Exactly what Larry was doing was uncertain. He said something about being at a party and losing shoes, although Larry's workboots were in the barrel. Oddly, the boots in the burning barrel looked perfectly fine to Roy, and it was cold and snowy outside.

Linda privately told us that Roy liked to embellish his stories, and we wondered whether he was exaggerating now. Roy promised he'd be around if we needed him and that he would have no problem repeating what he had told us. However, he refused to sign any statement about that day. Linda later explained that he could neither read nor write and didn't trust the court system.

Roy told us Larry had access to cars at the time of Gail Miller's murder, even though he didn't own one himself. That would tie in with the theory of Dr. Ferris, who concluded that the killer may have raped and murdered Miller somewhere else, then dumped the body in the alley.

"You didn't hestitate to lend him your car?" Paul asked.

"No."

Before we returned south, on March 10, Linda gave us a signed statement. All she wanted in return was the promise that we would tell her in advance before any information she gave us was made public. She just wanted time to take precautions so that Larry wouldn't hurt her or her family.

In her statement, Linda recalled life in the basement apartment of Albert Cadrain's house. Larry stayed out the night before the murder, and Linda was furious. He was a good-looking man, and she suspected he was running around with other women. He didn't come back in time to get ready for work that morning, which was out of character.

Linda woke up the morning of the murder to find Larry freshly showered and in his dress clothes, which included a pair of mod flowery pants. Linda looked at the getup and accused him of cheating on her. As they shouted at each other, news of the murder came on the radio, and Linda erupted, saying, "My paring knife is missing. You're probably the one who was out stabbing that girl."

She didn't really mean it. She was just trying to shock him, but he was stopped cold by the accusation. "He looked at me like a guilty person who'd just been caught," Linda said. "The colour drained from his face and he looked shocked and scared."

"Linda, did you ever see any evidence of a violent personality?" Paul asked.

"Oh, yeah," she replied quickly, between hard draws on a cigarette. There had been brawls. Once, when she was sitting on the couch looking down, Larry walked up and kicked her in the head. When a relative challenged him on it, he whimpered and backed down, suddenly a coward and not a bully. Linda told us that Larry kept a double-bladed knife in his truck for his work. Forensic testing had concluded that the final stabs to Gail Miller, after the paring knife broke off in her body, could well have been from a double-bladed knife.

During our conversation, Linda said something chilling: Larry was due for mandatory parole in 1994. That meant he would have to be set free, no matter how dangerous prison authorities considered him. "I wouldn't want Larry to get ahold of that tape," Linda said, nervously gesturing towards our tape recorder.

Everything we heard about Fisher suggested we were finally on the trail of the real killer. After we left Cando, we were able to track down one of Fisher's old foremen, who said that in 1968 Fisher worked at a potash mine about sixty miles east of Saskatoon. We heard a woman was raped there at that time, and that the attack remained unsolved.

Private investigators who were working for us thought some Saskatoon police officers could help us. I knew I had a better chance than anyone else of getting them to talk. After all, it's pretty hard to turn down a mother. I played on the fact that they should feel guilty. I know I blatantly played the mother card at times, and this was one of them. When I talked with some reluctant police officers, I said something like, "I know your mother would be doing just what I'm doing for my son, for you. I know you'd want the person she was talking to to help her. Won't you help me?" Basically, everyone is a decent human being, and if you can reach out to them on that level, you've got it made.

A police source let us see, but not photocopy, records of Fisher's attacks. We were somewhat fortunate to have had a couple of police insiders helping us out, and David Asper went to extreme lengths to both preserve and protect these sources. They gave us information not only about Fisher but also about how the Justice Department was conducting its investigation, using Bobs Caldwell and others involved in the original prosecution. This later proved to be great fodder for our "political campaign" to clear David's name.

The dissidents told us scuttlebutt about police incompetence and possible corruption. Once, before a raid of an escort service, the owners were tipped off. And apparently four murders in Saskatoon had been written off as suicides, since unsolved cases don't look good on police officers' records. It was clear that several careers within the Saskatoon force were boosted by David's conviction, including that of Joseph Penkala, who was now the new police chief.

∾

We got another break when Lorne Huff phoned the law office. Huff, a former Fort Garry police officer, did some occasional investigative work for the firm and, coincidentally, he was the detective who interrogated Larry Fisher after his capture in September 1970. Now a private investigator, Huff was shocked when he read coverage of David's case. Huff always had a strange feeling about the extreme reluctance of Saskatoon police officers to talk with him or his partner, Det. Doug Gilbert. "They gave us bad vibes when they were here," Huff later recalled. "They just didn't want anything to do with us. They were extremely standoffish."

Huff had no doubts that Fisher was capable of murder. "He's got the coldest eyes that I've ever seen and I was twenty-six years as a policeman," Huff later said. "He's like a senior Charles Manson . . . I'll never forget him as long as I live."

After Fisher's arrest, Det. Ed Karst was sent from Saskatoon to Winnipeg to interview him, rather than officers with the Saskatoon force's morality squad, who were in charge of investigating the rapes. That struck us as odd. We also wondered why morality squad officers were never told about Fisher's confessions. In some cases, their investigations continued, and in all cases, victims were never told that their attacker was finally behind bars. It also struck us as unusual that Larry Fisher's sentencing was delayed until all of David's appeals were exhausted. Years later, when we won access to more police files, we found many letters from Fisher's lawyer asking the Crown to hurry up with the sentencing. The delays continued, however. The irony was that Fisher would likely have done no more prison time if he had confessed to Gail

Miller's murder. However, it would have meant public embarrassment for Saskatoon police and prosecutors, since David was already in prison.

"Had we known about the murder, I think we could have got him," Huff said years later.

EIGHTEEN

APPROACHING KIM

"Mom, you told me, 'With God, all things are possible.'"
Susan pushes me to sing for David at a benefit concert

WE FORWARDED THE statements from Linda Fisher and her uncle Roy Pambrun to Justice Minister Kim Campbell as additions to our Section 690 application for mercy in David's case. Now we didn't have just an extremely powerful forensic case; we also offered up a possible killer who had lived just one and a half blocks from the murder scene and whose modus operandi fit the attack on Gail Miller. If the jury had known about Larry Fisher, wouldn't they have had at least a reasonable doubt? If police had checked Fisher's alibi — that he had gone to work the morning of the murder — they would have found he was lying. Wouldn't a jury have wondered why Fisher wasn't the one being investigated rather than David? Didn't the Crown have an obligation to put this new information forward? Surely our lawyer, Calvin Tallis, would have welcomed this as part of the Crown's disclosure, when they are obligated to put forward all relevant information. David was entitled to raise as a defence, "I didn't do it. He did it." If David had been given this opportunity, he could have added, "And the police think so too," referring to the headline in the *Saskatoon Star Phoenix* that read, "Killer Possible Rapist." Linda Fisher had no lawyer with her when she was grilled by Justice Department officials, but later Larry would be allowed to have his lawyer present. In the case of Donald Marshall, his lawyers made a Section 690 application only after they had a confession from the real killer. We prayed that Larry Fisher might confess, but we weren't holding our breaths.

We weren't expecting Kim Campbell to declare David innocent. All we wanted was a new trial, and a chance to put our new evidence before a jury.

In the spring of 1990, we heard that Kim Campbell was coming to Winnipeg for talks on the Meech Lake accord to restructure Canadian federalism. Those Meech Lake talks were crowding our case from the news pages and airwaves, but now they seemed to be working in our favour by steering Campbell in our direction. I was suddenly full of hope. Here was my chance to give her Dr. Ferris's forensic report, which, according to the rumour mill, she still hadn't seen.

I called up all the media to let them know that I was going to the hotel where she would be speaking so that I could present her with the Ferris report. I scouted the hotel and figured that she would have to arrive at the conference room either by a flight of stairs or an elevator, and then Maureen and I positioned ourselves in the hallway so that we would be ready for her.

I stepped out to see her when she got off an elevator. I had to quickly get out of her way as she breezed by, as a wall of reporters and camera people heard her curtly say to me, "Madam, if you wish to have your son's case dealt with fairly, please do not approach me."

I sat down and just sobbed. All I wanted was to hand her the Ferris report. We didn't even have to speak. That snub made the national TV news.

The next morning, I was on Peter Warren's *Action Line* radio show in Winnipeg. An indignant caller spoke for countless Canadians when he asked, "What can we do? Is there someone we can write . . . that would have an effect in some way?"

What sweet music to our ears, after struggling so long to get anyone to listen.

"Oh, boy," I replied. "You could write to the minister of justice."

Another caller suggested a petition, and soon that was under way, quickly drawing thousands of signatures.

All the callers seemed sympathetic towards me and angry at the justice system.

"As taxpayers, it's costing all of us a lot of money to have that kind of lousy justice," a female caller complained.

After *Action Line*, I went on CBC's *Newsworld* for more of the same, then off to Stony Mountain to visit with David for the afternoon. The night was capped with church. It was tiring, but I felt we had finally broken through.

Kim Campbell later said she was told by her staff that any contact with me would affect her impartiality or her perception of impartiality. However, I wasn't asking her to judge my son David. I just wanted to ensure she had all of the facts.

The encounter with Campbell was perhaps the turning point in the case. She had provided an image for television that didn't need words or an explanation. She became the embodiment of faceless, uncaring big government, and it galvanized our support across the country. David Asper knew the importance of this, because people could easily grasp a good-versus-evil story, and Campbell, by her actions, gave everyone a dose of evil on national television.

"Don't talk to Kim Campbell," David Asper now told me bluntly.

Campbell likened herself to a judge who could not be approached during a trial, not a politician who was accountable to the people. I respected David Asper immensely, but I also had faith in my intuition and I still wanted to approach her. I wondered how I could respect both Asper and my own feelings.

The answer came to me that night in a song, literally. All through the night, I kept hearing a melody, and every half-hour, I woke up with another line. By morning, the song was completed, with both the words and the melody, even though I am not a musician. It was called "Please, Madame Minister" and went:

Please, Madame Minister, listen to me
Please, Madame Minister, set David free
He is not guilty, you have the proof

How can you stand there so cold and aloof?
How many people must tell you so
How many years till you let him go?
Please, Madame Minister, listen to me
Please, Madame Minister, set David free

David is innocent, this they can't hide
Everyone knows that people have lied
Justice cries out to be done in his case
Justice cries out there's no time to waste
Please, Madame Minister, listen to me
Please, Madame Minister, set David free

Twenty-one years of torment and pain
Twenty-one years can't be brought back again
They made a mistake, that's plain to see
Please, Madame Minister, set David free
Please, Madame Minister, listen to me
Please, Madame Minister, set my son free.

At the time, I was staying with my friend Diana McIntosh in Winnipeg. Periodically, when I came into town, I would stay in her home. I was learning to become very organized, and I would organize her drawers and her cupboards, which she loved. Diana's a concert pianist who has played at Carnegie Hall, and she has a recording studio in her home. Her home was the perfect place to be when you're hit by a song.

That morning, I phoned David Asper. He sounded a little wary but also, I suspect, a little amused. If he didn't have a sense of humour, he would have been long gone.

"You said I can't talk to her," I said. "Can I sing to her?"

"Joyce, what now?"

"I'm serious. I wrote this song. Actually, God did."

I played a tape of it for him.

"Now it's your turn to sit down," Asper said. "Last night I was at the folk festival. A bunch of the musicians said they wanted to do a benefit for David. Now you're telling me that you've written a song."

Among Asper's friends was Mitch Podolak, who ran a recording studio and hall at the West Side Cultural Centre in Winnipeg. He was involved in the folk festival and he and David Asper had known each other for years. Before I knew it, David and Mitch had organized a group to play the new song. But when Mitch wanted me to sing it, I refused. Mitch was adamant. It had to be the mother singing the new song.

Susan was there encouraging me as I headed up to the stage where they were set to record. Suddenly, the place was full, with media people with cameras and tape recorders.

I began to get cold feet.

"I can't sing this," I protested.

"Mom!" Susan replied. "You told me, 'With God, all things are possible.'" I was so mad at her. We had raised a smart girl, and now it was coming back to haunt me. She made it clear she didn't just expect me to sing it. I had better sing it well.

"God, you sing the song," I said to myself.

Don't think I didn't feel pressure on me, as I saw all these figures moving around in the dark beyond the stage. We did four or fives takes. Each time the guy in charge said to the musicians, "You did this or that wrong." Finally he said, "You're the musicians, and Joyce is the amateur. She's done everything perfectly and you're making mistakes. Get your act together."

The next take was a wrap, as he called it.

NINETEEN

SCENT OF VICTORY

"This semen cannot possibly be from Mr. Milgaard."
Forensic expert Dr. Peter Markesteyn
on evidence used against David in trial

IN MAY 1990, WE approached Dr. Peter Markesteyn, chief medical examiner for the Manitoba Department of Justice. Ironically, he had been trained years ago by Dr. H.E. Emson, the pathologist who had testified against David. If the federal Justice Department wasn't going to respond to the Ferris report, we would give them another forensics expert.

I was ecstatic to read Dr. Markesteyn's report when it arrived on June 4, 1990. He shared Ferris's concerns about the alleged semen that was recovered from the snow four days after the murder. By that time, the scene had been extensively trampled and searched, and snow had melted. "Yellowish stains in snowbanks most commonly find their origin, not in human ejaculates, but in urine, most commonly of canine origin," Markesteyn concluded. "Human semen does not freeze into a yellowish stain at

−40°F. In fact, it is white and difficult to spot in snow other than through special techniques such as ultraviolet light exposures, etcetera." And dog urine, the forensic expert added, often contains semen.

It was so bizarre that we had to get a highly regarded medical authority to tell us that dogs peed in the snow. It was also mind-boggling to think that my son might have spent the past twenty years in prison partly because police mistook dog urine for human semen.

Even if the dog urine thesis was discounted, David still came out looking innocent. Markesteyn wrote:

> If this was uncontaminated semen, then this semen cannot possibly be from Mr. Milgaard as he was stated to be an "A, non-secretor." A-antigens can find their origin in non-human material such as animal blood and secretions, bacteria, and, again, soil.
>
> I agree with Dr. Ferris that the serological evidence presented at the trial *failed to link* David Milgaard with the semen retrieved from vagina, snowbank, and crotch of panties.
>
> If, to everyone's satisfaction, it was established that the origin of the yellowish patch was unadulterated, uncontaminated human semen, then the presence of the A-antigen in this specimen clearly, from a serological point of view, *could not be Mr. Milgaard's.* In my opinion, the serological evidence presented at the trial was on very shaky scientific grounds to a degree

that it may well have been erroneous. I do not know what effect, if any, this evidence had on the jury in order to reach a verdict in Mr. Milgaard's trial. Unless another trial were held, we will never know if another jury, properly instructed on the scientific merits of these forensic tests, would draw another inference.

Science stories don't generally have the news appeal of face-to-face confrontations. Kim Campbell snubbing me in the hotel hallway made good television, but a camera shot of dog urine didn't cut it. Still, this was so bizarre that we could see some news potential.

"What's your headline going to be, Dan?" I asked Dan Lett of the *Winnipeg Free Press*.

"Well, I'm not sure we can get dog piss in the headline," Dan replied, "but I think you're going to find that the guys who write headlines for Page One are going to have a field day with this one."

The story did make Page One, on June 6, 1990, but appeared under the rather restrained headline, "Milgaard Evidence 'Shaky,' Examiner Says."

There were other interesting things in Markesteyn's report besides his dog urine findings. His conclusions about the murder were horrifying. Markesteyn wrote that the killer stayed at the murder scene for at least fifteen minutes. Gail Miller had died over several minutes, and the killer continued to stab her even as she lay dead. We could only shudder at the thought of his extreme hatred towards women. Markesteyn could find no explanation why the knife blade had snapped, since no bones were struck by it.

Complicating things further was the fact that original police notes about the sample found in the snow were missing.

"Hah, I wonder why," I said to David Asper as he read the report aloud. We sent the new report off to Ottawa. As soon as the new forensics report reached a desk in the Justice Department, one of the department's investigators finally booked an interview with Dr. James Ferris, two years after we had sent them his report.

We braced ourselves for yet another visit with the parole board at Stony Mountain Penitentiary. We lost track of how many parole board hearings we had attended and lost. On June 4, 1990, the day before the parole hearing, we were planning to hold a press conference, when David Asper called. He had just spoken with Paul Henderson by phone from B.C.

"Wilson caved," David Asper told me. "Wilson caved in and told the story."

David Asper's voice was soft and he sounded shocked. Paul had just gotten a statement from Ron Wilson, David said, adding, "He hates you. He's afraid of you."

"Why?" I asked.

"He said that you had come on so strong. He really doesn't want anything to do with you. He wants David to phone him tomorrow if at all possible. He wants to speak to David. He came clean."

It had been ten years since I found Wilson, back in

1980. He refused to see me then, as well as every time I tracked him down since then.

"Don't go anywhere," David Asper said.

"All right," I replied, sighing.

As soon as we were off the phone, I called Maureen, crying, "Wilson has just caved right in."

"What's the matter?" Maureen asked.

"David's going to be walking free very soon," I said. "I can't believe it. It sounds as if it's really coming together."

"That's fantastic, Mom. You okay?" All she could make out was my sobbing.

Maureen was crying now too.

"I'm just praying."

Then I called Susan.

"What do you mean, he's caved in, Mom?" Susan asked. "Do you mean he's going to turn around and say it was all a lie?"

"Yes, yes."

Now she was crying too.

"Do you realize what this means?" I asked. "If Ron Wilson has caved in, with this other evidence, they've just . . . it has got to be the end."

"Oh, Mom."

There were plenty of sobs on both ends of the line.

Susan was thirty-five years old now. I couldn't help but think back to the horrible turn her life had taken with David's conviction, when she was just fourteen. From the time David was convicted, Susan had never had anything approaching a normal life. She had been a strong, popular student, participating in volleyball and gymnastics and working part-time babysitting and at a restaurant. Her IQ was well above average and she was particularly strong in mathematics and science, with ambitions of someday becoming a scientist. She had idolized David, and his conviction crushed her. Other kids were often cruel, shouting that her brother was a murderer and crossing the street to avoid her. She could also find no peace at home, where everyone seemed in shock, and crying and arguing were constant background noises. As I devoted myself to freeing David, Susan took over as the mother in the family, shouldering household duties like cooking and looking after Maureen. After the conviction, the children seemed to be constantly fighting, and Susan sometimes took out her frustrations on Maureen, then felt guilty for it.

This once-ambitious student dropped out after completing only grade ten, and was out of the family home by seventeen, working in various low-paying jobs like waitressing and telemarketing. She worked as a cab driver and dispatcher in Portage La Prairie, Manitoba, and was married from 1975 to 1983. She considered her ex-husband the finest man she ever met, and blamed their marriage breakup on her lack of self-control, and her preoccupation with David's case. Jobs were also tough to maintain, since so many mornings she simply couldn't get out of bed because of depression. The little girl who once dreamed of becoming a scientist now saw herself as a failure.

After I hung up with Susan, it was back on the telephone line with David Asper.

"I just had a very emotional conversation with Mr. Wilson," David said, his voice hushed. "He started reading through his statement to me . . . Paul gave him a copy. He broke down."

"I believe that David is innocent," Wilson's statement said. "My testimony was coerced by the police . . . I was seventeen. I was frightened. I felt the police were trying to pin it on me."

During Ron's interrogation, police officers wouldn't stop asking him if he had murdered Gail Miller. He kept replying that he didn't kill her and he didn't think David did either.

"It was like brainwashing," Wilson said in his statement. "I started to implicate David Milgaard to tell police what they wanted to hear." They used Shorty's statement against David to push Wilson to say that he also must have seen blood on David's pants. In truth, Ron said he had never even seen David with a knife in Saskatoon.

"He recants everything," David Asper said. "He is totally demolished. He is afraid. He is confused. He doesn't know what to do. He feels sick. He says that he has thought about this every day for the past twenty years and didn't know what to to . . . He felt afraid and a little intimidated when you were there. He says he wrote David twice and tried to explain everything, but the letters never made it. He is just really stricken by the enormity of what he has just gotten off of his chest."

"I think it's wonderful," I said. "I think it's just wonderful."

"He is really, really shattered," David Asper continued. "He wants to talk to David. He wants to personally
apologize to David. He feels sick . . . He said he will do
anything to help David but he wants to talk to David."

Ron was so shaken that he had to take the next day
off work.

"Would it help if I phoned him, and just thanked
him?" I asked.

"No, do not talk to him. He has bad memories."

"I really put the fear of God in all of them, didn't I?"

"Yep, yep," David Asper said. "Whatever Paul's
approach was, it worked."

Asper cautioned me again that we couldn't afford to
spook Ron Wilson. That meant saying nothing about his
statement to anybody except our family for the time being.

"You have to bear in mind, Joyce, we need this guy."

Ron Wilson was extremely concerned about his wife
and his job. He had spent the past decade growing out
of the person he once was. Would his statement ruin his
new life? "All of that goes down the sewer with this,"
David Asper said.

In their emotional telephone conversation, David
Asper had promised Ron Wilson that he would try to
form a wall between Ron and the people who used him
to convict David. Life can be so strange. We were now
the protectors of one of the people who had helped put
David in prison.

My son David wouldn't be able to hear the news
about Ron Wilson until the next day. He had already
written a nice letter to Shorty Cadrain, saying if Shorty

could help, that would be fine, but if he couldn't, David would understand. He signed it, "Peace, Dave." The letter suggested that they might even be friends again later on. For years, David didn't want anything to do with Shorty, but forgiveness was so badly needed here — for both of them.

I went into that parole hearing at Stony Mountain hoping that, at the very least, they would transfer him to the minimum-security Rockwood prison farm, which adjoins Stony Mountain Penitentiary. There, he could have a little space. It seemed he couldn't walk five feet in Stony Mountain without fielding a question about his now-famous case. Prisoners and guards often meant well, but David needed a break. He didn't want to talk about it anymore.

However, the parole board refused to even look at Markesteyn's report and the fax of Wilson's statement. They didn't see their role as retrying the case. What's more, David didn't do well at the hearing. It seemed as if the board officers were picking at him. They wanted him to explain how he had changed for the good since he was first locked up. They pressed him to admit that he had been a hippie, criss-crossing the countryside doing drugs.

"Yeah, everybody was doing it at the time," David replied.

"The picture that you paint of him as a long-haired hippie travelling the countryside is true," I told them. "But at one point, my son took a job with *Maclean's* as a salesman and that job satisfied his need to travel the country. Plus, it gave him good money and he was doing very well with it. The weekend when he was in Saskatoon, he was travelling with his friends while he was waiting for a licence for him to work in Manitoba. It subsequently came through a few days later. He worked quite successfully until September, a few days before he was charged. During that time, he displayed a lot of skills, made a fair amount of money, and even sent some home to the family. The picture that you're painting doesn't have that in it at all. You're just seeing somebody who was travelling the country committing crimes, and I just can't see that."

My proud-mother speech didn't sway them. Not even close. As they prodded away at him, David reverted to being a sixteen-year-old kid and hit back verbally. He still hadn't learned not to retaliate. "You seem pretty nervous about all of that," he said to the chairman after the questions about his hippie lifestyle. Things were going downhill fast. They asked David about drugs, and David turned the question around, asking members of the parole board, "Have you never smoked dope?"

David Asper and I just about died. I kicked my son under the table. Once again, David was showing absolutely no respect for authority. Of course, he was also being honest. How do you respect the authority of a system that has stolen the past twenty years of your life? It was ironic that his problems with the parole board stemmed from his honesty.

"When did you last have an illegal substance inside the institution?" a parole board member asked.

David admitted he had smoked some marijuana just a month before. As he later said to me, "It's not easy in here. I haven't touched anything in over a month. But sometimes, I'll see them all smoking up and they look at you like you're really weird if you don't have some and it makes you feel good for a little while, when you've been feeling terrible. Is it so wrong, Mom? Is it so wrong?"

I know it's wrong and illegal, but how quick would I be to judge if I were in the same situation? The parole board members are looking for applicants with a short haircut, a tucked-in shirt and "Yes-sir, no-sir" answers. That's what the real criminals do. That makes the authorities feel powerful. But David wouldn't play this game.

We hadn't even made it back to Winnipeg from prison when we heard on our car radio that, once again, David was denied parole. We had gotten used to that, although you always feel a certain amount of hope, nonetheless. He was also turned down on his application to be transferred to the Rockwood farm camp.

I was proud of how David handled this latest rejection. He pushed hard to get more speakers for his Justice Group to speak with inmates. He wanted speakers who had done something with their lives, who offered inspiration for the convicts. Despite the rejections, David was getting on with his life.

I was also pleased with the way he handled himself when Ron Wilson telephoned him. Ron was very emotional and badly needed David's forgiveness. I think that David also badly needed to forgive him, since bitterness can be so corrosive. "It's all right," David said. "I understand. You've been a victim too."

TWENTY

UNHAPPY HERO

*"I would not consider my brother to be
a reliable witness at that time."*
Dennis Cadrain on his brother Shorty,
star witness at David's trial

SHORTY CADRAIN WAS living in a treehouse in his brother Dennis's backyard in Port Coquitlam, B.C., when Paul found him. Paul went for coffee at a restaurant with Dennis and Shorty. Shorty's head was shaven now, and he had grown a moustache, while his skin had taken on an olive tone, giving him a reptilian appearance. Shorty began to rant and rave and said that David had snapped the antenna off their car, presumably to keep them from hearing news broadcasts of the murder. This was interesting because Ron Wilson had told Paul that the radio on the beat-up car had never worked anyway. Now Shorty was saying that David threw his clothing into a garbage can, which was immediately picked up by a garbage truck after the murder. He hadn't said this at the trial. Shorty said he worried that David would kill him and maybe even wipe out his entire family if he was ever released.

Dennis clearly saw his brother as mentally deficient and unstable, and pitied him. After drinking coffee for an hour in the restaurant, Paul, Dennis and Shorty went to Dennis's house. Dennis was a carpenter, and his split-level home clearly showed his success. When Shorty was briefly out of the room, Dennis told Paul that his brother had never been quite right since his police interrogation before David's trial.

As he talked, Shorty's mood turned mournful. He felt he was the dummy of the family; he'd dropped out of school after failing grade six three times. Shorty felt abandoned, and complained that he was the only child in the family who never got a birthday cake baked by their mother. He also still resented his mother not letting him take piano lessons. He said that, at fifteen, he was tying to impress a friend by drinking wood alcohol when he died. After Shorty returned from the dead, he said, he gained insights into the living by studying yoga. He felt that it helped him see auras around people, and what he saw around David was frightening. "I saw purple on Milgaard and that means he has murdered someone," he said. He also had memories of Larry Fisher, his former downstairs neighbour who was now serving time for knifepoint rapes. Fisher got him a short-lived job in masonry, and also tried to get him to "pick up sluts" at a pool hall.

Life held a seemingly endless store of bad memories for Shorty, which included getting a sexually transmitted disease from a lover. He had a nasty scar on his face from when his nose was torn off, then reattached. Exactly how this happened wasn't explained. Perhaps the only time he was taken seriously and held real power was when he was the star witness in David's trial. Shorty bristled at the suggestion that he testified for money, noting that he gave the $2,000 to his family, and fully accepted responsibility for David's conviction, saying, "I can't change my story for the devil."

It was bizarre to think that this sad, delusional, simple-minded man was the star witness whom prosecutor Bobs Caldwell, in his interview with Peter Carlyle-Gordge years before, had so heartily praised as the hero of the trial.

Years before, in his own interview with Peter, Dennis had compared my son to American cult killer Charles Manson. Dennis's view had dramatically changed now, as he knew that Shorty had been talking with police about the killing a couple of days before he came forward with his revelations about David. Shorty's grandiose imagination, combined with his desperate need for attention, was a dangerous combination in Dennis's opinion. Dennis wrote in a signed statement for us: "Knowing my brother as I do, I am certain that he would not intentionally lie about anything. But I also know that he is prone to exaggeration and suggestion, and that he could easily be coerced and manipulated by police. If ideas were planted in Albert's mind it is quite possible that he would come to accept them as true. Frankly, I would not consider my brother to be a reliable witness at that time.

And for this reason, I have had concerns that David Milgaard may not have received a fair trial."

Dennis added that his sister Celine was home the morning of the murder, and that she did not see any blood on David's clothing, as Shorty had described.

I was so excited, so hopeful, but I didn't tell all of this to my son. I couldn't tell him every time our hopes went up. That just set him up for a fall, and he could only take so many more of those. He had far too much idle time in prison to dwell upon things, and no power to do anything.

TWENTY-ONE

MANAGING THE MEDIA

"I have to start each day fresh."
I talk with reporter Dan Lett
about coping with the pressure of David's battle

DAN LETT OF THE *Winnipeg Free Press* was one of
the first members of the press to see the value in David's
story. As Dan's confidence in the case was borne out, he
found himself being sniped at by other reporters who
were just starting to wake up to it. Rather than praise
Dan, some of them accused him of being spoon-fed by
us. I had forgotten just how nasty the news business can
be, as it had been some time since I'd worked on the
switchboard at the *Toronto Star* as a teenager, in the
midst of its circulation wars with the *Toronto Telegram*.

"I hadn't realized that it was such a cutthroat business," I once said to Dan.

"I guess we're all starting to feel the wear and tear,"
Dan replied.

"I don't accept wear and tear," I said. "I have to start
each day fresh." I wasn't just offering a platitude. That

was how I kept from being overpowered by the seeming hopelessness of David's case. However, the sniping was clearly bothering Dan. "It can't touch you unless you react to it," I told him. "Just let it go. You have integrity and you are a quality person. Don't let it upset you. Hang in there."

As much as we liked Dan, we sorely needed to bring this story east, out of Winnipeg, and onto the front page of the papers read by MPs in Ottawa. David's plight was still largely a regional story. We needed it to be a true national issue so that politicians in Ottawa would be forced to take a look at it.

I had learned a long time ago that, as a family member of a convicted murderer, my voice didn't count for much. What I needed was the voices of other Canadians, and the way to get them was through the media. At first, our challenge was to get anyone interested in writing anything about the case. Now the problem was to decide how to get news out without getting the media angry at each other — and at us.

The *Globe and Mail* could have helped immensely at this stage, but we were told by its Manitoba reporter Geoffrey York that if we didn't give the paper information first and exclusively, it wouldn't handle the story at all. York had seemed angry at us from the beginning, and upset at Dan Lett's success with the story.

The national obsession with our constitution was also still getting in the way of publicizing David's case. All available reporters and all news space seemed devoted to the seemingly endless Meech Lake constitutional talks.

"That's a fact of life that we have no control over," David Asper said.

Dan Lett told us that his stories were being picked up on the Canadian Press newswire and transmitted across the country. This was true, but they were only getting mention in the back pages, if at all, in Ontario.

Cam Fuller of the *Saskatoon Star Phoenix* joked that the clipping service that collected news articles for the Justice Department must be going crazy now. I collected a stack of those articles and sent them to an editor at the *Globe and Mail*, and asked why they hadn't done anything. Meanwhile, hours were spent with reporters updating them and encouraging them to follow various lines of investigation. Our finances were running thin, and we needed them to carry the ball some. It was an easier sell now because they could smell a big story. Fortunately, *Globe* reporter David Roberts got the paper onside in a big and important way, as it fought with the rival *Toronto Star* for scoops on the case. There was a great deal of excitement when the *Globe* discovered that police files on the case had gone missing. Pushing for David's freedom was now a lot like running a political campaign — we had to keep his case in front of the public.

I wanted to keep the media on the story but away from Shorty. He just seemed too fragile, and I kept imagining how his mother must feel.

"Joyce, you can't contain this kind of stuff," Jim McCloskey said. "You're trying to put a cap on a volcano. You just can't do it. Shorty Cadrain is a major player in the original conviction."

David Asper calmed me somewhat, noting that there had been an unbalanced figure in the Donald Marshall case as well, and the media had treated him with kid gloves throughout that inquiry. "The individual wasn't exploited, the police were," David said.

Now we had Deborah Hall, Ron Wilson, Linda Fisher, Shorty and Shorty's brother Dennis giving us statements with new evidence backing our case, in addition to our two forensics reports.

"The Department of Justice will say, 'How come these people will talk to your guy and not us?'" David Asper said. "And, of course, our answer will be, 'Look in the mirror.'"

On June 14, 1990, I got a call from Hersh Wolch, and he was clearly excited. He told me to tune in to the local CBC-TV news that night. "Are you ready for this?" he asked.

"I'm ready," I replied. "Go ahead."

Hersh asked me to think about Fisher's other rapes. He told me that they had taken place within two months of the attack on Gail Miller. "Do you know where those girls lived?" Hersh asked.

"No."

The original newspaper story about Larry Fisher's rape conviction had been datelined Regina, because that's where his trial was held. However, CBC-TV had learned that the attacks had actually taken place in Saskatoon. It came as a huge shock to hear this, after our years of digging into the case.

"About a block and a half away. Do you know what bus they took?"

"Same bus?"

"Same bus."

"Wow. You think that might influence anybody?"

"Oh, I think it might . . . a lot."

The story was going to be aired that day in Winnipeg and Saskatoon, and the CBC-TV reports would also run the story June 17 and 18.

"The effect of it will be very large," Hersh predicted. "It'll be monstrous."

The CBC report noted that Fisher used a paring knife to commit those rapes, just like Gail Miller's attacker. It also pointed out that the Saskatoon police must have known about those other attacks. Saskatoon police officers had gone to Winnipeg to pick up Fisher after he had confessed to Lorne Huff in Fort Garry. Now we felt we could understand why they were so standoffish with Huff and his partner. Perhaps they had a queasy suspicion that a major blunder had been committed. Indeed, a number of anonymous police officers were often calling the *Star Phoenix*, urging them to dig a little deeper into the force. Their general message was, "If you only knew what we knew . . ."

David Asper was just flying with the news. At our next strategy meeting, we decided to play nice with the Justice Department and give them room to save face and reverse tack with dignity. If we felt the need to lambaste anybody, we would target the Saskatoon police, since we didn't need them for anything anyway.

CBC-TV's *The Journal* called, saying they wanted to push the story even further than the regional CBC reports. They planned to zero in on our new suspect, Larry Fisher, and hoped to interview him. An RCMP officer working with the Justice Department had talked with Fisher in a Saskatoon psychiatric centre, where he was being held in seclusion, and we heard that Fisher was going to make some sort of statement to him. Up to this point, we had heard, Fisher hadn't actually denied doing the killing, although he hadn't confessed either.

Now David Asper wasn't just a lawyer, friend and tactician. He was also an image consultant for the case. He, for instance, told me not to wear bright or flashy clothes when I appeared before the cameras. Nothing red or yellow, but greens and browns were motherly and fine. I had to laugh when one concerned supporter offered to buy me some new clothes because she always saw me wearing the same earnest-looking dress on the news. David Asper was particularly concerned that my son wasn't paying enough attention to his appearance.

"I tell you that when we next go to a parole board hearing, if I have to tie him to a wall, he's going to have a haircut," David Asper said. "I don't care. He's going to look like a thirty-eight-year-old guy concerned about his life and concerned about his future."

The CBC scoop came at a time when my son felt strong. Sometimes, he would stay up all night worrying, but at this time, he was sleeping well and looking good. We also tried to coach David in the presentation of his answers, although he wasn't one to be told how to do things. "Very often, he speaks to the reporter as opposed to the viewer," David Asper said. "It's a classic talent of a politician, to sit there and look at a reporter but talk to all of the viewers."

With David Asper, the marketing of David's innocence was in good hands.

TWENTY-TWO

RUMOURS OF JUSTICE

"At this point, hell, I'd be trying to escape too."
Bob Horner,
chair of the House of Commons Justice Committee

IN THE SUMMER OF 1990, Larry Fisher still hadn't cracked and confessed to Gail Miller's murder, even after three weeks of questioning from a Justice Department investigator. Years before, he had managed plea-bargains for his rapes, and maybe he expected to cut a deal now too. It was horrifying to think that he clearly had a sick attraction for women in medical uniforms; I was a nurse now too, and it bothered my son to no end that Fisher might decide to do something against me once he got the chance. In a strange twist, Fisher had remarried again recently, and Justice Department interviews with him about his sex crimes had to be scheduled around his conjugal visits.

We had strong doubts about the seriousness of the Justice Department investigation, and they only got worse after an August 1, 1990, *Globe and Mail* article in which William Corbett, a senior lawyer with the department's criminal prosecutions branch, was quoted as ridiculing the faith of David's supporters, saying, "Seventeen per cent of people still believe Elvis Presley is still alive."

In addition, Linda Fisher and Deborah Hall accused Eugene Williams, a Justice Department investigator, of not being impartial. We heard that Williams seemed to want to make their stories fit the government case, just as police investigators years before had succeeded in making the suspicions of David's friends match their own preconceptions. Deborah said she found Williams condescending and thought he was trying to make her feel like a liar. She left her interview with him in tears. It particularly enraged us that Williams was assisted in his investigation by Bobs Caldwell, whose reputation would suffer if David was proven innocent. So much for impartial justice.

On the bright side, more people in power took us seriously now. MP Bob Horner of Mississauga West, beside Toronto, called on his cellular phone as he drove through rural Manitoba with fellow Conservative Felix Holtman, who was David Asper's MP. Horner was chairman of the House of Commons Committee on Justice and seemed concerned, as he asked question after question for forty-five minutes. I told him that David was particularly depressed.

"Well, I can understand why," Horner said. "I promise you nothing except that I will do everything I can to get the justice minister and Justice Department moving on it. And I may even go so far as to talk to the commissioner of the RCMP."

I said I hoped Shorty Cadrain could be shielded from media ridicule. "He's another victim of the whole thing," I said.

"They're certainly all victims," Horner agreed. "Mrs. Milgaard, I'll do anything I can to help . . . As a parent of four, I know what you're going through, and my heart goes out to David."

In the short term, I said, it would be nice if David could be transferred somewhere better, like the Rockwood prison farm, although I knew his earlier escapes still hurt his chances of this.

"At this point, hell, I'd be trying to escape too," Horner said.

Time was weighing very heavily on David now, and my immediate hope was to somehow get him to the farm camp. Perhaps it would let his mind slip back to happier, more peaceful times, like when he was an adolescent spending summer days in the country with Pappa Milgaard.

In our calls for help, we now cast a broad net, literally from biker bars to the Oprah Winfrey show to Buckingham Palace. Oprah's staff wished us well and told us to keep in touch, but didn't do anything on David's story. The Section 690 procedure stems from the old royal prerogative of mercy, so approaching Buckingham Palace wasn't totally off the wall. I mailed the Queen newspaper clippings and a letter saying the Justice Department wasn't listening to us. We also prepared a video tape for her, which wasn't as easy as it sounds, since British video cassette recorders have a different format than those in North America. The first time I contacted the Queen's office, I was urged to write the Canadian Justice Department. The second time the response was a little more encouraging. I got a letter on impressive official stationery stating, "The private secretary is commanded by Her Majesty The Queen to acknowledge the receipt of the letter and enclosures from Mrs. J. Milgaard and to say that they have been passed to the Governor General of Canada." Every little bit helps. I also wrote to Percy Ross, a multimillionaire with a newspaper column who granted wishes, but he didn't want to get involved.

I was getting impatient as we approached July 7, 1990. That date would mark David's twentieth birthday spent in prison, his twenty-first if you count the time he served in jail before his trial. That was well over half his life, with no end in sight. We kept hearing rumours of major developments just around the corner, but had no way of knowing exactly what was true and what wasn't. Anything seemed possible. Everything already seemed unreal. Governments came and went, hopes rose and fell, and still David remained behind bars, with no release date in sight. There was now a rumour that the Saskatoon police commission might be looking into the city police department's investigation. If true, that would be promising, but we couldn't find out for sure. There were rumours that the RCMP investigators working for the Justice Department had gotten something substantial out of Larry Fisher. They had apparently interviewed him three or four times now. Of course, this sounded promising, but was it just more false hope? In the meantime, David was now a middle-aged convict.

Some things offered definite hope. The John Howard Society, which aided ex-convicts, was distributing bumper stickers marked "Free David Milgaard now, 21 years is long enough" and collecting money for his defence fund. They would eventually raise $40,000 from across Canada, mostly in $5 and $10 donations from average people who cared. Maureen and Susan went to the Red River Exhibition to sell bumper stickers and were turned away. They appealed their case to senior exhibition officials, and soon my daughters were at the front gates with their bumper stickers. They weren't allowed to actually sell them, so they took $2 donations, then gave out the stickers as a gift for the donation. It was hot work, and Maureen got sunstroke, but they pressed on.

My daughters got more than ten thousand signatures on a petition calling for a review of the case as they took the fight to virtually every street corner in Winnipeg and almost every hockey and football game, concert and bar. Maureen even appealed to the rock group the Tragically Hip, who recorded a song for David, "Wheat Kings."

Graham Reddoch, the Manitoba executive director of John Howard, had been a longtime supporter of David's right to a new trial, and now they weren't alone. The Church Council of Canada, which I had made contact with during my trips to Ottawa, and the Manitoba Mennonite Committee were also willing to help, and we even contacted Amnesty International in the hopes they would see David as a political prisoner. I wasn't too proud to take help from others. Far from it. The struggle to free David was never totally on my shoulders.

Meanwhile, David Asper explained just how serious it was for the Justice Department. If David won a new trial, the precedent would mean that every convict in Canada might start thinking of going after the same thing. "I'm just telling you the facts of life," Asper said.

I couldn't help but feel enormously frustrated and impatient, but Asper was convinced we were finally in the home stretch. "Over the past twenty years, you've fought like a dog, and we're now down to the last, it appears, three weeks of the fight, and I don't think you should tell David this, and we just have to bear down," David said in mid-June 1990. "I believe we are going to Ottawa on July 6."

"Not till July 6!" I replied. Just because David had been in prison for decades didn't mean that every extra day didn't hurt.

"All of the delays, all of the problems, all of the letdowns, all of the misrepresentations given to us by Justice — it'll come out in the wash," David replied. "But let's just back off."

"This is not the time to back off," I replied. "This is the time to push."

"This is the highest-level negotiations and it is not a negotiation about if they reopen," David said. "It's a question of when, where and how."

I should have felt happy, I guess, but I didn't feel any less frustrated.

"I'm telling you, Joyce, that you've got to bear down and you've got to let these last three weeks unfold," David

Left to right, front: *Susan, myself, David, Maureen and Lorne in front of Hersh Wolch* (l) *and David Asper* (r) *at the news conference announcing that the Supreme Court would reopen David's case, November 29, 1991.*

(KEN FAUGHT/ *TORONTO STAR*)

David with David Asper, December 1998.

(MAGNUS THOMPSON)

Hersh Wolch, who, along with David Asper, persevered in helping David and our family achieve justice.

(*WINNIPEG FREE PRESS*/CP)

David being put on a plane back to Stony Mountain Penitentiary in 1992.
He had been arrested during the Supreme Court hearings after missing curfew at a halfway house.

(IAN MACALPINE/*KINGSTON WHIG-STANDARD*)

David in a reflective moment during a press conference to announce his freedom. His sister Susan is in the background.

(MARC GALLANT/CP)

David in 1993, after he was finally freed, visiting Peter Edwards at the Toronto Star.

(DAVID COOPER/ *TORONTO STAR*)

Convicted rapist Larry Fisher tries to avoid the camera in Calgary, 1994.

(DAVID LAZAROWYCH/ *CALGARY HERALD*/CP)

Ron Wilson. His false testimony in 1969, along with that of Nichol John and Shorty Cadrain, led to David's 23-year long incarceration.

(FRANK GUNN/CP)

My English gentleman, Geoff.

(JOYCE MILGAARD)

David and Marnie at their wedding on Kitsilano Beach, Vancouver,
August 14, 1996.

(JOYCE MILGAARD)

I hug Maureen as David shakes Hersh Wolch's hand the day after DNA test results, announced July 18, 1997, clear David's name.

(KEN GIGLIOTTI/ *WINNIPEG FREE PRESS*/CP)

Receiving my 1997 Honor Roll Award from Maclean's *magazine.*

(*MACLEAN'S*)

Donald Marshall, another wrongfully convicted Canadian and former jailmate of David.

(ALBERT LEE/CP)

With yet another man wrongfully convicted of murder, Guy Paul Morin. His conviction was finally overturned on January 23, 1995.

(ROB ALARY/ *WINNIPEG SUN*)

Joking on the set of Milgaard, *the CTV made-for-TV movie about David's story. Gabrielle Rose plays me in the movie, while Ian Tracey plays David.*

(JOE BRYSKA/ WINNIPEG FREE PRESS)

continued. "The last three weeks in this whole ordeal are going to make it or break it. Everybody with the decision-making authority is on this case, and they're pushing this."

"All I can say is it would be one terrific birthday present," I said, thinking of how I'd like something good and concrete to be able to tell David by his July 7 birthday. I told Asper that my instinct was to recoil at the thought of another three weeks of delay.

"It's not a delay," he protested.

"That's lawyer talk, Asper."

"No, that's not lawyer talk. The fact is that we've finally broken through. It's like you chip away at a wall and finally you get a little bit of a hole and you keep chipping and the hole gets bigger. We're going through the wall now."

I said, "My problem is, when I get to the stage where I see it's getting big enough to get through, I want to break it down."

"I know. I know."

But the three weeks came and passed, and still nothing. Instead of things coming to a climax, there was just more delay.

On August 25, 1990, I was on stage at a musical fundraiser in Winnipeg, singing my song for his freedom, "An Innocent Man." One of the three verses went,

> I'm calling for Justice
> I'm calling for Truth,
> I'm calling for Freedom
> For they have the proof.

> I'm calling for people
> Across this great land
> To rise up and fight for
> An innocent man.

I had plenty of backup now, and the stage was full of musicians. People had risen up all across the country. I felt so supported and loved.

TWENTY-THREE

WEARY SIXTEEN-YEAR-OLD

"Mom, just tell me your life."
David grows weary of talking about his case in visits

WE SOMETIMES WONDERED what life would be like when David was finally free. There would be a fresh set of problems, but at least he would be with us, finally.

David Asper warned me, "David is going to have a problem accepting that he's going to have a structured life."

We kicked around the idea of getting David into an adult treatment centre for people with learning disabilities. Although David was bright, this would mean a place to stay, access to counsellors and a way of measuring his conduct, to reassure authorities.

"That's the type of thing that I think would win easy favour with the parole board," David Asper said. "It's going to be horrendous on you. You're dealing with your sixteen-year-old son, but worse, there's going to be a difficult transition period where he's going to rebel and he's going to act out."

I knew my son would balk at the treatment centre, since

he was very much against anything that labelled him as having mental problems. He simply could not stand being labelled a killer-rapist, and he wasn't about to be stamped mentally deficient either. At the same time, I could see the strains of the past two decades had left profound emotional scars. How could they not? "I know it's going to be a trial and I'm not minimizing it at all, but I think that we've got a strong family unit," I replied. "We can surround him and help him through this with our love."

I wondered how David and Lorne would get along once David was freed. There was a great deal of love between them, but love doesn't always mean peace. Lorne was strict, especially if David was giving me a hard time. Then he would come down on David like a ton of bricks.

"You've got to turn back the clock," David Asper said. "It's as though he's sixteen, and when he's sixteen, Dad's the heavy."

"When he was out, he functioned," I replied. "I think that he'll revel in it. He's not afraid of things."

"Boy, it's an interesting study, I'll tell you," David Asper said.

"This is no study. This is my life."

David Asper said his father-in-law Don Browne might be helpful when David finally got out. Don was a social worker, and David might relate to him. He was into peace, anti-poverty and native issues, all of which would appeal to David. I thought it might work if he visited David as someone interested in poverty and injustice, not as a professional social worker treating him as some kind of case study.

I was visiting David two or three times a week now, and it was clear he just wanted to bury himself in anything but his plight. He simply couldn't talk about the case anymore. It was too frustrating, too painful. "Mom, just tell me your life," he'd say.

David was often haggard for lack of sleep, but as the summer passed, he seemed to return to normal, and I was delighted to see the old David return. I kept reminding him and myself not to take yesterday into today and to start every day fresh.

As autumn 1990 began, there was still no time set for a decision, and David could hold back his depression no longer. He checked into a prison hospital ward and pushed us away. He fired David Asper and Hersh Wolch, only to quickly hire them back. It was as though he was being pulled in six directions at once and could only react blindly. He wanted to be an island unto himself, but also realized on another level that he was totally dependent on others. He knew he was getting paranoid, but also felt that he was the victim of a massive coverup. He knew he would be enormously fortunate to win a new trial, but he also knew that he deserved much more than that. What his doctors called his manic phases usually lasted about ten days, and then, towards the end, he would reach out for help. This time, however, his pain was particularly troubling. It was clear he couldn't last much longer.

The seemingly endless waiting was also getting to me. Sometimes I thought that the constant wait was worse than a negative decision would be. If our appeal was denied, we could start planning something else, although I had no idea what that might be.

It was comforting to know that we weren't alone. We learned that the speaker of the House of Commons, John Fraser, planned a dinner with Kim Campbell for November 5, 1990. They were both lawyers from B.C., and Fraser had considerable influence. An impeccable source said that Fraser planned to put a three-page letter by Campbell's dinner setting outlining reasons that David was the victim of a grave miscarriage of justice. Because of his role in the government, Fraser couldn't go public with his concerns about David, but behind the scenes, he wielded significant clout. Constitutionally, the speaker of the House was above the prime minister himself.

Our high hopes for Kim Campbell had long since passed. We were intensely frustrated by her now, but knew we had to tread lightly. We had to allow her to reverse her decision and save face at the same time. We were unsettled by her reputation of reacting against things, or, as David Asper put it in a moment of extreme frustration: "She's this right-wing, stupid airhead . . . Why would you toy with somebody like that, because this is who we have to deal with? . . . This person has enormous power. So, it's like, tread delicately until we had got what we want, and then launch nuclear war on her. That has always been the plan."

TWENTY-FOUR

STRAIGHT
AND NARROW WAY

"No cross, no crown."
Untitled hymn number 289

HOPES FOR A DECISION by David's birthday in July 1990 were a distant memory now. The United Nations responded to information I had sent them, and that fall there was a strong chance that David's case would be aired at a meeting in Geneva. I thought of how wonderful it would be to get a favourable decision from the UN. If they moved ahead with it and called attention to the case, I would call Kim Campbell's office and tell her she had forty-eight hours to give us a decision. I didn't want to embarrass Canada, but my first responsibility was to my son.

I was nursing at Tenacre in New Jersey when, on February 27, 1991, Susan phoned me to say a decision was coming through on the fax machine at the law office and would be available within twenty minutes. That wasn't much time, but the wait was agonizing. The phone rang again a couple of minutes later. David Asper told me the decision of the Justice Department was negative. I felt absolute disbelief. We had no warning this might happen, although all along we knew we were up against a system that just doesn't want to admit it has made a mistake. It wasn't justice. It was politics.

I immediately asked to be relieved from work at Tenacre, then made arrangements to fly up to Winnipeg right away. A friend of mine, Karen Haire, drove me to Newark airport. As we drove, I reached out to the Father, saying, "How can this happen?" I was so angry and full of disbelief. I felt like such a failure. We had everything we needed in that appeal, yet Kim Campbell had turned us down.

Hymns can pick you up when you're down, and so I opened up the hymnal as we drove. It opened to hymn number 289. The words were perfect:

> Press on, dear traveller, press thou on,
> I am the Way, the Truth, the Life.
> It is the straight and narrow way
> That leads to that eternal day,
> That turns the darkness into light,
> That buries wrong and honours right.
>
> Press on, and know that God is all;
> He is the Life, the Truth, the Love.
> It is the way the Saviour trod,
> It is the way that leads to God.

Think of the words: No cross, no crown;
Though tasks are sore, be not cast down.

When I read those words, I started to cry. That was exactly the message I needed. I flew back to Winnipeg, and when I met Susan at the airport, I again burst into tears.

"I failed him," I cried.

"You didn't fail him, Mom," Susan said. "*They* failed him."

The press was there in full force to record that searingly emotional moment. When I looked at it later, I saw what looked like a broken woman, but even then I knew that somehow God would give me the strength I needed, and I said to the reporters, "I'm kind of aching. I don't want to even see David. I feel I have failed him, but I know I will feel better tomorrow and I'll start again."

The next day I went on national television with a more aggressive approach to the government.

In her decision, Kim Campbell wrote that David's case had been given a full review by Justice Department officials. Despite the two scientific reports, she was unimpressed, writing, "In the final analysis, the forensic evidence presented at trial proved nothing. With the benefit of hindsight, it may have been preferable had the evidence simply not been tendered . . . The information provided by Deborah Hall does not detract from the evidence led at trial, and Mr. Wilson's present recollection of the events in question is palpably unreliable.

"The suggestion that the forensic evidence exculpates

David Milgaard overstates the value of that evidence, which established neither guilt nor innocence. Further, there is no reliable basis to believe that Larry Fisher was connected in any manner with Gail Miller's death. The submissions concerning the location of the offence and Mr. Milgaard's opportunity to commit the offence were fully canvassed by trial counsel and by the judge who properly charged them on that point. There is no body of new evidence which constitutes a reasonable basis for believing that a miscarriage of justice likely occurred in this case, or, to adopt the test suggested by you during submissions, there is no basis to conclude that a miscarriage of justice may have occurred here. Accordingly I am not prepared to refer this case back to the courts."

Had they even studied the case? How could they dismiss the forensic evidence when that formed two pages of prosecutor Caldwell's address to the jury? Caldwell had made a point of telling the jury that the forensic evidence *didn't* exclude David. That was clearly false. Those were the last words the jury heard from him before they convicted David.

Susan and David Asper drove up to Stony Mountain to break the news to David, and Susan was numbed when prison authorities refused to let her inside, saying she had not booked an appointment. She had so badly wanted to be able to hold him and hug him and say everything would somehow be okay, but now she had to wait outside as Asper went in alone. David was in solitary confinement, trying to get a break from the general prison population, when David Asper appeared at his cell door. My son could see what was coming from the look on David Asper's face. He didn't need to hear him. Just as when the guilty verdict was read in court more than two decades before, the face said it all. I was so proud of how David took the news. He comforted David Asper, instead of the other way around. When I saw David, he was the same, hugging me and telling me it was going to be all right. I wanted to crawl into a hole myself. I felt I had somehow failed my son. I broke down, but David held me and that made me feel proud.

But after we left, David melted into a deeper depression. The staff and inmates at Stony Mountain who resented his media profile were tough on him now. Hope was so dangerous in prison. It could so easily blow up in your face, leaving you utterly vulnerable. No wonder so many prisoners preferred to be numb and to shuffle through life as unfeeling zombies.

"Mom, let's just give this up," David said in another visit. "You go back to England. Start a new life. I'll get out somehow."

"David, even if you were not my son, I'd have to fight this because what Kim Campbell has done is wrong," I told him. "It's political."

David wanted to be alone in solitary confinement to deal with the decision. He was devastated and later said, "It was like somebody just smashing all of your dreams." Something died inside him with the decision. He wanted nothing whatsoever to do with the case. When I did come to visit, we played backgammon and talked about family matters and left the case alone. He couldn't handle it now.

I knew something bad happened to him in prison after the decision, but David didn't want to tell me and I didn't want to pry. I knew he wasn't much with his fists, although he would stand up for himself verbally, often taking a beating for it. His missing front teeth spoke to that. I knew he beat his fists and his head against the wall, and I could understand his feelings only too well. We had been so sure he would finally be getting out. That hope, that carrot, was dangled in front of him for so long. Then it was pulled away.

I clung to the fact that God is all powerful. It was not the Kim Campbells of the world that were supreme. God was supreme. The rejection just highlighted this truth. Justice is mine, saith the Lord. That thought enabled me to get up and start all over again, just as the biblical David had done against Goliath. I once again claimed that the battle was the Lord's and continued to expect good. We learned from testing times, as hard as they might be.

Beyond that, we had to figure out a new strategy. The problem was that we didn't know how or on what basis the decision on the Section 690 application was denied. Campbell had referred it to a retired Supreme Court of Canada justice, William McIntyre, but we weren't allowed to see what he had seen or been told. We didn't even know what Kim Campbell had heard about the case. In the United States, if you can make a strong case before a judge, you can have a case reopened. Here, it was like flying in the dark.

Paul Henderson had returned to the United States and was working on a new case. He was, however, ready to get back on the trail for us. He had several leads about corruption within the Saskatoon police force, and maybe they would indirectly point us to something that might free David.

"How's David taking it?" Paul asked on the telephone, his voice weary.

"I was so proud of him."

"Of course, everybody's going to be trying to sanitize the police department's role in this."

"If we can come up with a dirty police department right now, that would be a great advantage."

Our phone was ringing constantly. People said things like, "Hello, Mrs. Milgaard. I'm a concerned citizen. I wonder how we might help."

"Keep up the fight," another caller said. "What they did to him is just terrible."

TWENTY-FIVE

TRAIL OF VICTIMS

"You're the only one they'll let in,
because you are David Milgaard's mother."
Rev. Jim McCloskey talks to me about interviewing the
rape victims of Larry Fisher

JIM McCLOSKEY WAS adamant. We now had to create a profile of Larry Fisher, a profile of a serial rapist capable of murder. To do this, I would have to visit all of his victims and get every detail of their attacks so that the similarities of the crimes to the attack on Gail Miller could be stressed. The idea was repugnant to me.

"I can't do that. Maybe Paul . . . ," I said.

"No, Joyce, you're the only one who can do it," Jim replied. "You're the only one they'll let in, because you are David Milgaard's mother."

I knew he was right, but that didn't make it any easier. It was obvious that the Justice Department did not understand the significance of Larry Fisher's crimes and they had not fully followed up on him. We would have to do it for them. The key to David's freedom seemed to lie in Larry Fisher and his eight known rape victims, not including Gail Miller. There were likely even more victims we didn't know about. So we set out to interview the ones we knew about, tracing them through court records and a skip-tracing agency.

On April 24, 1991, Paul and I rang the doorbell of a woman in Winnipeg whom Fisher had raped back in September 1970. She was hungover, and totally without pretense, as she invited us into her apartment without hesitation at 9 a.m. that morning. She was pasty and bloated, sitting half-dressed on her couch. Years ago, she was a dentistry student, but her promising future was long gone now, like the liquor from the empty bottles that seemed to be everywhere. She now lived off $500 a month in disability allowance, and existed in squalor, among dirty laundry and cigarette butts. She braced herself with a slug from a two-litre bottle of 7-Up and started to tell her story.

She was in her first year of dentistry school in Winnipeg in September 1970. The dental school was near the Health Sciences Centre, close to downtown. She wore a white lab coat in school, but the night of the rape, she was dressed casually to go dancing with a boyfriend. When the bars closed, they went their separate ways, and she took the bus south to her home.

She was a block from her door when suddenly there was a hand over her mouth and nose. She couldn't see her attacker as he grabbed her from behind. She struggled to tell him to just take her purse. He warned her that he had a knife, then dragged her between two houses, yanked down her panties, pulled her sweater over her face and ripped off her bra. Fisher bit her nipples so hard it felt like he was going to tear them right off. "You've had it before," he said as he raped her. She screamed loudly and lights came on in a nearby house. Police were on the scene quickly. Larry Fisher tried to run but couldn't get far with his pants down. The next day, the woman returned with police to the rape scene, where detectives found a paring knife in a flower bed and Fisher's pickup truck parked nearby.

Paul wondered whether Fisher had stalked her on a previous occasion. Since it was a remote, residential street, it seemed hardly the kind of area where a rapist would wait, after midnight, just in case a victim came by. It also seemed a huge coincidence that she wore a medical uniform much of the time.

We thought back to a conversation with Linda Fisher when she was describing visiting Larry in Winnipeg. It was just hours after Linda left Winnipeg for Saskatchewan that he raped the dentistry student. Did he feel angry and abandoned? Or did he finally have the opportunity to attack now that Linda was gone?

The woman's life careened downhill after the rape. She felt it was her fault. Her father rejected her, blaming her for being out drinking the night of the rape. She said she wouldn't have reported the rape if Fisher had gotten away. She had tried to kill herself twice, once by attaching a vacuum hose to her car exhaust and the other time by trying to hang herself. Now, it seemed she was doing it slowly but surely with alcohol.

It was so hard to picture her before the attack. She had been an honours students in high school, a finalist for Miss Blue Bomber and training for a profession. She was still her daddy's sweet little girl. Her sister had gone on to become a successful doctor. "I think it's affected my whole life," she said, dramatically understating what Paul and I strongly felt in the pits of our stomachs.

Three days later, Paul and I paid an unannounced visit to another of Fisher's Winnipeg-area victims. "Oh, my God," she muttered as we introduced ourselves, dropping to her knees as the terror of twenty-one years ago flooded back. She shook, sobbed and gasped for breath. Her husband rushed to her side to offer support. But rather than chase us away, they agreed to help. They had heard about David's case and were extremely sympathetic. The woman had absolutely no doubt that Fisher could have also murdered Gail Miller.

It was obvious that she and her husband badly wanted justice, and they drove Paul and me to the rape scene, where she walked us through the attack. It took place on August 2, 1970, not long after Fisher and co-workers from his masonry contracting company in Saskatoon arrived in Winnipeg to start a job. She was taking a nursing course at the Health Sciences Centre, near the dentistry school, and often wore a medical uniform. At that time, Fisher lived nearby at 613 Minto Avenue.

The woman left the Health Sciences Centre around midnight and caught the last bus to her house in the far south end of Winnipeg. The bus took her only about two miles from home, and she had to walk the rest of the way alone. She got within a block of home when Fisher approached her and asked for directions. He walked on, then grabbed her from behind, with his hands over her mouth and warning her that he had a knife. She could feel its sharp blade against her neck, but screamed anyway.

Fisher dragged her to a vacant lot, which was heavily overgrown with brush and scrub trees, then ripped off her skirt and short-sleeved sweater. He smashed her in the face several times, making her "unrecognizable." He raped her, then made her lie on her stomach and hog-tied her with her clothes. He promised to let someone know about her location but also threatened to kill her if she yelled for help before ten minutes had passed. Much of what happened next was a blur. She doesn't know how she got to the sidewalk, with her hands and feet still bound behind her back, but somehow she worked her way out of the brush, screaming for help. A passerby stopped to help. Curiously, he was also armed with a knife, which he used to cut her free. Her father arrived on the scene and tried to chase the passerby away until she was able to explain that he wasn't the attacker. Her parents sent her to Bible college for two years shortly after the attack, hoping to shield her from humiliation and further emotional trauma.

Despite the horror of her memories, we were impressed at how she had gotten on with her life. An attractive woman, she obviously took care of herself. She and her husband ran a business together, and their richly furnished condo suggested they were doing well at it. Still, some things clearly hadn't been resolved. The police never told her the name of her attacker, and she and her husband vowed to demand that police give them her 1970 statement and reports. As we left, we could see that they, just like the other Winnipeg victim, badly wanted to help David. Such help from strangers was indescribably inspiring.

On April 30, Paul and I drove to see a woman who had lived on Avenue V South, in Saskatoon, just a few blocks from where Gail Miller's body was found. She was now the wife of a Saskatchewan wheat farmer, and no one was home as we drove up to the farm. An in-law who lived across the road told us she had an appointment that day at the doctor's in town. We found her in the town café, and at first she didn't want to talk with us about the attack. Eventually, she agreed to come outside and talk with us in her car, where her two-year-old son looked on, strapped to his car seat.

In 1970, she was an eighteen-year-old high-school student working part-time in the canteen at City Hospital in Saskatoon. This was the same hospital where Gail Miller was employed. Larry Fisher sat across the aisle from the student as she took the bus home from the hospital that February 21. She wasn't sure whether he followed her onto the bus, but recalled he was wearing heavy boots, which she could still see in her dreams. She also still couldn't escape memories of his dirty hair, even after all of these years.

Fisher followed her as she got off the bus on 20th

Street. She was walking on the sidewalk when he bumped into her, grabbed her from behind and dragged her into a yard. She screamed as Fisher hit her in the face what seemed to be at least a dozen times. Then he threatened to kill her and forced her to take off her sweater and skirt. She fought back ferociously, and bit Fisher, who warned her, "I could easily break your neck."

It was hard for us to tell how badly the attack hurt her. She seemed to be blocking it out to a point, and insisted Fisher didn't penetrate her vagina. However, Paul had managed to get a look at police records on the attack, and they suggested otherwise. She was never told of Fisher's arrest and confessions, and for years she lived with the horror that her attacker might return some day. Even now, she kept the door to her house locked day and night. Every window and door was fastened shut, as if her farmhouse was a small fortress. She knew this wasn't the norm for rural Saskatchewan, but did it anyway. The farm was so isolated that she might as well live on Mars, but she still felt more secure keeping a German shepherd ceaselessly roaming the yard.

Interestingly, she recalled a detective saying the rape was "similar to the Gail Miller case." Her attack came more than a year after Miller was murdered and a few weeks after David's conviction. David was in custody then, providing him with an alibi that even Kim Campbell couldn't doubt.

On May 1, yet another of Fisher's victims agreed to help us. Compared to the others, she handled our visit well, although it was still clear that Fisher's 1970 attack had changed her forever. She lived near Saskatoon, not too far from where she was assaulted. She still had trouble sleeping and was afraid to walk anywhere alone. Like the others, she was never told by police when Fisher was finally arrested. One evening around seven-thirty, she was returning to her home on Avenue H South when Fisher came out of nowhere. He flashed a large knife, put his hand over her mouth and threatened to kill her if she screamed. "You do as I say or else."

Fisher dragged her into a nearby alley and forced her to remove her own clothes. As she lay naked on the ground, he stuck the knife into her vagina, and she recalled the sensation of the knife tearing her skin. "I didn't think I was going to get up alive," she told us. She didn't think Fisher penetrated her with his penis before something scared him away. She pulled her jeans back on and ran to the nearest house. No one was home. She ran to a house where a light was on. No one answered the door, and so she ran to the safety of her own home, one and a half blocks away.

Paul and I left wondering whether the bus was a common denominator between her attack and that of Gail Miller. They both caught their bus to work on West 20th Street, and lived about a mile apart. However, this woman left for work at a later hour. Did Fisher stalk her to learn where she lived? Or was he prowling the neighbourhood looking for a random victim? Fisher probably knew Gail Miller, since they lived less than two blocks apart. He likely saw her at the bus stop and on the bus, since they each took it to work at the same stop and at the same time each morning.

On May 2, Paul and I approached Fisher's youngest known victim. She wasn't quite seventeen back on November 13, 1968, when she was walking from her house to meet her boyfriend sometime between six-thirty and eight. She was less than two blocks from where Gail Miller's body was found when Fisher walked past her on the sidewalk, saying nothing. Then he grabbed her from behind. "If you want to live, do as I say," Fisher ordered as his hand shot over her mouth. She recalled that he smelled like oil.

Fisher dragged her into a darkened yard and ordered her to undress. "Lie still and don't move," he demanded. She never saw his knife but felt its blade at her throat throughout the rape. "I just laid there and obeyed. All I told him was, 'Don't kill me.'"

She went to the police station several times to see suspects in a lineup, but never found her attacker. Not knowing Larry Fisher was ever captured, she had lived the past two decades in fear. That evening years ago had left her overly protective with her own teenaged daughters. She said to me, "Can you imagine, Mrs. Milgaard, how many times I have been at a party and I've looked across the room and some guy has been looking at me strangely and I have wondered, 'Is he the one?'"

I especially dreaded the thought of talking to a victim in Fisher's hometown of North Battleford. She was fifty-six, close to my age, when Fisher raped her, and this attack was particularly brutal, even by his standards.

I knocked on her door on May 3, expecting her to quickly tell me to leave. Instead, she was courageous and totally cooperative. She was rock solid. We didn't have to convince her that Gail Miller was murdered by Fisher. She had suspected this ever since Fisher's name surfaced a year ago in David's case.

She was attacked a block from her home on March 31, 1980, when Fisher was out of prison on parole after serving time for the Saskatoon and Winnipeg attacks. They lived in the same neighbourhood but didn't know each other. Larry Fisher had been free for only two months when he struck. She shook and sobbed as she told how he slit her throat, stabbed her chest, tried to suffocate her and left her for dead. I felt sickened as I looked at a large scar that ran across her throat. She said Fisher told her he'd done the same thing before and that he'd slit her throat. "There was no doubt in my mind then, and there is no doubt today, that Fisher was confessing to having murdered another victim before the attack on me," she continued.

This woman lived a few blocks away from Fisher's mother, Marceline, and was terrified Fisher would return to her later that year, when he was eligible for parole. She was willing to do whatever she could to focus attention on David's case, saying, "I feel that it is outrageous and despicable that the government would release Fisher without conducting a thorough and honest investigation into mounting evidence that he murdered Gail Miller, as well as trying to murder me."

The telephone caller told David Asper he was a lawyer respresenting a woman who was attacked in the Yorkton, Saskatchewan, area in May 1968. The caller wouldn't identify the woman, and when challenged by David, he admitted he wasn't really a lawyer either. Still, we thought his story was worth checking out.

As Paul and I drove towards Yorkton on May 5, I called in for messages and learned that the woman had telephoned my Winnipeg home just after I'd left. I returned her call, and she told me that police had said it was David who raped her. Recent publicity about David's case triggered ugly flashbacks for her, and now she was determined to resolve the matter.

We arranged a meeting in a Regina motel, but she didn't show up. During the telephone conversation, she had mentioned that she would be taking a bus to Yorkton, so we went to the bus station. The Yorkton bus was to leave at 6 p.m., and at 5:59, a short, overweight aboriginal woman carrying a small suitcase showed up. I approached her and she admitted she was the caller. She asked to see a photograph of David. I gave her a photo, which she studied and said, "It could be him but his hair was longer and dirtier."

The picture I'd showed wasn't of David but of Larry Fisher.

When I told her that, she was taken aback. She told the bus driver to leave without her, and we went into the restaurant to talk. The attack had taken place in a resort near Esterhazy, about thirty miles from Langenburg, in

1968, the year David dropped out of school and hit the road. She was cleaning up in the kitchen when someone grabbed her from behind, just as all of Fisher's victims had been. At first, she thought it was her husband and laughed, but the attacker pulled out a paring knife and dragged her by her hair into the bedroom, yanking off her jeans, shirt and bra and popping buttons in his haste. She wouldn't say exactly what the attacker did after that, just that she screamed and fought. At one point, she broke free and fell, then scrambled on her hands and knees into the kitchen and crawled into a floor-level cupboard. The attacker chased her, stabbing her in the back and slashing her bare legs with the paring knife.

The attacker stole four steaks and a blanket, then left. He was part native, like Fisher, wore a red headband, as Linda had said Larry often did, and work clothes and boots, again like Fisher. He drove a red truck, and we believed Fisher's company trucks were red. Around that time, Fisher's construction company had a site at a potash mine near Esterhazy. (Unfortunately, the company went out of business in 1978, and all its records were long gone.) The attacker was slightly taller than his victim, who was five-foot-four. That was about Fisher's height. David didn't match the description at all. He wasn't native, and at the time was just fifteen, with no vehicle or driver's licence. The attack site was secluded, and inaccessible to anyone without a vehicle. She said that later, when the RCMP returned her clothes, which had been taken for evidence, they told her the case had been closed with the arrest of David Milgaard. She thought seeing

David locked in prison would help set her mind at ease. "I relive it every night," she said of the attack.

The same day, Paul and I saw yet another of Fisher's victims. Back on November 29, 1968, she lived in Saskatoon on 12 Street, about six blocks from where Gail Miller's body was later found. She was a student at the University of Saskatchewan and was walking home from the library with a handful of books that evening. Hers was the final documented attack by Fisher before Miller's murder. It was different from the others in two ways: it was on the east side of Saskatoon and Fisher may have used a vehicle. This didn't surprise us, since we had been told by Fisher's old foreman that his company had a construction contract at the University of Saskatchewan at this time.

The rest of the attack fit Fisher's pattern, though. Fisher asked the woman for directions as she walked past him on the sidewalk. She wasn't able to help, and was aware that he was now following her. She crossed the street and Fisher crossed too. He grabbed her from behind and put his hand over her mouth. She dropped her books and screamed. He said he had a knife and would kill her if she wasn't quiet, but she ignored his threats, and kept yelling and fighting as Fisher dragged her into an alley. He pushed her to the ground and held her there, ordering her to come with him to his vehicle nearby. Suddenly, there were headlights on them from a car in the alley. Fisher jumped to his feet and fled, while she ran to the car and safety. She was deathly afraid that she was going to be killed, and still keeps her doors locked, even in daytime. Like Fisher's other victims, she felt lucky to have escaped alive.

None of the women he attacked expressed any doubt that he was capable of murder.

TWENTY-SIX

SUPPORTIVE PUBLIC

*"Do you know how guilty I've felt as a mother
that I have failed my son?"*
I talk to listeners of Roy Norris's radio show

DAVID'S STORY WAS NOW attracting countless ordinary Canadians who couldn't stand to hear about an injustice and do nothing. On July 15, 1991, I was on the Roy Norris radio talk show and the phone lines lit up. With me was Neil Boyd, a professor from Simon Fraser University. He was studying Section 690 applications for mercy, and was conducting a study on David's case with Kim Rossmo, a former Saskatoon police officer who was now a Ph.D. student in criminology in Vancouver. Rossmo was an expert on serial killers and sex attackers and was sometimes called to act as a consultant with the FBI. Rossmo had first heard about David's case when he lived in Saskatoon.

Boyd and Rossmo approached me, and I was thankful. If private researchers took a hard and honest look at the case, I was confident they would come away supporting

David's innocence. That's the way it had been with Peter Carlyle-Gordge and everyone else who had taken time to look at the case. Ironically, the fact that Rossmo was a police officer was appealing. It would make his research with Boyd more convincing.

"We don't have an axe to grind," Boyd told callers to the radio show. "We're in no sense anti-police. Obviously, one of us is a police officer."

I begged listeners who might know anything about the case to come forward. There was a strange call from a woman who said there was blood on the floor of her house, and that a nervous police officer covered it with two inches of cement. "I could show you where the blood of Gail Miller is under the cement," she said.

Rev. Bob Hussey of Sydney, Nova Scotia, phoned in to say he knew how tough it was to get a case reopened. It took two years from the time they had a signed confession from the real killer before Donald Marshall's case was reopened. Marshall was adjusting well now, we heard. He had a new girlfriend and a rambling home. Still, he felt an intense need for privacy, and was hiding out from people and the media spotlight.

"The greatest power that we have is the power of common people," Hussey remarked. "In all the cases I have been involved in . . . without the public and without the media, we wouldn't have moved anything."

Things were finally coming together in our struggle to bring the story east from Manitoba. We made the front page of the *Toronto Star* on August 11, 1991, with photos of Gail Miller, David and Larry Fisher accompanying the lengthy story. A Toronto reader looked at the picture of Fisher and suddenly felt ill. "I got a terrible feeling in my stomach and started crying because I recognized this person," she later recalled.

Her mind lurched back to January 31, 1969, the morning Miller was murdered. The woman was attacked by a man in Saskatoon a couple of blocks from where Miller's body was found. Her attacker was short and swarthy, and she had no doubt he would have raped her if she had been wearing a dress and not jeans that morning. She hadn't followed David's trial closely and knew only that there had been a conviction. "I assumed that the person that was convicted was the person that attacked me," she later said.

Now, the faces stared out at her from the newspaper. She tried to read the article, but every time she looked at Fisher's picture, she started to sob. "My stomach just started thumping and I started shaking and started to cry," she recalled. "On the telephone to my friend, I said, 'My God, this is the person that did this to me in 1969.'"

It was clear that Fisher was on the prowl that morning, hunting a victim. Boyd and Rossmo would later conclude that the attack on Gail Miller had gone wildly out of control for Fisher, ending in the murder, and that he left her bleeding body feeling an urgent need to re-establish his pattern, his order. That was when he met his second victim of that morning, the woman who now came forward after reading the *Toronto Star*. Immediately after the attack, the new witness had gone to police. It should have got them thinking. The assault was just minutes after Gail Miller was murdered, near railway tracks that run directly between Fisher's home and the home of his in-law and boss, Roy Pambrun. Someone in the Saskatoon police must have seen a connection between this attack and the Miller murder, but this evidence was never disclosed to our defence team.

The woman's story underlined the cavalier treatment the rape victims had received from police. The Manitoba Action Committee on the Status of Women demanded to know why Fisher's rape victims were not told by police that he had been arrested. Once again, we were reminded that David wasn't the only victim in this story.

TWENTY-SEVEN

OPENING DOORS

"We all have mothers."
Prime Minister Brian Mulroney
shows an interest in David's plight

EVERY TIME I TALKED about Gail Miller, I felt sorry
for the pain that her family must feel, first from the
horrible loss, and then from the media attention that we
were generating. Television news reports inevitably
showed film clips of Gail lying face down in the snow,
and usually also included a school yearbook photo of her
looking young and cheerful and full of promise. I hoped
that the Millers understood that I also felt a deep responsibility to my son. I knew that sooner or later, I would
have to talk with the Miller family face to face, and in
August 1991, it seemed like the right time. We were
launching our second bid for a ministerial review, offering the new evidence Paul and I had found about similarities between Miller's murder and Larry Fisher's sex
attacks. It was twenty-two years now since the murder
that bound the Milgaards and Millers together forever,

but we had never talked until I knocked on the door of one of Gail's brothers in Saskatoon.

"I always knew that one day I would open that door and you'd be on the other side," the man who answered the door told me.

"Really?" I said.

"Yep," he replied. "I don't think that I can help you."

"What do you mean?"

"Well, my family doesn't really want to get involved in this."

However, despite his reservations, he politely listened as I told how Rev. Jim McCloskey was helping and had some evidence he would like the family to consider. I think the fact that Jim was a minister helped the Millers realize they weren't going to be pushed around. So the man at the door agreed that he would call his family together and they would watch a tape of interviews we had put together.

After they watched, they did something remarkable: they issued a written public statement saying they joined our call for a fresh look at the case. "We are making this statement simply because we want justice to prevail," their statement said.

Around this time, Dan Lett of the *Winnipeg Free Press* felt a need to visit Gail's grave. I went with him. I felt an overwhelming sadness as I stood where she was buried. There was such a strong sense of tragedy and waste. Two young lives had been ruined, hers and David's. I thought of Gail, "If only you could tell us what happened that day. If there was only some way." Later, in a television interview, one of Gail's friends said she often wished Gail could tell the world the truth about what happened that morning. Then Gail's friend said that she thought Gail's way of telling her story was through Mrs. Milgaard. Now, as I stood there at the gravesite, I felt such a sense of responsibility. I owed it to Gail Miller, as well as to David, to do my job right.

David was clearly desperate as the summer of 1991 wound down. "Mom, you've got to talk to the prime minister," he said during a visit. It was touching that he thought his mother could simply approach the most powerful politician in the country and appeal for justice. It was also heartbreaking. A couple of weeks later, some of his support group and I went to see him. He looked simply awful, and accused me of lying, which had never happened before. David knew how important the truth was to me. His accusation was the culmination of a sad, steady decline that had been accelerating since the previous February, when he got the news that his 690 application had been denied. David badly needed to know that people still cared for him.

On the spot, we decided to stage a candlelight vigil the next day, September 6. We were going to hold the vigil at the prison, but freelance reporter Leslie Hughes told us that Prime Minister Brian Mulroney was going to be in Winnipeg the next day, so we moved the vigil to outside the hotel where he was going to speak. We lit twenty-two candles, one for each year that David had lost behind bars. There were only slightly more people than candles, since the vigil was hastily organized, and was held at noon, when many people were at work. Political science professor Alan Mills of the University of Winnipeg gave a wonderful speech that roused everyone as he told them how horrible and unjust it was that David was behind bars.

I approached one of the prime minister's staff to say he didn't have to worry about us. I wasn't going to throw myself at Mulroney's feet, or do anything to embarrass him or myself. The man from the Prime Minister's Office floored me when he replied, "He's planning on speaking with you."

I was stunned, but quickly informed reporter Alan Habbick. "No way, Joyce," he said, but, just in case, he had the station's camera person change his position, as did others. It spread like wildfire through our group that the prime minister was going to speak to me. I quickly arranged for someone to tape the conversation.

"Please, God, don't let me cry," I said to myself. There was a carpet laid out from the street into the hotel for the prime minister, and a rope to separate his walkway from our group, the curious and the media. The prime minister stepped out of his car, went halfway up the carpet, then turned and strode directly towards me. He took my hand and addressed me by name, looking me squarely in the eye.

"Thank you," I said, my voice trembling. "I've been trying to see you to just ask you . . . His mental situation is not good right now, and anything that you can do to help toward getting him transferred would be so helpful. We just feel he needs to have some peace of mind and I'm afraid that the case will not be reopened before David has lost his sanity. It's so important. And, of course, the other question is, anything you could do for a speedy review? Because now the Saskatoon police have apparently admitted they haven't given full information to the Justice Department, that really the minister was working with just half of the things she should have had, and I find that so . . . difficult."

"That was the most recent . . . information?" the prime minister replied.

"Yes, yesterday."

"Yesterday, and I've just checked in Ottawa and I gather that information is either en route or has just been received down there so they'll be taking a close look at it very, very soon. What about . . . you mentioned his health? . . ."

"He's been in the hospital."

"I know he's been hospitalized but . . ."

"You see, he's asked for a transfer to Rockwood or a transfer to Collins Bay . . . It's not that the other inmates are against him: it's just that they're constantly questioning him and saying . . . , 'How are you doing, Dave?' It's friendly but he just needs some peace of mind."

Prime Minister Mulroney could have easily turned away at that point. We had chatted a couple of minutes, and he had shown his concern for the cameras. However, he kept on talking.

"It's hard on him?" he asked.

"It's very difficult on all of us."

"How are you getting on?"

"Just the fact that you're talking to me makes me feel better."

"I'm happy to do it. Happy to do it . . ."

"And anything you can do to help, we would just be so appreciative of."

"Well, Ms. Campbell is going to take a look at the new information that's come in and . . . I'm sure that . . . the minister of justice will be back to the attorney-general."

"A speedy review?"

I didn't tell him that David Asper had written three times to the Justice Department trying to get some idea of when a decision would be made but still had received no answer. Perhaps this meeting with the prime minister might speed things up.

"Well . . . I can't speak for her, but I will be talking to her when I get back . . . I hope you're well."

"I'm trying my very best."

"I know you are . . . You're working very, very hard . . . You're very courageous."

"Thank you for that."

"And I'll . . . I've taken note of your other request and we'll do what we can."

"We . . . are just asking for justice. But now. It would be terrible for me to have justice for David in Canada and not have him able to know he's got it. Okay?"

"Is . . . is . . . is he . . . ?"

"It's that desperate."

"Is he that sick?"

"It is that . . . desperate."

"I didn't realize . . . I knew he was ill. But I didn't realize he was that sick."

"It is exactly. I would never be coming to you otherwise."

"I'll look into it right away."

Prime Minister Mulroney could have walked away at any point in the lengthy conversation, but he didn't. David had been right. Perhaps a chat with the prime minister was just what we needed.

A little while later I was on the phone with my son, asking, "Did you see the headlines?"

"Yeah, I saw you on TV," David said, sounding mellow and proud. "I think you did real good."

"Well, David, a lot of prayer. I didn't go and tag him. He came and talked to me."

"That's good."

"Isn't that incredible? It was just an incredible day. A wonderful vigil."

David had been depressed, but that meeting with Prime Minister Mulroney put a smile back on his face. It was his idea, and now there we were, Brian Mulroney and I, together on the front pages of newspapers across the country.

Mulroney would recall our meeting in an interview with the *Winnipeg Free Press* in 1997: "There was just something so forlorn but very loving about a woman standing alone on a very cold evening in Manitoba on behalf of her son. But in that brief meeting I got a sense of Mrs. Milgaard and her genuineness and her courage. We all have mothers. But even the most devoted and loving of mothers would not continue their crusade for twenty-two years if there was any doubt in her mind. So I went back to Ottawa and had a much closer look at it."

Actually, it was noon, sunny and 27°C when we met,

but who's quibbling? More important, he said that his subsequent review of the case convinced him that a mistake had been made. "So I did what I thought was appropriate as prime minister . . . ," Mulroney continued in his *Free Press* interview. "I told the appropriate people I thought a review of this particular case was warranted and I wanted appropriate action taken to bring this about."

When we first started our fight, it was us against the world, but now the world seemed to be coming onside. Our cause was further boosted in mid-October, when Neil Boyd and Kim Rossmo released their independent study on the case. It was just what we expected, another reasoned but strong voice for David's innocence. They concluded that David was probably innocent and Fisher probably guilty. Whoever killed Gail Miller was a psychopath with no empathy to women, and David hadn't shown any history of this type of deviation. They concluded that Saskatoon police probably wouldn't have looked at David as a suspect if they had known about Fisher early on in the investigation.

Boyd and Rossmo added that they were frustrated by the high number of closed and missing files on the case, ranging from police reports on Fisher from the early 1970s to information used by Kim Campbell during her department's review of the case that year.

They weren't the only ones who weren't getting the full picture. That fall, the Saskatoon police had acknowledged that they hadn't disclosed all of their files to the Justice Department when Ottawa reviewed the case. Also, files on polygraph tests of Ronald Wilson could not be located for Wilson's lawyer, Kenneth Watson of Vancouver.

The Simon Fraser researchers had some unsettling interviews. Dr. Harry Emson, the Saskatoon doctor whose testimony had hurt David, told them cryptically that he would not testify the same way if the trial was to be held again. Ron Wilson told of a telephone call he received from Nichol John, after I had contacted her in the early 1980s. Nichol was crying when she told Ron that she didn't want to talk with me because she didn't want to admit that she had lied in court against David.

The strongest sections of their report were their chilling conclusions about Larry Fisher. Even in a world inhabited solely by psychopaths, Fisher would be particularly feared. They slotted him into the least common but most violent category of rapist, whose "purpose is to punish, debase and degrade their female victims, for whom they have a great deal of anger. These victims are often symbolic, the rapist transferring his anger from some other woman he feels has hurt or wronged him." There was a methodical, scripted pattern to his attacks, and the Miller murder neatly fit that pattern. True to his controlling, orderly nature, Fisher committed his rapes in a comfort zone, which in the winter of 1969 was alleys in the working-class Saskatoon neighbourhood where he lived and Gail Miller died. Boyd and Rossmo offered a terrifying prediction. Given the chance, Fisher would very likely commit more rapes, and he was due for mandatory parole in 1994.

A month later, I was flown to Prince Edward Island for a taping of the television show *Front Page Challenge*, which was great for publicizing the case and lots of fun too. Author Pierre Berton recognized my voice, so I didn't stump the panel, but it showed that the message was being heard, and I got to meet a lot of influential and interesting people at a reception, including former Conservative leader Robert Stanfield, P.E.I. premier Joe Ghiz, Liberal party power-house Sheila Copps, panellist Betty Kennedy, and Marion Reid, the lieutenant-governor, who was very supportive. Ironically, I was filling in a spot on the show that originally had been held for Kim Campbell, who had cancelled. As a result, I had Campbell to thank for the publicity and the plane tickets, and I took full advantage of both.

On the way back to Winnipeg, I arranged a two-day stopover in Ottawa. Once there, I phoned the Prime Minister's Office.

"I'm going to see the press," I said. "I know they're going to ask me what has the prime minister done. What *has* the prime minister done?"

Minutes later, I got a telephone call from someone in the Justice Department saying the Prime Minister's Office asked him to call and explain how it was going. He said they were extremely busy, and that the file would soon be with the minister.

"Let me be 100 per cent clear with you," I said. "I am not out to embarrass the minister, Kim Campbell. I am out here to get my son out of prison. I'm willing to give her as much space as she needs to bring this new decision out, but I need to know what's going on. Now that you have communicated with me, my position with the press will be that the lines of communication are open and that we are talking about it and that I am happy with it."

"We really appreciate that, and I will pass your message on to the minister," he said.

Within an hour, I received a hand-delivered, signed letter from the prime minister, which stated:

> Thank you for your letter of September 9 . . . I can well understand your concern for the well-being of your son. Rest assured that your request for him to be transferred to another institution and for the review of the second application for a new trial to be completed quickly have been communicated to the Solicitor General and the Minister of Justice respectively.
>
> As you know, the minister of justice has the statutory responsibility under Section 690 of the criminal code. I am confident that the minister of justice will discharge her duties impartially, objectively and promptly. I am also confident that the solicitor general and the officials of Corrections Service Canada will take whatever measures are appropriate. I know how difficult this matter must be for you and I admire your strength and commitment.
>
> Yours sincerely,
> Brian Mulroney

I couldn't help but think that the prime minister wouldn't get involved if there wasn't going to be a favourable outcome for us this time around. However, I had been wrong before and hope was such a scary thing. I knew from Lloyd Axworthy's office that he was going to continue to hit the government with questions about David and delays in David's transfer to Rockwood farm. I had to tell Axworthy about the letter from the prime minister so that he wouldn't be blindsided by it.

During my two-day visit in Ottawa, it became apparent that we now had a broad base of support for David's case from Liberals, New Democrats and Conservatives. Among those who approached me was Liberal leader Jean Chrétien, who was very kind. Even in that cynical capital city, the issue seemed to rise above party politics.

Kim Campbell was, however, still hard to understand and more than a little frightening. It seemed the harder we pushed, the more intransigent she became. Shortly after the 1991 meeting with the prime minister, she downplayed its significance, saying Mulroney expressed humanitarian concern about David's health but was "too good a lawyer" to try to influence a legal review by Justice officials. Interestingly, she later adopted a different tone in her memoirs, *Time and Chance: The Political Memoirs of Canada's First Woman Prime Minister*. There she said the news of my meeting with the prime minister hit her staff "like a bombshell . . . We were all floored. We just couldn't believe it. The PM had blindsided me on one of my most difficult issues."

Whatever was going on behind the closed doors of

Justice, the tide was turning for us now. A month after I met Mulroney, the Stony Mountain warden was dispatched to talk to David about his case. The warden told us the Prime Minister's Office was calling the prison every day for updates on the case. Typically, David initially refused to meet with the warden. They had been at odds since the warden took over in 1985, when David was trying to get his Justice Group going. David had been a real thorn in his side since then, and David wasn't about to pretend otherwise now. However, when he found out the purpose of the meeting had been to discuss a transfer to Rockwood, with the help of Lloyd Axworthy, a supportive MP, a new one was quickly rescheduled.

Life in Rockwood promised so much. The thought that David would be allowed outdoors to work was also thrilling, and now he would be getting to work in a greenhouse. He would see the sun and the clouds, things he had been denied for so many years.

Twenty-eight

Legal History

*"Mom, do you realize that I can go out
and take a walk in the field?"*
David tells me about life in
minimum-security prison farm

It was decision time in Ottawa and the stress was almost unbearable. We had been waiting three years since filing the application. Now, in the fall of 1991, Justice Department officials were flown into the capital to discuss David's case. "Just try to relax," said David Asper, who was doubly nervous himself because his wife, Ruth, was about to go into labour any day.

"Relax?" I asked. The uncertainty had done so much emotional damage. I was so run down that Susan phoned a Christian Science reading room to find a nurse to work with me. Susan was terrified that I might die before a decision was reached on David. The person answering the phone at the reading room gave Susan the name of someone to call. Unfortunately it was my name, which was funny in a way. Susan kept calling around and finally found someone to stay with me. Meanwhile, Maureen was constantly on the phone asking people to pray for me. Lorne's gout flared up, and I'm sure that was also a result of the stress. Maureen was suffering from bronchial pneumonia, and Susan couldn't sleep properly and was just tearing herself apart. "I just can't handle it, Mom," Susan said. "I'm going crazy." I had never seen her like this before. She even thought of calling a press conference to ask everyone to leave me alone. I temporarily stopped answering phone calls and letters, and David Asper asked the media to direct calls to him, not me, until I got better.

Once, when I visited David in prison, he playfully butted up against me and I almost fell over. He was so shaken that he insisted on supporting me from one side while Chris held me up on the other side. David hadn't seen me display such weakness before, and this left him white as a sheet.

Part of what was wearing on me was the constant worry about shielding him. I didn't want him to get his hopes up again, because I wasn't sure he could take too much more disappointment. It was such a volatile situation now. The media was shouting for action, and we had to keep David muzzled from the press now, or things could go right over the top.

I got a telephone call from an aide in Kim Campbell's office, only to be told he couldn't tell us when the waiting would end. "Mrs. Milgaard, I would sincerely love to be able to tell you there was some specific date . . . All I can tell you is that the minister is very much considering the application and is taking it extremely seriously."

"Can you ballpark it?" I asked.

Not within the next few days. Perhaps within the next few weeks. "She is considering the matter and she is taking it very, very seriously."

I told him again that it would mean so much if we could narrow down the time frame, and then I started to cry over the phone to this stranger in Ottawa, as I said, "Some kind of time would help."

I couldn't help but think that Kim Campbell was taking her time so it would appear that she was carefully considering new evidence and not bowing to pressure from the prime minister. The fresh evidence in our new application was basically the old evidence of our previous application in a new package, but obviously we were not saying this, so that she could have room to reverse herself. We knew that senior officials in the Justice Department were advising Campbell that the debate should be about how to reopen the case, and not about whether the case should be reopened.

So many crazy thoughts went through my head. What if David wasn't freed by the summer? Should I lead a march on Ottawa? What if Kim Campbell was going to make a surprise announcement on a weekend, to catch the media off guard with a negative decision? What if the case was referred back to Saskatchewan for a final decision? David would be totally against this, and for good reason. Serge Kujawa, the Crown attorney who had handled his appeal and the Larry Fisher file, was a politician now and could end up as Saskatchewan's minister of justice after an upcoming provincial election. If we did get a new trial in

Saskatchewan, and we won it, some people would say it was a tainted victory because our old lawyer, Calvin Tallis, was now an appeal court judge there. It would also be extra hardship for us as a family to have to take time off our jobs and go back to Saskatchewan for a trial, at considerable expense. The waiting meant there was plenty of time to second-guess things. What else could we have put in our submission? What else could we have done?

David Asper was hurting now too. He complained of a constant burn in his stomach. Now he could understand how my David would get so upset that he just couldn't talk about the case anymore. Being ribbed about being "David Milgaard-Asper" had stopped amusing David Asper a long time ago. We had been front and centre of our local and then national media nearly every day for almost two years. It consumed all of us, and Asper's anger at the Justice Department had reached a boiling point. Containing the emotions was a constant struggle.

My son was also taking out his frustrations on those who cared for him most. He was particularly incensed when David Asper made negative comments on CTV's *The Shirley Show*, saying that he doubted the Justice Department would take our application seriously and reopen the case. Asper's pessimism and bluntness upset my son in the way you can only be hurt by a true friend or family member. From his prison cell, David announced that he had once again fired David Asper. Asper later said his comment was a deliberate attempt to arouse more public sympathy and outrage. It worked, as he received tons of mail.

Hersh Wolch knew that the relationship between the two Davids was light-years beyond the norm of a lawyer–client relationship. For starters, we hadn't been able to pay our bills for years now, and they still worked like sled dogs. The two Davids clearly shared more than the same first name, and each saw our struggle as nothing less than a battle between right and wrong. Whatever their differences, they always shared this bond. My son saw David Asper as his champion in the legal world, and after so many years and so many setbacks, naturally, emotions were running high.

"As far as I'm concerned," Hersh told David Asper, "you guys are good friends and friends have a right to get mad at each other. And I have no doubt that we'll win this thing. Keep it together and we'll get there."

Much of the problem was that my son was so isolated in prison. "He's got to have some input on this case," I told Hersh and David Asper. "He's screaming for control. He feels that he's being abandoned out there."

Hersh tried again to convince me that we were almost at the top of the hill, saying he was eager for the chance to argue legal fine points. "I'm salivating at the chance of getting at these people," Hersh said. "The lawyering is mine. I can't wait."

In the meantime, Hersh wanted me to clean up my son's appearance. It was time to buy him some nice clothes and fix the dental plate that had been broken in prison. "I hate to say this," Hersh said. "I never say this, but we can't lose."

Hersh normally made a point of not seeing his clients

too much, so that he could maintain a professional detachment. But here we were, in his shiny office, talking about "Free David" T-shirt designs and frayed emotions. "Joyce, this is not a normal case," Hersh said, profoundly understating the obvious.

My personal funds were exhausted once again, and I wasn't sure whether I should stay around Winnipeg and wait for a decision or fly back to the United States and make some more money Christian Science nursing. With the intense publicity, we had raised some $5,000 for David's fight over the past month, but that money was for the fight, not for my personal expenses. I took out an ad to sell my mink coat, my last reminder of the salad days of the mid-1980s. It was a glorious coat, with a high shawl collar and high, full sleeves. I had already sold my car, and the mink was the last thing of material value that I had. At the time I bought it, the mink was the culmination of a dream of a poor little girl rising up to be a rich little girl. It was my pride and joy.

A distinguished-looking man in his late fifties showed up at my door after the story ran and gave me $2,000 on the understanding that I would not sell the mink. I had never seen him before and have not seen him since, and he refused to give his name. Then someone from Family Optical in Winnipeg offered me free glasses, but Charleswood Optical had already donated a pair. A Winnipeg grandmother named Florence offered me a Persian lamb coat. They weren't alone in their generosity. There was Janice Kay from Oakville, Ontario, who bought David a new television for his cell, and the manager of

Sunrider jeans, who donated a thousand T-shirts, which we used for fundraisers, and Valerie Mikula, who has a restaurant a hundred miles north of Winnipeg, where she held a social to raise funds for David. There were so many wonderful people like that, like support group stalwarts Alan Mills, Bob Bruce, Barb Degan and Bessie-Marie Hill. Even the computer I used for writing roughly forty letters a day to supporters was donated. Things like this meant so much more than money. I was never poor.

Transfers from maximum-security prisons like Stony Mountain to minimum-security prison farms like Rockwood, which adjoined it, were almost unheard of, but now, after the meeting with Prime Minister Mulroney, David was getting one. The dramatic change in David's day-to-day life took some adjustment. A parole board member had asked David how he would like living on a farm. "I don't know," David replied. "I haven't been on a farm for twenty-three years. But I'm sure going to like to try."

David now had a room instead of a cell. Oddly, the fact that he didn't have a door on his dorm room really rattled him. If you're used to having a heavy door shut behind you, at least you feel that no one can get in to harm you. Now David felt vulnerable without a metal door to shield him from the outside world. On the prison ranges of the maximum-security prisons, David could see far off into the distance by holding something reflective between the bars and looking down the corridors. When he got into a room at Rockwood, there were solid walls, and he felt claustrophobic. The walls pushed in on him. This was something we had never considered. We just thought how wonderful it would be for him to be in a house instead of in a little jail cell. We missed the bigger picture.

However, there were many wonderful things about freedom. Shortly after he arrived in Rockwood, David strolled around the grounds, and ended up in the tiny chapel, where he heard a couple of inmates strumming guitars. Now, if he wanted a break from others, he wouldn't have to go into solitary confinement or the hospital. He could simply walk out in the fields and look out at the cattle. "Mom, do you realize that I can go out and take a walk in the field?" he told me during a visit, a look of wonder on his face.

One evening, David was wandering about outside, looking at the stars and thinking how great it was to look at the stone walls of nearby Stony Mountain from the outside instead of the inside. Lost in thought, he strayed past some markers that set the limits of how far he was allowed to walk, and a prisoner told him he had gone too far. David rushed back to where he was supposed to be, saying, "I don't want to get into any trouble." His attitude towards authority was changing, a little. "You know, lots of times I made loud noises at the pigs," he said of the guards. "But they're not like that here. There's a caring. They're really trying to help me." David was learning to reciprocate, to take the chip off his shoulder and give something back. It was as if he was allowed to be human again.

He was also learning how to make choices. Rockwood prisoners were allowed to buy a parka to wear on temporary absences, and a kind man who knew of David's story called him up and said he would like to buy a parka for him. What style would David like? Having a choice, even on something mundane like the style of his coat, threw David for a loop. For so long, his decisions had all been made for him. "I don't know. What do people wear now?" David replied.

He was still off balance, but at least now he could articulate it. That was a step towards coping with things. To cut the pressure on him, David did not allow any media in to see him. He didn't want to make waves with any of the inmates or staff, and he did not want to stand out. For us, it was such a nice feeling, knowing we could finally visit him without having to book appointments in advance. While he was in Stony Mountain, we were allowed only nine family visits a month, although we were able to stretch this at times, since we were working on his case. Now we were even allowed to park right in front of the facility and walk in the front door. Once inside, there was a lovely lounge with soft chairs to sit in while we waited for David. He could also have three passes outside Rockwood a month.

We hoped this move was a sign of something far better in the near future. We heard from a source in the Justice Department that towards the end of Donald Marshall's prison time, there was a process of deinstitutionalization. Was this newfound freedom a very important — and positive — signal for David as well? Whatever the decision, it was coming soon. A frequent word we were now hearing from Ottawa was "imminent" for D-Day, or

David's Day. I couldn't help but think that maybe it would be over soon, and I could go back to just being a mom. Oddly, Larry Fisher was already in minimum security, so David was now on a par with him in the eyes of the justice system.

That fall, David had a hearing for full parole, as he had every two years since 1979. I tried to be practical and not get my hopes up, but I couldn't help but think that maybe, just maybe, this would be the last time that I would have to walk up to see David in custody. At the parole hearing, we started to talk of his wrongful conviction, but a woman on the parole board held up her hands, as if to fend off the question. That wasn't their role. They had to assume that everyone brought before them was guilty. We pointed out that David had support in the community and job offers, and that we had a plan for him to take some university courses. We would be there to help him integrate into the community. However, we were told that although he had had six passes for escorted absences since last March, he had not completed them, thus ruining his chances for parole. The warden had cancelled his passes from Stony Mountain when David went voluntarily into solitary confinement after our original Section 690 application was denied. David had badly needed some quiet time back then. He was like a wounded animal that just wants to crawl into a cave and recover. At least, at this latest hearing, there was no nitpicking or rehashing of his escapes. Even the rejection seemed a little positive. There was no question in my mind that the regular calls from the Prime Minister's Office were being heard.

Meanwhile, the delivery date of the second baby of Ruth and David Asper was fast approaching. Ruth was in considerable discomfort, while their little tot Daniel was running a high fever. David Asper was also preparing to defend someone in a murder trial, and the media was constantly phoning his home when they couldn't reach him at the office. If he wasn't there, some reporters would grill poor Ruth about our case. She was reluctant to answer her own phone now, for fear they would try to squeeze her for information she simply didn't have, or wasn't about to discuss. Even when the media did reach us, what could we say? We felt in the dark ourselves. It was so different from a few years before, when we had to go on bended knee for media coverage.

I couldn't pull back on pushing David Asper, even though Ruth was now in labour. Looking back at it, I am amazed at their patience, like when I unsuccessfully urged him to drop a hospital visit to work on the case. "We can take care of this for you," I told poor David Asper. "You don't need to be here. We've got work for you."

The Aspers had a beautiful baby girl, and I thought back to how David Asper's life had changed since we had started working together. Back then, he was single and hadn't even met Ruth, and now he was married, with a two-year-old and an infant. At the same time, I was still waiting for my boy to come home, and my boy was seven years older than David Asper.

Soon the snow was starting to fly as winter set in once again. The thought of going to visit David in custody through another Manitoba winter was simply horrendous.

Finally, on November 29, 1991, Kim Campbell made headlines when she referred David's conviction to the Supreme Court of Canada for review. This was only the third time in the past forty years that the government had referred a case to the top court. The first case was the conviction of Quebec prospector Wilbert Coffin of the murder in 1953 of three American hunters. The other case was for the murder conviction of Steven Truscott, who was just fourteen in 1959 when he was found guilty of killing twelve-year-old Lynn Harper in Clinton, Ontario. Ominously, the high court upheld both the Coffin and Truscott convictions. Truscott was later paroled, but Coffin was hanged.

David heard the good news about the Supreme Court hearing by cellular phone from Hersh early in the morning after a sleepless night. Lorne, Susan, Maureen, David Asper and I were with him to share the moment. He had no laughter or tears of joy. Just silence. Then he couldn't understand why he couldn't quickly get bail. The thought of another Christmas behind bars wasn't something he wanted to face. His mood had changed again a couple of hours later, when he was giddy at a press conference in Rockwood's chapel. Susan presented him with a gold ring of his she had been keeping for him all the years he was in prison. He noted that his handsome green shirt was sent to him by a supporter named Barb, one of many people to write him hopeful letters, then said, "If I'm not home [on bail] for Christmas, I'll probably run home for Christmas."

"He won't do that," I responded immediately, laughing. I would have kicked him under the table, and it was lucky for him my legs weren't long enough.

David always knew how to get a laugh and a reaction out of me.

David stepped into a whole new world when he was allowed out on day passes to help us work on his appeal. One day, he spent hours simply riding the shiny elevator in the chrome-and-glass office building where Hersh and David Asper worked. My son had planned to go up to their law office, but was overwhelmed by the elevator. It was something he had never experienced before. People kept getting on and off, giving David fresh folks to chat with. And he was surrounded by bright metal and lively colours. In prison, all the tones are drab, as if anything too cheery might overly excite the inmates. Later, when David Asper was driving David back to Stony Mountain after one of his office temporary absences, a police officer pulled him over to give him a speeding ticket. My son thought it was just hilarious to see his lawyer in the hands of the RCMP.

We knew that the Justice Department was finally taking a serious look at Larry Fisher. On January 16, 1992, David Asper interviewed a man in Saskatchewan Penitentiary who had a story to tell about Fisher. The prisoner had a nasty record that included assault, attempted rape and kidnapping, and was locked up in the Prince Albert prison in the early 1980s, at the same time as Fisher.

The prisoner told the Mounties that Fisher once called him to his cell, asking, "Can you help me with this?"

The prisoner said he walked into Fisher's cell, and Fisher slammed him against his locker and choked him, saying, "We'll have sex." The prisoner said he briefly lost consciousness, and when he recovered, Fisher was holding something in his hand, saying, "I killed a woman before and I went like this, and like this, and like this," making stabbing thrusts into the air.

"You ever control someone's destiny?" Fisher asked his prison victim. "Do you know what it feels like to kill?"

The prisoner submitted, sure that if he didn't, he'd be killed. When the rape was over, Fisher said, "Get out of here before I kill you too." The prisoner told the Mountie he had nightmares about the attack, and that he had seen Fisher the previous month on television during coverage of David's case. In his nightmares, the prisoner could see Gail Miller lying in the snow, as she was raped and stabbed by Fisher. In those awful dreams, Miller would struggle to her feet, but Fisher would continue stabbing her. The man told the Mountie that he was willing to testify against Fisher, for "the sake of an innocent man."

Five days later, the first time I walked into the Supreme Court of Canada in Ottawa, I felt a sense of awe. The RCMP escorted us to special quarters, which had been set up just for us. They're not used to hearing cases, and so it was all new and remarkable. They even had to build a witness box because they had never heard from live witnesses before.

It took no time for things to get nasty at pretrial

Supreme Court hearings. David Asper immediately had a testy exchange with Eugene Williams of the Justice Department, when Asper caught sight of my son's prison files on a table in front of Williams. "Wait a second," David Asper said. "I've been trying since 1986 to get this stuff . . . What's it doing here?"

Williams said something about the Privacy Act, and David Asper angrily pressed ahead, asking, "Do you have Fisher's files?"

"What do you want with Fisher's files?" Williams replied. "We're not going to allow you to go on a fishing expedition with Fisher's files."

"What the hell are you doing with Milgaard's files?" David continued. "You're fishing in Milgaard's files."

The meeting had barely begun and already it was degenerating at quantum speed. Williams walked out, and the tone was set for the days ahead.

It was an imposing, frightening sight when the five Supreme Court judges in their long robes walked out in front of the courtroom, with its high oak walls and vast visitors' gallery. There just seemed to be so many judges up on the bench. At first, we could get no one to listen to us, and now we had the five most powerful judges in the country.

The very fact that he was being heard strengthened David. He had not testified at his first trial, and now, nearly twenty-three years later, on January 21, 1992, he was the first witness called before the Supreme Court. It was such an emotionally charged moment, as I looked at him and saw how good and how strong he looked. I could see the truth was on his face and I thought the judges must be able to see it too. I felt so proud of him, as I thought of how he had refused to take the easy road and give a false confession, even though it would have bought him freedom. His voice was firm and strong when it was finally heard in a court of law, as he said, "I did not kill Gail Miller."

Ron Wilson was on the witness stand shortly afterwards. He didn't expect an easy ride from the judges, and he didn't get one. Chief Justice Antonio Lamer was visibly frustrated, noting that Ron had now given at least four versions of what happened the morning of the murder. What was the truth? Were Ron Wilson and David ever apart that morning? Was David gone for fifteen minutes? Were they two and a half blocks from the murder scene or five blocks, as Wilson said another time? For all of his vast education, Lamer clearly didn't see the need to hide behind legal mumbo-jumbo as he cited Ron for contempt, accusing him of "lying through his teeth."

I felt sorry for Ron. He had finally come forward to tell the truth and they were raking him over the coals for it. Ron perhaps hadn't been paying close enough attention to the questions, and he got tangled up in his answers, becoming more frustrated and frightened by the moment. I looked at him and I looked at my son, and I thought, "David's been in prison for all of this time, but look at Ron Wilson. He looks in worse shape than David." All of David's old friends looked worse than David. They had all obviously suffered a great deal.

Wilson wasn't the only witness who didn't get an easy ride. Jail guard Ben Douzenko testified that David had confessed to him about the Gail Miller murder several times while at Stony Mountain. It was quickly clear that Douzenko had severe personal problems, magnified by alcohol abuse. He had never once mentioned David's alleged confessions to other Stony Mountain staff, even when David's case was being discussed. He also made no written reports about the supposed confessions, and no other staff members ever reported overhearing similar comments from David. It was notable that Douzenko had been in charge of David the day he escaped on his day pass from Stony Mountain, back in 1980. Understandably, Douzenko didn't appreciate that.

During this time at the Supreme Court, it meant so much to us to have the company of my niece Anne and her husband Eric Augstman, and their children Larissa, Shawn and Ashley. They would bring us fresh home-cooked meals at our hotel when a day of court was over, and on weekends we would visit them. David could play with the children, who ranged from four to eleven, and relax, while we would work on the case. Eric was skilled with a computer, and this helped immensely as we tried to compare exhaustive details of Fisher's sex crimes to find a pattern that tied in with the Gail Miller murder.

There were other times, during breaks, when David and Maureen would wash each other's faces in the snow and have snowball fights. They also lay on their backs and made angels in the snow. It was as if David was a teenager again, with years of play to catch up on.

One night, David Asper and I were prepping Hersh
when Hersh read a police document and looked startled.
"Joyce, do you know what this is? Don't you realize the
significance of this?"

"No. What's the significance of it?"

"Look at this," Hersh said. I looked at a police report
we had received in the late 1980s, after we started pressuring the Justice Department to make sure Saskatchewan
provided us with all available documents on the case. I
had seen it what seemed to be a thousand times, and so
had David Asper. It hadn't struck us as particularly
remarkable, perhaps because we were buried so deeply
into the case.

"This is incredible," Hersh said. "They did this before
they talked to those kids."

Hersh was marvelling about a Crown document that
set out the prosecution's game plan. What was shocking
was its timing. It said what witnesses were to say *before*
they had said it. At the bottom of the document, the
police were ordered to get David's young friends, inter-
rogate them and get them to make statements that
conformed to the Crown's theory, which they did in
May 1969. Everything that was outlined in the Crown's
theory was what they eventually got those kids to say
later. It was an absolutely dynamite piece of paper.

Hersh had waited years for his chance in court, and
he wasn't about to waste it. Eddie Karst, one of the key
police investigators in the case, was on the witness stand
on February 17, 1992, when Hersh produced the Crown

"game plan" document that targeted David. Hersh absolutely rocked the packed courtroom when he said, "A senior officer laid out a whole theory and told you to go get it from these people." It wasn't so much a question as a bald statement of fact.

"If there was, it's completely out of my memory," Karst answered, adding that he was unaware of the report. More questions didn't improve Karst's memory. He said he never even thought of reopening the Miller murder investigation after Fisher's confessions to committing a number of rapes in Miller's neighbourhood.

That night, David had dinner with us at a restaurant, then returned at 10:10 to the Ottawa halfway house where he was staying. That was twenty minutes before his curfew, and he asked staff if he could take a walk. He was told he could, if he had an escort. However, David left alone, walked about half a block up the street by himself, and returned to sit on the backyard patio alone. He was still rattled by Karst's testimony, and he just wanted to get away from the world.

At three in the morning a staff member on rounds looked out the back window and saw David sitting alone on the deck. David had been behind bars for so many years that being outside, even when it was freezing, was reassuring. The staff member didn't talk to David but instead called police, who arrested him. "I didn't go anywhere," David protested as he was taken away. "I was just sitting on the back step. They seemed to think I took off. I didn't go anywhere."

I was devastated. I could understand David's emotions.

He had been jerked back and forth like a yoyo, and it was no wonder he was upset. The appearance in court of Eddie Karst was what finally set him off. In David's mind, Karst and his partner, Keith Mackie, were instrumental in putting him away. David felt a couple of times he was going to throw up in the courtroom as he looked at Karst.

The back porch debacle meant that David was shipped back to Stony Mountain in custody, missing the rest of his court proceedings. Coincidentally, he was up for another parole hearing early that February. Once again he lost.

～

In many ways, the Supreme Court experience was like watching an intricate, well-acted play. Another former inmate who knew Larry Fisher in Saskatchewan Penitentiary told of an altercation with Fisher during an inmates' hockey game in 1977. This new witness, a convicted murderer, got into a fight with Fisher, who screamed, "I'm going to shank you and stuff you in a snowbank, and the guard will find you in the spring."

"You and whose army?" the prisoner replied.

"Listen, I've done it before," Fisher replied. "I've got no problems doing it again."

The prisoner told court how he overheard Fisher and a convicted killer chatting during lunch in 1977. They were talking about the movie *Last Tango in Paris*, which depicts anal sex, and Fisher bragged that he knew what it felt like to rape a victim as she died. His lunch companion accused him of one-upmanship, and Fisher replied, "I'm serious. It happened a long time ago. It was the best . . . I had in my life."

Court also heard from the Prince Albert inmate who had told the RCMP that Fisher raped him in prison in the early 1980s. He sounded a lot like the female rape victims of Fisher as he described the pattern of the attack, as Fisher approached him for information, then suddenly turned violent and attacked him from behind. Yet another prisoner, convicted killer Brett Morgan, told of a conversation he had with Fisher in prison in 1980. Morgan was convicted of killing a prostitute, and perhaps Fisher felt some sex-attacker-to-sex-attacker bond as he offered him some free advice — try to pin it on somebody else. "He did mention a few times to me that he had in the past beaten or sloughed off a murder beef by having somebody else wear the beef for him," Morgan said, quoting Fisher as saying: "I killed somebody in Saskatoon but I never got any heat because I confessed to some crimes in another city and it happened at the same time or near the same time as the murder in Saskatoon."

There was such a sense of sadness about Nichol John when she took the stand. Seeing her in court was a reminder of how much of our lives this case had consumed. She was a mixed-up kid then, but now, on the witness stand, she looked weary and middle-aged. She continually referred to her nightmares about the case, and when Hersh asked her to show what she saw in them, Nichol made a stabbing motion in the air, raising her right hand high. David was left-handed, and we couldn't help but feel that he was that much closer to freedom as she re-enacted her dreams.

She also said something about hearing church bells in Gail Miller's neighbourhood the morning of the murder. She had never said this before, so I immediately telephoned Doug Groat in Saskatoon, whose parents, Jackie and Jim, had been so supportive for me throughout the ordeal, to find out whether there had been any church bells there at any time. Doug talked to the neighbours and was told there hadn't been any ringing in the neighbourhood for as long as anyone could remember.

I was rather taken aback when Larry Fisher stepped in front of the high court. I didn't expect him to look as nice as he did. He looked very distinguished and well dressed, and his hair was carefully styled. I hoped that nobody would be fooled by his appearance. Hersh had talked with a psychiatrist about how to handle Fisher, and was told to encourage him to explain things. "You've got to get him helping you," the psychiatrist had told Hersh.

It worked. Hersh's tone was measured and unthreatening as he drew Fisher to explain his technique as a rapist. The judges had made it clear to him that he was simply a witness, not someone on trial, and Fisher carried himself as an expert witness of sorts. He was so polite it was eerie as he explained what went on inside the mind of a serial rapist.

Fisher described a definite, precise pattern to his attacks — a pattern wholly consistent with the fatal attack on Gail Miller.

"And in your pattern, sir," Hersh said, "what you do is you grab the lady from behind and put the knife to her throat, cover her mouth so she can't yell and drag her or force her into the alley, lane, whatever it might be. That's your pattern."

"From the side, sir."

"From the side?"

"Yes, sir."

"So I'm a little bit off. It's a side grab? You can tell us . . ."

"Yes, sir."

"You tell her she can't yell, hand over her mouth."

"Yes, sir."

"Exactly the same way every time."

"Yes, sir."

"Because it works."

"Yes."

These attacks weren't about sex; they were about power and control. You could almost feel the pride in Fisher's voice as he described how he hurt women.

"Now, in your pattern," Hersh continued, "when you take her down the lane, in order to establish control, what you do is, you order them all to undress. Isn't that your general pattern?"

"Yes, sir."

"You want the clothes off. Correct?"

"True."

"And the reason you want the clothes off is because that shows you're in control."

"Yes, sir."

"Because when you do it, you don't take your clothes off, do you? When you rape?"

"No, sir."

As Hersh led Fisher deeper into his explanation of his attacks, it became clear that things could quickly get far worse if Fisher's pattern was broken.

"You pull the sweaters up over their face, don't you, inside out?" Hersh asked.

"I can't tell you what kind of a garment it was, sir, but I did do it."

"That's what I'm getting at. Those that were wearing sweaters had the sweaters pulled up inside out over their face."

"Yes, sir. I don't know whether it was a sweater or blouse or whatever."

"But the clothing ultimately is covering the face."

"Yes, sir."

"Because you don't want them to see your face. I mean, you're very professional at what you do, sir."

"I just said yes, sir."

"I mean, I'm not criticizing you, but that's very clever and very proper because you don't want to be forced to commit violence. Correct?"

"If you say so, yes, sir."

"Because if the party can identify you, if the party can see you, you may be forced to seriously harm them, isn't that right?"

"Yes, sir."

Fisher's rape victim from North Battleford sat in the courtroom as he testified. She was in her sixties now, and the slash mark across her neck from Fisher's knife was still visible. She was such a strong woman, and I was so deeply impressed by her. We weren't the only ones who wanted justice. She sat quietly as Fisher spoke of how he was abused and ignored when he was young.

"As a child, you were controlled," Hersh said to Fisher. "You didn't speak out. The nurses wouldn't listen to you. Now, you were in control."

"Yes, sir," Fisher replied.

"And when a lady walked by the alley, you'd grab her, with a knife, and drag her in," Hersh continued. "That was the real thrill, the power."

"I was looking for that power," Fisher replied.

"It was the power," Hersh said. "The sex came later."

"That's right," Fisher replied. "To fulfill it all."

In the courtroom the atmosphere was electric, almost as if we were all holding our breath.

I felt sadness for what Larry Fisher had gone through as a child. He claimed to have been sexually abused by a female relative, and I had no reason to doubt him. However, I think I would be more inclined to feel sorry for him as an adult if he decided to admit all of what he has done. I feel that if someone tries to make things right and repents, then you forgive. However, you don't forgive someone if they continue to lie and continue to do the wrong thing.

When Fisher's testimony was completed, he glared directly into my face as he walked out of the courtroom. His eyes were cold, just like pebbles. I felt hot, then I went icy cold. I was chilled to the bone. His eyes just penetrated. I felt that he raped me with his eyes. They were like a knife. I have never, ever felt someone look at me with such hatred. I stared right back at him, but I was shaking inside. When I got out of the courtroom, I was still trembling.

TWENTY-NINE

CALL IT LOVE

"You're leaving a shadow over my brother."
Chris tells Saskatchewan justice minister Bob Mitchell
that David's name must be cleared

AT FIFTEEN MINUTES PAST noon on April 16, 1992, David was finally a free man. It was such a wonderful moment. As we walked down the narrow prison corridors and squeezed through the front door into fresh air and sunlight and freedom, Maureen said it was like a butterfly leaving a cocoon. We could fly, finally, after so many years of confinement. There was clapping and smiling and I felt total exhilaration. Here we were, a family together again, doing what we had dreamed of doing for so many years. You could see from David's face that everything was a little out of focus, and that he would love to run down the hill and away from the crowd of reporters and well-wishers, but he also knew that, in a sense, it was their moment to share too. In the parking lot of the prison, Hersh and David handed him a special birth certificate that another family lawyer, Greg Rodin, had made for him, with the birthdate April 16, 1992. In David's pocket was some $240 from wages he had earned doing jobs in prison, with which he was to start his new life.

The Supreme Court of Canada had ruled that David should have a new trial. In the meantime, the high court ordered David released. The phones rang all day, and every few minutes, flowers, balloons and telegrams arrived. It was Easter, a time for new life, and our family was reborn again. We celebrated that wonderful weekend at the Marigold Chinese restaurant, where the house and various guests provided free champagne. We had asked the press to give us some space, and they honoured that, which I thought was a great tribute to the respect that we had developed. David had champagne, filet mignon, egg rolls and chow mein. He was finally savouring his victory meal, although it wasn't the one he and his grandmother Milgaard had planned so many years before.

After the meal, Maureen, her boyfriend, Darryl, and David went out on the town, while I retired home and thanked God once again for finally bringing my boy home.

Sometime after midnight, David stumbled home. Behind bars, prisoners can get hooch made from fruit and potatoes and almost anything else, but outside it was different. David had tried that night to make up for twenty-three years of not being able to visit bars. He had decided not to drink heavy liquor on his first night of freedom, but certainly managed to get quite smashed on "just" beer. How he was able to stagger down the stairs to his area in Lorne's basement I'll never know. As he collapsed on his bed with his clothes on, he looked up at me with a bleary grin, slurring his words as he said, "Guess what, Mom? I'm home!"

I slipped his shoes off and covered him up, and said, "Yes, you really are." I can laugh at it now, but at the time I didn't think it was particularly funny. What could we expect? I realized that one set of hard times were over and a new set were only just beginning.

I cooked him four eggs for breakfast around eleven that morning. He tried to hide his hangover, but it didn't hurt his appetite. He got a haircut and Lorne prepared dinner, as he had so many times in the past. I was able to keep up such a heavy workload in part because Lorne took care of me, making sure I was getting proper food. Lorne was such a solid, good man.

This time, however, Lorne started shivering badly just as the meal was ready. We put him to bed and called the doctor, who asked us to take him to the hospital. Lorne's fever was high and he stayed in hospital overnight for observation, but our fears passed and he was soon released. I'm sure he was badly run down from what he had gone through with David. It was just too much for him to take.

Freedom took some adjustment. Shortly after his release, David wanted to go out for a walk. "Can I go out alone?" he asked, sounding more like a nine-year-old than a man of thirty-nine.

"Of course you can," we replied.

Here he was, almost forty, and having to ask if he could go outdoors alone.

The Province of Saskatchewan refused to prosecute again, but at the same time, it did not register an acquittal and refused to award compensation or hold an inquiry.

"There's simply nothing left to inquire into," Saskatchewan justice minister Bob Mitchell said. "This is a very cold trail and it just doesn't seem productive at all to try to go back and inquire into it further."

So, to our frustration, Mitchell was content to leave a cloud over David's head. David was free, but in the eyes of the law he had not been cleared of the horrible crime. It seemed strange to us that Mitchell could talk of cold trails at the same time that Kim Campbell's Justice Department was helping prosecute Nazi war criminals for crimes that were committed overseas and years before David was even born. What's more, former senior Crown attorney Serge Kujawa was a politician now, sitting in the provincial legislature as a government member alongside Mitchell. Kujawa had handled the files of both David and Larry Fisher. How fortunate for him that his government did not see the need for an inquiry that would undoubtedly zero in on his conduct. The cold trail wasn't just aiding Larry Fisher.

Michell was quoted in the *Globe and Mail* saying he still believed David was guilty, which left us wondering how we could ever expect a fair hearing for him in Saskatchewan. It was David's brother, Chris, who took action this time. I was so proud of him when he approached Mitchell in the halls of the provincial legislature, in front of the media, and told Mitchell that his treatment of David wasn't right.

Chris was always the shy one of the family, and seldom showed up in media interviews.

"You're leaving a shadow over my brother . . . I feel this cloud should be cleared up."

"With respect, I feel the air is clear," Mitchell replied.

Chris felt that he hadn't suffered as much as his sisters. He left school after grade eleven, when the family moved to Winnipeg, but returned later to earn a degree in computer science. He benefited enormously from his marriage in 1977 to Kathy, but David's ordeal had left him extremely introverted and emotionally withdrawn. Despite Chris's ability to pull into himself, there were inescapable painful moments, like when he would present a credit card and the recipient would ask if he was related to the murderer. When Chris had visited David in prison, David tried to give the impression that everything was fine, but Chris could see he was deteriorating. Now that David was finally freed, Chris sometimes wondered whether his brother hadn't been better off in prison instead of being out and hounded by police. It was as if, in their minds, he was still guilty.

It bothered Chris and the rest of the family that David was denied a complete victory. The Supreme Court made clear from the outset that the system was not on trial. It was never the intention of the top court to hear evidence about the conduct of police or prosecutors. The high court exonerated everyone who put David behind bars, as if no one or nothing was to blame. No fault was found with police or the prosecution. Kim Campbell now seemed to be claiming victory, saying the decision showed that the system works. She didn't mention that it had cost us all the family assets and that our lawyers worked years for free. No mention was made that David lost almost twenty-three years of his life behind bars before the system finally worked. No mention was made of the things we had to deny our other children so that we could channel more money and time towards freeing David. There was also no mention that a real killer had been allowed to roam free while David rotted at taxpayers' expense. No mention was made of the memory of Gail Miller. When Campbell dismissed the need for a public inquiry, she ignored the request from Gail Miller's family for a deeper look at the slaying. If David's case was a victory for the system, I shudder to think of a failure.

Whatever the legal system's response, however, we clearly had public support. David was mobbed by well-wishers wherever he went. Strangers approached him on the street just to shake his hand and wish him good luck. Those were glorious days, with lots of smiles, happiness and huge amounts of eating. David, Maureen and Susan were able to escape to a friend's cottage outside Winnipeg, where they enjoyed quiet walks by the lake. Sometimes I had to stop and remind myself that this was really happening. It just didn't seem real, even though I'd always known it would happen eventually.

David had come out to such a different world. Just being able to use everyday appliances around the house was foreign to him, and he had a very short attention span. While others his age were entering the height of their careers, David wasn't trained to do anything. In prison, everything is done for you. There were also adjustments for the rest of us. We would be cooking side by side or eating or doing normal everyday things together, and then suddenly realize that we weren't being watched by a prison guard. There were odd feelings, like shopping for groceries and wondering what David liked to eat. Does he like broccoli? Does he like this salad dressing? It all seemed so ordinary, and yet it was all so new.

Now that David was out of custody, Susan felt she could finally leave Winnipeg and the seemingly never-ending publicity surrounding the Milgaard name. She moved to Calgary, where she lived alone, and from time to time, David would drop by to visit her. Often, he appeared unstable, and Susan would feel horrible waves of guilt, since a part of her did not want to be with him when he was like that. Often she would wake up in the middle of the night, haunted by nightmares.

In Winnipeg, Maureen felt constant pressure on her, as everyone around us always said she had the best rapport with David. A constant phrase within the family was, "He will listen to Maureen," and while she loved him enormously, she hated being his keeper.

Doing volunteer work helped David adjust. The John Howard Society in Winnipeg allowed him to use an office, and from there he called up prospective employers about giving ex-inmates jobs. David couldn't just turn away from prison, even though he had prayed for so many years to be released. He was like a survivor who walked away from a horrible crash, thinking, "Why am I here when there are still people in there? They should be out too." He wanted so desperately to help the others he left behind. Helping others had helped sustain him while he was a prisoner, and now it was a part of his healing.

It took a couple of months for David to shake the unsettling feeling that a return to prison was just around the corner. On June 19, 1992, he felt comfortable enough to appear on Peter Warren's Winnipeg radio show to thank his supporters: "They believe in what's good and what's right and they see it as a struggle for what's good and what's right and maybe that's what people have to keep inside them — a sense of what's good and what's right."

The next day, he was on *The House* radio show, trying to find the right words to express his immense gratitude. "There's always something there," David said. "I don't know what word to say. Call it love. I don't mind using that word . . . I hope it's a safe word. It's nice to feel the love of Winnipeg and people when they talk to you and they come up and they pat you on the back and they congratulate you . . . It means a lot to us."

David wasn't really sure what he wanted to do eventually, but guessed it would be something quite simple that involved helping people. In the meantime, he accepted honoraria for speaking engagements, including some at high schools. He felt that, as Canada's longest-serving prisoner, he could speak with some authority on the failures of the justice system. "Prisons should be used as a last resort, but people are regularly sent to prison without any adequate consideration of sentencing alternatives," David said in one of his speeches. "I also think it is fair to say that a lot more thought these days is given to the basic needs of animals in zoos than is given to prisoners in jail. The recidivism rate suggests that prisons have not had any success whatsoever in rehabilitating prisoners."

He also tried to make it clear that prisons aren't healthy places where people can learn better ways. The first thing a prisoner notices behind the walls, David said, is the abundance of drug pushers. "When men are making drug deals or gambling on credit or borrowing money as a way of life inside a penitentiary, this is where the trouble begins for the family. It makes life miserable for everyone. The living atmosphere of all penitentiaries revolves around this . . .

"During my prison days, I at one time lived in a cubicle. I was right next to all the institutional telephones. I could hear men treat their wives, girlfriends and others to the very cruellest abuse over these issues. It made me sick. I had to move away from the telephones. I just couldn't listen to it. There was nothing a woman could do right for her man if she couldn't get him some money or get him some drugs or if she couldn't get up to the visit. She wasn't worth anything. How many relationships, how many people's lives, have been destroyed like this and will continue to be? It has to stop."

David did some volunteer work with young offenders and visited with groups that had helped him over years, like the Mennonite Central Committee, the John Howard Society and the Native Service Agency. His appointment book was filled a month in advance. While in prison, David had converted to fundamentalist Christianity, and one week he attended services at three rural churches. He had also grown close to native spirituality through native inmates he had befriended, and loved the sweatlodge ceremonies for native cleansing as well as native singing and prayer. Trying to describe the feeling it gave him, David said, "I felt completely what I was." The first time he did the sweatlodge ceremony, David ran outside onto the snow and felt an exhilaration that he could never experience behind bars. "I felt really, really strong. I felt all of me." A native friend, Shirley Flamonde, took him to some traditional ceremonies, which he loved. David was particularly well treated on the reserves for standing up to the legal system, and was swamped by well-wishers at powwows, where he was quick to get up and dance. As Shirley joked, his celebrity status made the experience "a bit like travelling with Elvis."

Despite the joy and good wishes, everything was far from perfect, especially when David decided to drink. I felt sick in the pit of my stomach when I heard that he was arrested in July 1992 after police pulled him off a bus in northern Ontario. A woman passenger complained that he made some disturbing remarks. No charges were laid. Later that month, he was arrested again, this time in Vancouver. He was allegedly being drunk and disorderly in a public place. He admitted he was tipsy but saw two officers chasing a young native woman and felt they were being too rough. David stepped in and ended up handcuffed with his nose pressed against a police cruiser. Also in Vancouver, he was caught skinny-dipping at Wreck Beach, which brought more news stories and headaches.

In both cases, police took the unusual step of phoning the media to tell them.

He made the news again when he was picked up in Kingston, Ontario, and accused of shoving a teenaged boy in a convenience store. I had moved to Kanata, just outside Ottawa, to be close to politicians so that I could continue the push to totally clear David's name. Now, David was put in my custody while on bail for about a month, but it seemed more like ten years. He constantly tested all of his boundaries with me again, just like he was a sixteen-year-old trapped in the body of a forty-five-year-old. He blared his music. He slopped food on my clean carpets; he wasn't used to having carpets, and spilling food in a prison is no big deal. He opened a tin of soup by hacking at it with my best butcher knife, rather than using a can opener. He chewed with his mouth wide open, which was just atrocious. These were things we had taught him not to do decades before, but he had forgotten.

If I touched any possession of David's, however insignificant, he became agitated. I remember moving something of his to dust the apartment, and he was so upset. "Why did you touch my things?" he asked. "They're my things. You can't touch my things." That was the prisoner in him talking. Possessions, however small, were something to be prized and guarded. Anything that belonged to him really belonged to him.

At eleven o'clock at night, when we were ready to go to bed, David was compelled to go out even when he was desperately tired. We later learned this was because at eleven at night for all those years, he had been locked down, and this was his way of saying, "I am free."

To take a break from everything, at one point David hitchhiked to Thompson, Manitoba, about four hundred miles north of Winnipeg, arriving at the Maw-We-Tak native friendship centre without a penny to his name. He was seeking out his own treatment for his very deep spiritual wounds.

Ironically, if David had been released on parole as a convicted murderer, he would have been helped by a parole officer and been eligible for job training. Instead, he was on his own.

A lot of people thought the story was over now, but we weren't about to let it die. We kept pushing for an inquiry so that David's name could be truly cleared. Something had gone horribly wrong in the legal system, and it needed to be fixed if we were to salvage any meaning out of almost a quarter century of hell. We couldn't just pretend it didn't happen, and let the same thing happen to others.

I knew I was still getting on the nerves of some people in power. In September 1992, Saskatchewan justice minister Bob Mitchell held a news conference to hit back at my allegations about a coverup in his province's legal system. Some fresh information I had gathered particularly stung him. I had been told by a former Justice Department employee that when Premier Roy Romanow was provincial attorney-general, he and his former chief prosecutor Serge Kujawa went into meetings with David's file and those of Larry Fisher. Mitchell lashed out at my coverup accusations, saying that neither Romanow nor Kujawa, now his government colleagues, could recall any such meetings. "I think this is scandalous," Mitchell said. "She'd better be prepared to back this up with better evidence than she has to this point."

Serge Kujawa remained dismissive and utterly unapologetic, saying, "I thought these guys [Milgaard supporters] were silly little jerks up until now . . . I know that I am proud of my handling of all criminal cases that I have appeared in." He had earlier compared David Asper and Hersh Wolch to prostitutes, ignoring the fact that they had worked for years without pay.

I wasn't happy when David decided to go back to live in Saskatoon, thinking that he could somehow improve his case in the wrongful conviction lawsuit we had launched against the provincial government. David Asper was mortified, saying that the city's police would love to arrest him for anything, to make him seem like a convict. "That would be the end of everything that everybody's doing," Asper said in April 1992. "And Serge Kujawa would get up and say, 'I told you so.'"

"If you just got out of jail, would you want to be home with your mother?" I asked him.

"He's sixteen," David Asper replied. "You can't talk to him because he knows everything."

"Just think of it this way," I said. "It's a real lesson in what you'll have to go through with your son."

"Don't you ever say that again," he replied. His tone

was firm, but we were joking now. "In sixteen years I'll worry about it."

"This is practice for you, David."

"I can't ever discipline my kid without smiling because he's so cute."

"When they get older, David, you have to discipline them and they're not cute."

David's move to Saskatoon was short-lived, as he didn't have a security deposit for an apartment, and I wasn't about to lend him money for that. He was upset about it, but I couldn't help heaving a huge sigh of relief when he left the city.

The first Christmas when David was truly free was wonderful. He had been out on passes for a couple of Christmases, but those celebrations were always clouded by the realization that he would be going back behind bars at the end of the day. Our family felt so grateful during this holiday season for all of the people across Canada who had helped us free David. Many of them were people we had never met, and probably never would meet, but they were certainly in our prayers.

We tried to keep that Christmas much the same as previous years, but just having David there was so special. We always decorated our tree on Christmas Eve, and each member of the family had a different role. For far too many years, someone had to do David's job, but this Christmas, David finally got to do his own part.

Chris gave David a camera for that first Christmas of freedom, and that was the first present opened. Of course, David didn't know how to operate a camera, but once he figured it out he just had a ball snapping pictures of everyone and freezing the joy of that day on film.

David was forever restless, having to keep moving constantly. It was like he was sixteen and on the road again. In May 1992, just a month after his release, librarian Marnie Froberg was on a coffee break from her job at Vancouver Community College when a man started speaking to her. The conversation lasted for about an hour, and when it ended, they exchanged names and addresses. It was only then that she realized that the man was David Milgaard. She had heard his name for years as she grew up in Saskatoon, and she always believed he was guilty. That criminal in the news was so unlike the man she had just met. Through that summer, David called Marnie from time to time, and she wrote him care of Lorne's home. At first her parents were concerned, but they grew to know David and love him themselves, to the point that David would stay at their home when passing through Saskatchewan.

David and Marnie were married on August 14, 1996, at Kitsilano Beach in Vancouver. It was a unique union, since Marnie well knows about David's intense need for space and independence, and how he wanders, both verbally and physically. Some nights, David feels the need to sleep on the beach, and other times, he wanders off into the woods alone for two or three days. He and Marnie have an agreement that he will make contact with her every forty-eight hours, wherever he may be.

Marnie understands David's deep reluctance to trust

others. After fighting for so many years to prove his innocence, he now has trouble believing people are on his side. Many nights she was awoken by his screaming, when he was not sure where he was or who Marnie was. The thought that someone was sharing his bed filled him with panic, since he had grown so used to being alone in prison. Now someone else's presence seemed abnormal and dangerous.

David could talk to Marnie about his ordeal, although she knew he was still holding back much. And while she knew he needed counselling, she also appreciated his suspicion of psychiatrists and psychologists. Most of the psychiatrists who had worked with him in prison seemed only to want him to confess, and he had felt they were also using him as a human guinea pig. She heard of times he was locked in quiet rooms, naked with other nude inmates who also had psychiatric problems. They could earn back pieces of clothing and furniture through good behaviour. For reasons he didn't fully explain, David also has an enormous fear of being subjected to shock therapy, and made Marnie and me promise that we would never consent to such procedures upon him.

Marnie taught David how to work a VCR, transfer from bus to bus and do his banking. Her new husband had no idea about how to lease a home or about credit ratings. To improve his social skills, they acted out various situations, and she also worked to help him speak without using prison jargon. Normal things, like watching television together, simply were impossible for now. David didn't have the attention span to read or watch TV for any length of time, and the mention of the news, law, police, hospitals and medicine all made him agitated. It took him two years before he was able to watch a sympathetic Global television documentary on his case.

THIRTY

CLEAN SLATE

*"It wasn't the justice system.
It was science that saved me. I love science."*
Guy Paul Morin, wrongfully convicted of murder

PRIME MINISTER JEAN Chrétien seemed so friendly, like the boy next door, when he sat down with me in his Ottawa office to discuss David's case in May 1996. I had been constantly pressuring Justice Minister Alan Rock for a meeting, and member of Parliament John Harvard was able to arrange it. I felt off base in the meeting, to be sitting down with someone with the prime minister's power, in his private office. I also felt a sense of history, since John Harvard, who through the years had always been there for our family, told me it was the first time that a prime minister and a justice minister have met with someone in my situation, appealing a sentence.

The prime minister tried to put me at ease and talked freely about his own adopted son, who was in prison for sexual assault. "I know how you feel. I know what it's like to have a family member wrongly convicted."

He asked, "Why do you need an inquiry? Your son's slate is clean."

"People don't believe it is," I replied.

Alan Rock jumped in. "Mr. Prime Minister, there's no way that we can get into this. It would set a precedent. So many cases would flow from this."

"Alan, I want you to do whatever you can do to help this lady," Prime Minister Chrétien said. "Do you understand?"

"Yes, I do, Prime Minister," Rock replied.

I had thought the meeting would last only a few minutes, but we talked for about an hour about David's case. On my way to the door, Alan Rock asked me how it felt to be in the prime minister's office. That was the first time I actually stopped to take a look around the room. It was beautiful, really beautiful. I had been so intent on the meeting that I wasn't aware of anything else.

Not long afterwards, in the spring of 1997, we decided to take yet another run at scientific testing to prove David's innocence. So far, there had been the tests after his original arrest, the truth serum in the 1970s and inconclusive tests done in the U.S. around the time of the Supreme Court hearing. Also, in 1992, an RCMP scientist in Ottawa identified what she believed was a semen stain on Miller's underpants, but no follow-up testing was done to confirm this. Dr. James Ferris and Dr. Peter Markesteyn had done fine work, but science had advanced since then, and perhaps we could finally get strong proof of innocence. Toronto lawyer James Lockyer arranged the testing, as he had with Guy Paul Morin.

On January 23, 1995, Guy Paul Morin of Queensville, north of Toronto, was declared a free man after DNA testing overturned his wrongful conviction for the murder of a schoolgirl neighbour. That happy day, I beamed outside Osgoode Hall law courts in Toronto as I watched Guy Paul happily chatting with reporters. I relived my own joy when I met with his mother and father that morning.

The new DNA testing for David's case was conducted in England and involved American, British and Canadian scientists. Both the Justice Department and our side would monitor the testing. Although I was never told so, I strongly suspected that the testing was a result of my meeting with Prime Minister Chrétien. If the scientists found anything, they would be making history, since it was believed that Gail Miller's garments were the oldest to be subjected to DNA tests for court purposes. The scientists were trying an advanced method of analysis known as short tandem repeat, which is capable of yielding an even more exact result than the one that had cleared Guy Paul Morin. There was, however, a high level of risk. The tests on Gail Miller's underpants, bra, half-slip, other clothing and coat could use up entire samples, making future testing impossible. Yet David desperately needed a sense of closure. He needed people to know he was innocent beyond any doubt. On July 14, 1997, the tests began. A stain on Miller's underpants was ruled out as semen, but semen was detected on both her slip and coat. It was amazing that no one had found this before. Four days later, the results were in.

When I flew in for the news about the testing on

July 18, I was greeted at Pearson International Airport in Toronto by Guy Paul Morin. "I want to put your bags in the car and then I want to come around and stand beside you," he said coyly.

"What's the problem?" I asked.

"I just need to be there where you are," he replied, still smiling.

For an instant I worried something had gone wrong. "Paul, what's going on?" I said.

"Come, let me get you in the car," he continued. By now, the bags were put away and he came over.

"Well, the test is done and guess what?" Guy Paul asked.

"David has been exonerated."

"Yeah, that's right. The best part is, it implicates Fisher."

I must have been the happiest woman alive. I started to cry and laugh at the same time. Then I asked Guy Paul why in the world he wouldn't let me in the car.

"Because I couldn't have an unconscious woman in my car, in case the cops pulled me over," he answered. I assumed he was joking. It's sometimes tough to tell with Guy Paul.

I just wanted to shout the news from the housetops. Instead, we held a press conference, where the public was told that state-of-the art, unbiased DNA testing cleared David's name and overwhelmingly suggested that Larry Fisher was the real killer. There were only sixteen people on the entire planet — including Fisher — whose DNA was a match for that sample found on Miller's clothing. Of those sixteen, I would imagine that some were women, some were very old and some were very young. And I highly doubt any of them, besides Larry Fisher, was in Gail Miller's Saskatoon neighbourhood that fateful morning.

The new federal justice minister, Anne McLellan, put it nicely, saying, "I would like to express my admiration and compassion for David Milgaard's mother, Joyce Milgaard, without whose tenacity and unwavering belief in her son's innocence, this result would not have been achieved."

There was, of course, a bittersweet feeling to this news. David was forty-five when his name was finally cleared. He had been just sixteen when he was first locked up. So much had been lost between those ages, and so much was damaged forever. So many dreams had quietly died.

The next day, on July 19, 1997, Saskatoon police questioned Larry Fisher, who had been living in a Fifth Avenue North apartment for the past three months with a woman, presumably his wife. Also that Saturday, Saskatoon police released him, saying they didn't have enough evidence for charges. Then the RCMP took over the case from them. Apparently, Calgary police got the results of the DNA testing by July 25, when he was arrested without incident.

I often felt like sitting down with Larry Fisher and asking him to tell about the deal he cut back in 1970. I honestly think he was told that someone else had taken the fall for the Gail Miller murder and that he could get away with that if he kept quiet. Now, he was finally facing charges, which meant he faced the prospect of another lengthy stretch in prison. If he had pleaded guilty to the Miller murder back in 1970, they would have folded the rape convictions in with it, and his sentence wouldn't have been any longer than what he served. He would have been able to seek treatment in prison, instead of always trying to bottle up his secret. He had been set up and used, like so many others in the case, including David.

On July 21, there was an amazing press conference in Regina. Serge Kujawa, former head of prosecutions who had handled David's appeal, and Bobs Caldwell, who had prosecuted his trial, flanked their lawyer, Si Halyk. Kujawa and Caldwell were mum, letting the pleasant Mr. Halyk do all the talking. "They both extend their sincerest apologies to David Milgaard, his family and all others directly affected for the failings of the system that resulted in his wrongful conviction," Halyk said. "They fully understand that there is nothing they can say today that will ease this horrible injustice and pain that has been inflicted on Milgaard and his family by this wrongful conviction."

Halyk stopped short of saying that his clients admitted to any wrongdoing, saying the failure was strictly that of the legal system. That was still progress, since back in 1991, Kujawa was quoted in the *Winnipeg Sun* saying, "It doesn't matter if Milgaard is innocent . . . I'm not primarily concerned with his guilt or innocence. What I am concerned with is that you [the media] and the lawyers are selling us down the river. The whole judicial system is at issue — it's worth more than one person." Now,

Caldwell and Kujawa sat silently as their lawyer called for a full public inquiry. Maureen turned to me with a look of bewilderment on her face. She had always thought of Caldwell and Kujawa as such powerful men, but now, as she looked at them on television, she turned to me and said, "Mom, they're nothing but old men."

However, that same day, Saskatoon police still weren't prepared to offer an apology. They had been accused of tunnel vision during the case, and they weren't prepared to take off the blinders just yet. They said they still hadn't officially received the DNA test results, even though they were sent three days earlier to the head of appeals for Saskatchewan.

Making it look even worse for the Saskatoon police, the British scientist who ran the DNA tests, Dr. Edward Blake, said there was enough semen left on Gail Miller's clothes for police to do blood tests that should have cleared David back in 1969. The problem, Blake said, was incompetent investigators, not poor technology. He said that Saskatoon police could have tried matching David's blood to the type of semen left on Miller's clothing. Then they could have discounted David as a suspect and zeroed in on the real killer, instead of waiting twenty-eight years. No tests were done, however, partly because two large stains weren't even found until mid-July 1997. "We kept asking how this could be, and the answer is simply that the examinations done in 1969 and 1992 were done incompetently," Blake told the *Saskatoon Star Phoenix* on July 22. Blake also said that there was more than enough genetic material available to clear David in 1992, when the Supreme Court called for DNA tests from an RCMP lab. Those tests had also been inconclusive.

As this embarrassing news appeared in the newspapers, Saskatchewan justice minister John Nilson turned the investigation over to the RCMP for "a fresh set of eyes." Unfortunately, those eyes belonged to Insp. Murray Sawatzky, who had headed a twelve-member task force that investigated the case from 1992 to 1994. Back then, Sawatzky dismissed allegations that police and investigators had mishandled the case. The RCMP report also found no basis for allegations of a coverup involving police, prosecutors and Saskatchewan premier Roy Romanow, who was the province's attorney-general back in the early 1970s. Sawatzky's report went even further, saying, "There is no new evidence which would exonerate David Milgaard, or that would inculpate any other person, including Larry Fisher."

My main goal now was to win an inquiry. I didn't want another family to have to endure what our family went through. In Ontario, the inquiry into the wrongful eighteen-month confinement of Guy Paul Morin was helping shed light on some unsavoury police tactics, such as a reliance on jailhouse informants, who have much to gain by lying. I could have used Guy Paul to catch me when, on July 18, 1997, I heard Justice Minister Nilson offer our family "the most heartfelt apology." He then went on to say he was considering the questions of compensation and a public inquiry. I didn't believe I'd ever, ever hear that. It was marvellous.

The wonderful week after the DNA testing cleared David ended in true storybook fashion, with a wedding. Maureen was getting married very simply, at our newly acquired camp. There were supposed to be only a few people, but lots of others came. I had requested that the media respect the family's privacy and only one reporter showed up, and he left rather quickly after I explained that he would never, ever get another interview with the Milgaard family if he stayed. The ceremony was simple, rustic and quiet; the perfect end to a perfect week. David wore sweatpants and a baseball cap, and as we expected, sometime during the celebration, he became flustered, apologized and then slipped away into the trees and grass for some quiet time alone. He had been doing a lot of that lately, and we knew he would do a lot more in the future. He loved to sleep alone under the stars and feel the wind against his skin.

This was the first full family celebration since back in 1968, when Gail Miller was still alive. We had lost so much since then, but in some ways we had gained as well. I think we all have learned from David, and the sense of innocence he safeguarded through all of his years in prison. It was as though we had lost our innocence and yet he retained his, and could see beauty where we could not.

I thought back to when he phoned me once from the Rockwood prison farm. From the sound of his voice, you would have thought he saw the face of God as he said, "Mom, I've just been outside and I've seen a sunset." When I asked what he meant, he said, "You don't understand. I could see the whole sky, every bit of it. Not just a little bit through the bars. I felt it was so wonderful." I started to cry, thinking, "How many times have I not looked at the sky?"

We know that David is not alone and that there are other wrongfully convicted Canadians in prison. The Association in Defence of the Wrongly Convicted was able to win a new trial for Chris Bates of Cowansville, in the Eastern Townships of Quebec, in May 1998. Ex-boxer Rubin (Hurricane) Carter, who had served twenty years in American prisons for murders he did not commit, crusader Win Wahrer, lawyer Lon Rose and private investigators Bill Joynt and Sean Gladney all joined in to fight for Chris after his parents, Janet and Doug, lost their entire life savings to legal bills. On June 25, 1998, Peter Frumusa, dubbed the "Mob Milgaard," was freed from custody in Welland, Ontario, after eight years in prison for a double murder he did not commit. It was whispered in the Niagara Falls mob that Frumusa was set up to take the fall for a pair of double murders to shield more powerful criminals. For the Frumusa conviction, the Crown relied on a jailhouse informant, even though the informant had a sordid criminal record, included thirty-seven convictions, one of which involved murder. Frumusa, a low-level cocaine dealer, got something David and Guy Paul Morin were denied: an apology from the court, as Mr. Justice Paul Forestell told him, "To you, Mr. Frumusa, on behalf of the court and our justice system, I apologize for what you have gone through."

I joined the Association in Defence of the Wrongly

Convicted in large part through James Lockyer's trickery. The association was hatched over James's kitchen table, when he tried to capitalize on the momentum of Guy Paul's release on bail in February 1993. James called me to ask if I could attend a vigil for Guy Paul. He was hoping I would be a drawing card for the press, but I declined, feeling too swamped with our own problems. James immediately got Guy Paul's mother to call me. How could I turn a mother down? I had played the mother card with others, and now she was giving me a strong taste of my own medicine. How grateful I would be to share in Guy Paul Morin's great victory and become part of a group that would be there for people when they are wrongly convicted. God helped get David out of prison and I had promised Him that I would help others once David was freed.

In February 1998, I met with Canada's justice minister, Anne McLellan, to discuss how we could keep David's ordeal from ever being repeated again. Her time was portioned out in fifteen-minute segments by her advisers, and we were able to get about an hour.

We told the justice minister that the Department of Justice has the moral duty to amend the appeal process and to create an independent review process to review and correct wrongful convictions. We told her the jurisdiction of appeals courts must be expanded. As it stood, a court of appeal had no choice but to uphold a conviction about which it has real doubt, as long as procedural rules were followed. As we stated in our brief, "Appellate courts must be given room to get at the truth . . . Amendments to the appeal process are not enough. No matter how procedurally correct a trial, no matter how rigorous the appellate review, there will always be victims of grievous miscarriage of justice."

Because of this sad inevitability, we called for a review process that could kick in after the appellate review process. It's important to remember that all of David's legal appeal avenues, short of the Section 690 mercy application, were exhausted twenty-one years before he was finally released, and that it took another five years after that to clear his name. The current system of having to appeal for Crown mercy is far too slow, too secretive and has failed too many times. Crown attorneys are trained to be prosecutors and aren't the people to take a fresh look at cases. We told the minister we wanted a *completely independent* commission with the powers and funding to investigate wrongful conviction claims. To bring a case to the commission, you would have to already have exhausted all appellate court avenues, and you would have to be arguing true innocence, not legal technicalities. In that sense, it would share common ground with Rev. Jim McCloskey's Centurion Ministries criteria. When the commission finds that there's a serious chance of wrongful conviction in a case, it would be referred back to the provincial courts for a fresh verdict. We weren't arguing that the gates of prison should be thrown wide open, but we did want to allow for some light on cases of those who might be wrongfully trapped inside, like Donald Marshall, Guy Paul Morin, Peter Frumusa, Chris Bates or David. This was something that was recommended in the Donald Marshall inquiry, and if it had been followed through with, David's time in prison would have been shortened.

I have never said that the entire legal system is corrupt. I believe in the basic system that we have in our country. However, I decry justice behind closed doors. Why must an application like the one prepared for David have to pass over the desks of so many bureaucrats? Couldn't important new evidence simply go before a judge, as it does in the U.S.? The problem with the current 690 clause is that there is no adversarial system. Lawyers for the accused can't see the prosecution's case, so they are forced to operate in the dark. Our civil lawyer, Greg Rodin, broke legal ground when he won the right to sue the Crown over their handling of the case, but other families in the future should not be forced to go to this extreme for justice.

We left the meeting with Anne McClellan feeling as if we were growing in strength. We felt part of something much bigger than ourselves. As a family, we needed to feel there was some greater purpose to the struggle. Maybe our role is to improve the justice system in Canada.

I feel uncomfortable when people say that I am a heroic person. Circumstances create heroes, and David's ordeal forced me to grow up. So much has happened since the police officers showed up at our door in Langenburg and asked, "Are you David Milgaard's mother?" I had to put aside my own self-will, which had once been so strong, and rely on God. I learned to do my very best and leave the rest to God, so that I could wake up fresh every morning, ready to start again.

I'm not nearly as materialistic as I once was. During our struggle, funds, which had always been in such short supply, became enough for the task. As I learned to love people, my needs were met. I also learned to recognize innocence in others besides David. I firmly believe we are all made in God's image, and that God is an irresistibly powerful agent for good. I know God as a Father and Mother and I know that I can talk to Him or Her, as can anyone else. I also learned that the truth is an extremely powerful and important thing. David and Guy Paul Morin were wrongly convicted because of jailhouse informants and the suppression of evidence. Those practices aren't based on the truth, and so they are doomed to failure. As it says in the good book, "I will overturn, overturn, overturn." (Ezekiel, 21:27.) I've become more patient through this. We just have to know that love is in His hands and show this love every day. That's what I do to the best of my ability. In the big picture, I feel that God is supreme and I feel that I didn't win by going to the Supreme Court. I went to God and He got David out.

It wasn't Canada that hurt our David. It was a few people who held power in the province of Saskatchewan. I remain intensely proud of being Canadian. Canadians from coast to coast joined me in praying for David's release, and I still feel that outpouring of love and it makes me strong. David's future won't be easy, but I am optimistic. We loved David through all of those years in prison, and we'll love him through the rest of this, and he'll make it.

AFTERWORDS

ON JANUARY 12, 1999, the week before the hard-cover edition of this book went to press, I spoke at a student law symposium at Queen Elizabeth Park School in Oakville, Ontario. The high school students had clearly put a lot of work into organizing the event, and impressed me with their genuine concern for making things better. One of them asked me an interesting question that made me pause for a second. He wanted to know if I regretted anything in particular during the prolonged fight to free David. I replied that I deeply regretted the pain that the publicity surrounding our struggle has caused the family of Gail Miller. Inevitably, television clips would run shots of Gail's body lying in the snow. I can't imagine how much this must have hurt her loved ones. I wish there had been some way of getting publicity for David's plight without hurting them like that, but I don't think it was possible.

I told the students how impressed I was with Gail Miller's family, and how they had agreed to watch a video presentation on the evidence prepared by Reverend Jim McCloskey. I thought it was just tremendous that they considered our evidence, then issued their press release saying they supported a new trial. Their strength and concern for justice deeply moved me. That picture of Gail Miller lying in the snow is deliberately not in this book.

I told the students that the issue of compensation remains unresolved, and that any inquiry must wait until the murder trial for Larry Fisher has passed. They were also interested in an upcoming television movie on David's story, which has been delayed from running by a court injunction, won by Larry Fisher's lawyer, Brian Beresh. The movie is a powerful production, but if delaying it guarantees Larry Fisher a fair trial, I can easily live with that. I told the students how Brian Beresh would be my first choice as a new lawyer, if we did not have the wonderful legal team we did. If I've learned anything through this battle, it's that justice in the courts isn't something you're guaranteed. It's something that must be fought for and won, and Beresh is a fighter.

When students asked what I thought about Larry Fisher, I told them I wasn't prepared to call him guilty of the murder until I have heard all the evidence in a courtroom. We've come too far in our fight for justice to deny anyone a fair trial. It's important that everyone is fairly judged, even the Larry Fishers of the world.

IT IS NOW DECEMBER 1999 as I write this update for the paperback edition and reflect upon another year of our struggle for justice. David still hasn't read all of this book or watched *A Mother's Love: The Joyce Milgaard Story*, a CTV documentary about his case. It's simply too painful for him. It may always be, even though we purposely tried not to sensationalize the worst of his prison horrors. In fact, we kept graphic details of what David suffered behind bars to a minimum in this book.

Since the publication of the hardcover edition of *A Mother's Story*, I have come to realize more fully the degree to which we had sheltered David from the pain the rest of the family felt during his ordeal. For example, while I was promoting the book in Vancouver, David heard, I think for the first time, that after he was convicted his sister Maureen, then a little girl, was encircled and taunted by her schoolmates. This caused enormous pain — and guilt — for David, as did other family experiences he has since learned about. There are so many other stories of family suffering that didn't make it into the book, because the pain remained too personal and raw, even years after the events.

As David heard how his family had suffered following his conviction, he started to spiral downwards. It was so devastating for him. Unfortunately, he didn't direct his anger at the justice system. Instead, he took out his frustrations on himself and retreated into himself, for a time almost cutting off all contact with the entire family.

The book promotion tour in the spring of 1999 came when we had waited almost two years to begin negotiations over a compensation package, and there was still no end in sight. This wasn't just frustrating for David. It was hard for the whole family, as all of us felt that our lives were again on hold. It seemed as though the pain would never end. It was almost as if we were reliving everything. We were waiting for letters from the government and lawyers, lawyers, lawyers. At every stop on the tour, there were at least two or three people who would tell me their own horror stories. I got a sense that so many people I did not know wanted us to win. They saw it as their victory as well. This helped me, but the rest of the family waited.

In April 1999, the government of Saskatchewan announced it had given us another cheque for $150,000 as part of the compensation package. Our lawyer told them that the money wasn't going to David or to the family but to lawyers and the accountant for fees involved in a study the government itself had requested. It wasn't for us. They must have known the public would think everything was going fine, but that was a lie. Normally, I'm pretty good about following the Bible's admonition to do good to those who despitefully use you and persecute you, but at that moment I lost it. I was so incensed. Seeing my family torn apart and everyone stretched so thin, I became violently angry, and then of course, as a result of the rage, I became physically ill. I had a high fever and could barely stand up. I started to re-read my Bible lesson and to think back to the things that had carried me through David's struggle: "Don't bring yesterday into today" and "Love, be nothing but Love." I knew I had to quell this corrosive feeling within myself or I would not be able to go on. I really had to use my faith.

Then I phoned for an appointment with the Justice Minister and the Speaker of the House. I had met the Speaker, the Honorable Gilbert Parent, in January 1999 at the film première of the movie *Milgaard*. He enveloped me in his arms and said, "Mrs. Milgaard, I would like to have your entire family come to Ottawa and introduce them to the House."

"Well, that would be wonderful, but I can't afford to bring the entire family out here," I replied. He obviously thought that our compensation package had been settled, as did so many others. I could only wish that were true. Now I would ask for his help because at the première he had offered help, "If there's ever anything I can do." I met with him and Justice Minister Anne McLellan but once again, I decided it would be wise to take my concerns to the top.

I asked for a meeting with Prime Minister Jean Chrétien and it was arranged within a day. I really wasn't surprised when I got the appointment, which struck me as odd afterwards. You would think I would have been, but somehow I wasn't. It was hard to be surprised by anything at this point. However, I must admit it was an incredible moment when it came time to meet with Chrétien and I was directed to his residence on Sussex Drive. In 1996 I had met with him in his office but now, here I was knocking on the door to his home (after a security check, of course). His butler showed us in and asked us to sign the guest book, then ushered us into the living room. It felt like an historic moment.

When the prime minister came in he seemed distracted. He had been travelling long hours the day before and just that morning he had been under attack by the opposition in the House of Commons regarding the war in Kosovo. Still, he was making time to see me. I had hoped the prime minister would enlist Saskatchewan Premier Roy Romanow's help in making a compensation offer. He told me that he couldn't tell the Saskatchewan government what to do, but that he would do the best that he could. Before our talk ended, I handed him a letter, which he slipped into the inside pocket of his jacket. Later, I told the *Toronto Star*'s Tracey Tyler what I had written and she described the letter as "a dose of encouragement and motherly guilt." It reminded the prime minister that he had the power to nudge Romanow into finalizing compensation and referred to the "Just Society" that Chrétien had set out to create as a young cabinet minister serving under Pierre Trudeau in the 1960s.

My letter reflected my growing concern for David. I knew at the time that he wasn't doing well, but I had no idea how bad things were for him. He was just in despair, wandering alone in the interior of B.C. He went without his medication for a couple of days, before appearing on the steps of a small town doctor, hoping for another prescription. The doctor was so alarmed by what he saw that he feared David might hurt himself. The doctor immediately called an ambulance, and David was committed to a psychiatric institution. I could only pray that everyone would do the right thing and that the ordeal would soon be over. Although I could fully understand why the caring doctor did what he did, it was so horrible to think of David locked up against his will once again.

Meanwhile, I announced to friends in the media my plans to set up a tent in front of the Saskatchewan legislature, starting over the Mother's Day weekend, and cancelling the book tour so I could protest the tortuously slow pace of talks. Soon, other Canadians were offering to camp along with me, which was heartening. I also received an immediate offer from a Toronto Christian Scientist to provide me with a suitable tent and gear. I felt that the inaction of Saskatchewan government officials had pushed David to his latest low point and I wasn't about to stay quiet while my son suffered.

I called the Prime Minister's Office and spoke to his aide. I told him that I had said to the prime minister that I feared for my son's sanity if someone didn't do something and now that fear had been realized. I was sobbing as I asked him to please speak to Mr. Chrétien and tell him what had happened and to ask him to call Premier Romanow.

The protest camp outside the Saskatchewan legislature was going to start on May 4, 1999, but instead, the Saskatchewan government broke months of silence and announced that officials would like to meet with me. This announcement on April 28 represented a reversal of the government's position. I had previously called trying to talk with someone, but I had been told that it would be totally inappropriate for the minister to speak with me. Now, he wanted to talk. (We found out afterwards that prior to the announcement at the news conference, the Saskatchewan Premier had been called out of a meeting to take a call from the prime minister. I was so thankful that once again Mr. Chrétien had helped us.)

When Saskatchewan Justice Minister John Nilson called me, I said I would be happy to meet with him, but only on one condition: he must bring figures to the table. It had been too long already. It was time for plain talking. They called our lawyer, Hersh Wolch, and he flew east to meet with Alan Gold, the retired Quebec judge who was acting as a negotiator for the province's NDP government. Now they were talking numbers. I called the provincial Justice Minister to inform him that I would not be going to Saskatchewan to meet with him, since things were progressing well. However, I would keep my pup tent handy, just in case I needed to camp out on the lawn.

The compensation offer followed shortly thereafter, and it was for a record $10 million — $4 million from Ottawa and $6 million from the province of Saskatchewan. We wouldn't agree to any settlement until Saskatchewan and Ottawa agreed that there would be an inquiry into David's wrongful conviction, once the trial of Larry Fisher for the Gail Miller murder was completed. It was important that lessons be learned from the tragedy, and steps taken so that it would not be repeated.

The government agreed to our conditions, then sent a cheque to me for $750,000 and one for the balance to David. Of course, out of that money all the expenses and the legal fees for years of hard work and dedication by the lawyers had first to be paid, and David being David, made sure each member of the family received a share as well. He had been the one to make the final decision of what to accept. I did not take part in the negotiations, which was difficult for me as I had been so deeply involved in everything up to that point. But I felt it was important that after all the years of others making decisions for him, David be allowed to make this one himself.

David's spirits lifted greatly with the settlement, and one of his first purchases was a Harley-Davidson motorcycle for David Asper, our lawyer friend. My two Davids had fought bitterly at times and my son David had fired my lawyer David more than once, but there was a love between them and the shiny Harley symbolized this. David Asper isn't a Harley kind of guy, but he looked so proud as he wheeled about on it. It was a freedom machine for both of them.

Shortly before the settlement, David sent me a book on the Beaver airplane. He asked me to read it and other books about planes and then to choose one. He wanted to buy me an airplane. I was thrilled. Years before, when I was learning to fly, I used to share my experiences with David during our prison visits. I loved the idea of taking to the skies again. Even before I selected a plane, I had a name for it, the "Easy Spirit." At first I wondered why in the world David wanted to buy me an airplane and then it came to me. I recalled a conversation he had had with a friend, offering to buy him a motorcycle *when* he got out of prison (we always said *when*, never *if*) and jokingly I had said, "Well, if he gets a motorcycle, I should get an airplane," and David agreed. Now, he was making good on that promise. A small part of me couldn't help but wonder, however, if he didn't also want me to have a plane so that I could fly him places. Recently, we had talked about that and I told him that he had promised me an airplane but I hadn't promised to fly him anywhere. Instead, I suggested that he learn to fly himself. He said he had always wanted to and one day I got an excited phone call from him. He told me he had taken his first lesson and he loved it. David is now also finding a special freedom in the sky, as I do.

It has also meant so much for David that his father Lorne could finally retire, at age seventy. Lorne had cashed in his retirement savings years before to help finance the fight to clear David's name. Our other son Chris and his wife, Kathy, continue to live in Saskatchewan. Maureen bought a lovely house with her family and Susan has bought a wonderful home, has a new puppy and has also gone back to school.

I thought seriously of attending law school, but after a chat with the Dean of the University of Manitoba Law School, I decided instead to audit courses that would bolster my work for the Association in Defence of the Wrongly Convicted.

After watching a glorious sunset over the beach at Maureen's, as the children sat on the dock fishing, Lorne and I decided to look for a home in the area to share. We found a very special house about a half hour's drive from Winnipeg. Once a railway station, it was now totally renovated, with a new second floor and even a ground floor Jacuzzi. The house had been moved to a 220-foot beach site and had a cement boat launch. It was more than we had ever dreamt of owning, and Lorne and I agreed to share expenses.

For David's part, he and Marnie continue to live in Vancouver, although they have a little bachelor apartment they use in Winnipeg when they're in Manitoba. They have been travelling a lot, often by bus. David can finally afford to fly, but he loves to see the countryside up close. On one trip, he rented a new car, then reconsidered and returned it, deciding instead on a Rent-a-Wreck at a cheaper rate. He later broke down and actually bought a car — a five-year-old red Corvette, being a little extravagent and a little penny-pinching at the same time.

Not everywhere David planned to go was accessible by Greyhound. There was a three-week Mediterranean cruise with Marnie, and they particularly enjoyed the canals and cafés of Venice. "We felt like we were in one of the ads on TV," David later told me, smiling.

On October 14, 1999, David was in Winnipeg to read his poetry at the Winnipeg International Writers Festival, then take a tour of our new house outside the city. It was a day for poetry and family, but soon the telephone lines were filled with calls from the media, asking about what was going on in Yorkton, Saskatchewan. The trial for Larry Fisher had begun but we had deliberately stayed away. It just didn't seem like the right place for us to be. The irony of David reading his poetry while Larry Fisher finally stood trial didn't escape the eye of *Winnipeg Free Press* columnist Gordon Sinclair Jr., who called it "Poetic Justice."

Reporter Les Perrault of *The Saskatoon Star Phoenix* kept us up-to-date with regular telephone calls during the six weeks of the trial in Yorkton. The trial opened with Fisher's lawyer, Brian Beresh, pointing the finger at David and me. I cannot explain the sick feeling this gave me. Beresh suggested that DNA evidence against his client was suspect and that I may have influenced the case against him. I felt as if *we* were on trial. Beresh charged that I had offered money for evidence and "harassed" potential witnesses. This greatly disturbed me as the reward for information that we offered was no different than rewards the police routinely offer. When Linda Fisher did come forward with her important evidence, our reward funds were long-since exhausted and she knew this. What she did was brave and commendable, not even remotely sleazy, as Beresh suggested. His strategy was particularly upsetting for me because he had once been a lawyer I deeply admired.

Beresh noted that the evidence room where vital exhibits were stored was loosely guarded and that lawyers and officials were allowed to examine items privately. "If contamination occurs or if (exhibits) are manipulated in any way, then it directly affects the final result," he said. He also said that some experts "ignored DNA evidence which pointed to individuals other than Larry Fisher." The suggestion was that I somehow took part in framing Fisher to free David. It was an absurd notion, since for it to be true, I would have had to extract semen from Larry Fisher while he was in prison, sneak into the court evidence room with it, scrub clean any incriminating evidence and then replace it with the Fisher semen. It was ridiculous.

This defence strategy really bothered me at first, but then I just decided that we were not going to allow ourselves to get pulled into it. I felt that I had done nothing wrong. I certainly didn't tamper with any evidence, and I was not technically capable of this. I was buoyed by reaction on Winnipeg call-in shows to the comments. It seemed that people were just as incensed by Beresh's attack as I was.

Conversely, David's poetry reading was wonderful.

He told the audience at the writer's festival how having a pencil and paper in prison helped lift him to a better place. Writing poetry freed him to think about abstract things, and better things, like the nature that existed outside the gray walls that confined him. David was wonderful as he read, "The sky opens to a small bird's sun song, breaking the rain puddle day."

David did his best to simply ignore what was going on in court, although I knew it bothered him. After the festival, when David saw our new house by the water, he just fell in love with it. He was like a kid. Above the garage there is a one-bedroom suite. "This is mine," David said. "We don't need to camp anymore. We're going to come over here."

He and Lorne bought tools for building lawn furniture. The girls and I talked about what dresses we would wear to the Gemini Awards, since the CTV movie *Milgaard* was nominated for eleven awards. Life was wonderful again, regardless of what was being said in the courtroom.

I couldn't help but feel a little concerned about what effect the movie might have on David. He never did watch the documentary *A Mother's Love*, since it simply hit too close to home, but he did sit down to watch the film *Milgaard*. It was somewhat easier for him, as it featured actors and not actual family members. His reaction to the movie made me laugh. He commented that he only wished he had a body as great as that of star Ian Tracey, who portrayed him.

The Geminis were pure Hollywood, or Hollywood North. The programmers weren't allowed to show any clips or images from the movie during the broadcast, since the awards were being aired in Saskatchewan, where the movie was banned, pending the outcome of the Fisher trial. *Milgaard* won six awards, including Ian Tracey for best actor and Stephen Williams for best director. The final award of the night was for best TV movie or dramatic mini-series, and it was such a burst of emotion to hear that we won that too. Producer Lazlo Barna called David and I on stage to share the award with him, and David looked like a movie producer as he calmly walked up with us, dressed in his tuxedo. The ceremony had taken two hours, but he showed no signs of the nerves he often felt in crowds. The emotion was so intense and loving when the audience rose as one and David stepped up to the microphone to say, "I think the people know the difference between right and wrong . . . I think that's what the movie was about. Thank you very much." Following his remarks, the standing ovation intensifed. It was so moving.

It seemed everyone around me was crying with joy, and David later hammed it up, hugging and kissing me for the cameras. It was such a mother moment, one of those joyous times when you step back and see your child all grown up, in magical surroundings. I will cherish a snapshot of that in my mind forever. It was one of the rare moments in my life when I couldn't have spoken, even if I'd wanted to.

Meanwhile, Larry Fisher's trial in Yorkton continued. The jury heard from three of Larry Fisher's seven rape victims. Two of these women were raped by Fisher within months of the Gail Miller attack, in alleys near the one where her body was found. Jurors didn't hear from a woman whose throat he slashed, because the judge found the attack so similar to the Gail Miller murder that it might be prejudicial. This victim was seventy-four now, and I was so impressed that she found the courage to step forward and testify at Fisher's preliminary hearing. She had such quiet dignity, as did Gail Miller's family, who sat through the trial testimony. It was awful to think how so much pain had been caused by the sickness of one man.

The DNA evidence against Fisher was nothing short of overwhelming. Anne-Elizabeth Charland, an RCMP DNA expert from Ottawa, told the court that Fisher's genetic code perfectly matched semen found on Miller's clothing. Asked to quantify this, Charland testified that the odds were 950 trillion to one that DNA in the semen on Miller's underpants and dress was from someone other than Larry Fisher.

Beresh presented a number of alternative theories: that a stalker, a possessive ex-boyfriend, a person with a nurse fetish or my David had killed Gail Miller. As his first witness, Beresh called Thomas (Bobs) Caldwell, who had prosecuted the case against David three decades before and who had fought so hard to keep David from getting parole. Caldwell, who was now a relief provincial court judge, told the jurors that David was convicted after a twelve-day trial, despite having been defended by one of the finest defence lawyers in the province, who had also gone on to become a judge.

A big question throughout the trial was whether Larry Fisher would take the stand in his own defence. If he did testify, he would leave himself open to cross-examination. Fisher had looked awful before the Supreme Court of Canada when he was cross-examined by Hersh Wolch back in 1993. He almost sounded proud as he described his technique in committing rapes, and perhaps because of this, Beresh chose to keep him off the stand.

Les Perrault told me that the Larry Fisher who appeared before the jury was clean-shaven and dressed like a professor in a nicely tailored suit. He was a man of fifty now, with gray hair, and for most of the testimony, he appeared calm, but apparently the stress was eating at him. Three times during the trial, proceedings were stopped as he complained of severe stomach pains. The third time was immediately after Justice Gerry Allbright started giving his final instructions to the jury. The judge said that he could be found guilty of first- or second-degree murder if he was found guilty beyond a reasonable doubt. The first-degree conviction would come if jurors found he intentionally killed her during a rape or indecent assault.

I heard that the courtroom was totally silent as Crown attorney Al Johnson closed the government's case against Larry Fisher. "I suggest to you, ladies and gentlemen, the man who raped and murdered Gail Miller left behind for thirty years his seminal fluid and DNA," Johnson said. "I say this simply, ladies and gentlemen: It's time to leave David Milgaard alone. Finally, let's leave him in peace."

Strong as the evidence was, I couldn't help but feel tense as we waited for the verdict. As the jury began their deliberations, my old friend Dan Lett of the *Winnipeg Free Press* wrote a wonderful article about the defence effort. "Ironically, Beresh's tactics are quite similar to the strategy that leads to many wrongful convictions. In the landmark inquiry into the wrongful conviction of Guy Paul Morin, commissioner Fred Kaufman commented on the propensity of prosecutors to heap worthless evidence until the jury is lulled into believing the accused is guilty," Dan wrote. "Beresh has played the same game by trying to seduce the jury with heaps of evidence on Milgaard's involvement in the crime, much of which has already been proved erroneous."

When I got news that the jury had found Fisher guilty of first-degree murder, I phoned David. He was asleep in his Vancouver condominium and I was happy to hear from Marnie that he was getting some rest at last. He called me back a little later and sounded relieved when he heard the verdict. It was finally the right decision, although it came thirty years late.

Once again, I found myself thinking a lot about the Miller family, and how considerate they had been from the start of the ordeal, back when Gail's father Mick walked over to Lorne after hearing the verdict against David and said, with tears in his eyes, "I'm sorry." It was painful to think that Gail would have been a woman of fifty now, had she lived. I have no doubt that she would have been a decent person, like the rest of the Millers.

The lives of my family and that of Gail Miller's family have been entangled since that horrible morning when Gail was slain. I know the Larry Fisher murder verdict has freed our family in a sense, and I can only hope it did the same for them. They deserve that peace. My deep love and prayers are with the whole family.

David Asper had very mixed emotions about the verdict. While he was happy at the result, he was seething with anger about the system and how it had not really changed in the eleven years since we put Larry Fisher's name forward to justice officials as a possible suspect. We were told then that Fisher was investigated and cleared. Later we read in the *Globe and Mail* of a justice department official comparing our belief in David's innocence to the belief some people have that Elvis Presley is still alive.

"There are other Davids out there," David Asper said after hearing the verdict. "They've got no money, no family support. They've got no capacity to redress a wrongful conviction."

He is right of course, which is why a public inquiry and changes to the system remain so important. Our legal team of David Asper, Hersh Wolch, Greg Rodin and James Lockyer and our family remain passionate that changes to the system must be made to prevent further suffering. An outside review mechanism, like that in Britain, Australia and New Zealand, for cases in which all appeals have been exhausted, would fit the bill. I pray that the legacy of my son's story will include changes to the system so that no one else has to go through what he endured. People may think it's all over but we know the inquiry must still be faced — and that could take years.

Throughout this whole experience, I have been so grateful to all the loyal volunteers who stood by me in the fight to clear David's name and also the many Canadians who continue to support and pray for us. I can't thank them enough. David's victory is also theirs.

On January 4, 2000, Larry Fisher was sentenced to life imprisonment for the murder of Gail Miller.

INDEX